ANGEL
&FAITH™

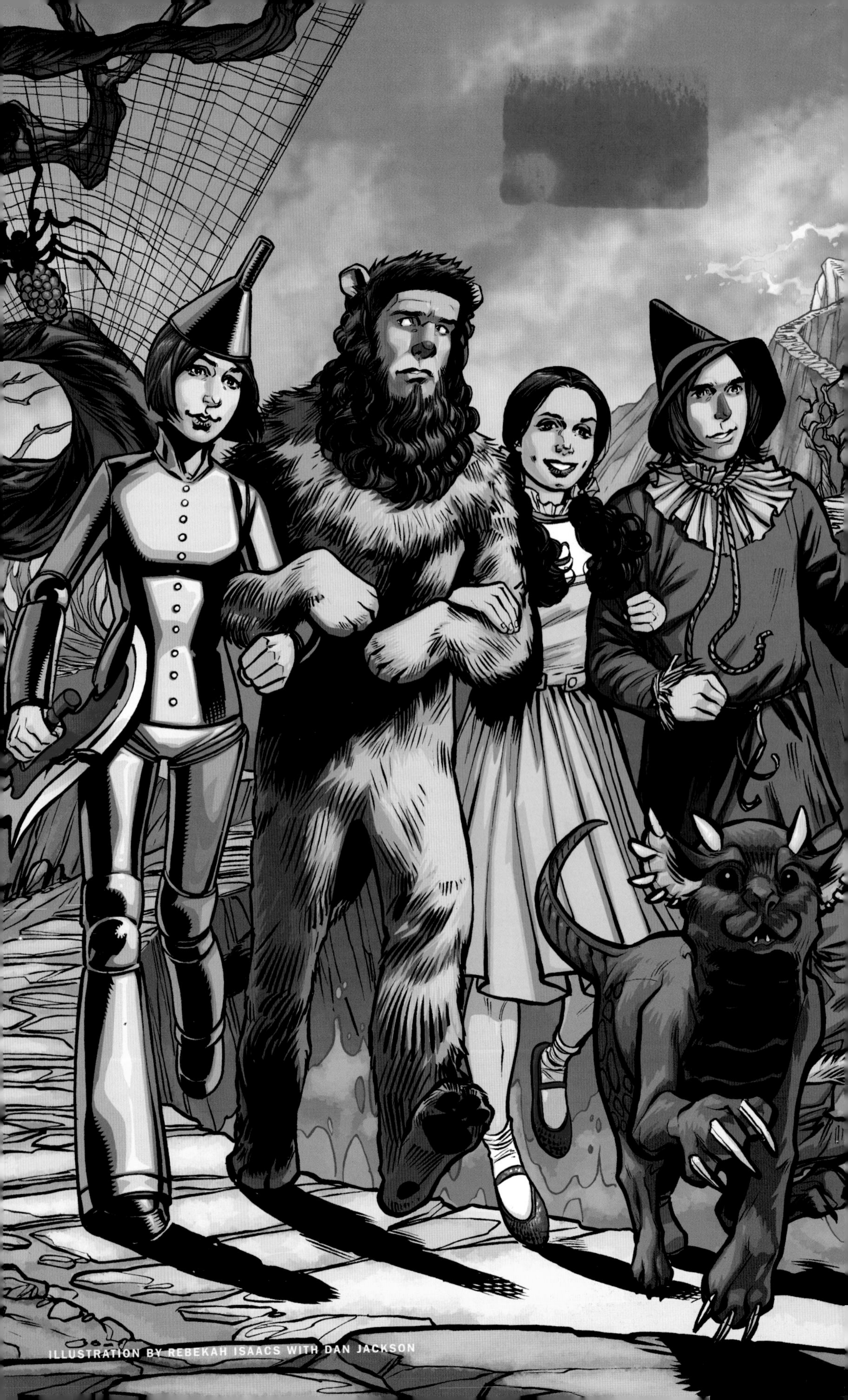

ILLUSTRATION BY REBEKAH ISAACS WITH DAN JACKSON

ANGEL & FAITH™

SEASON 9 · VOLUME 3

SCRIPT
CHRISTOS GAGE

FAMILY REUNION

ART
REBEKAH ISAACS

THE HERO OF HIS OWN STORY PART 1

PENCILS
LEE GARBETT

INKS
DEREK FRIDOLFS

THE HERO OF HIS OWN STORY PART 2

ART
DAVID LAPHAM

COLORS
DAN JACKSON

LETTERS
RICHARD STARKINGS *& Comicraft's*
JIMMY BETANCOURT

COVER ART
STEVE MORRIS

EXECUTIVE PRODUCER
JOSS WHEDON

DARK HORSE BOOKS

PRESIDENT & PUBLISHER
MIKE RICHARDSON

EDITORS
SCOTT ALLIE & SIERRA HAHN

ASSISTANT EDITOR
FREDDYE LINS

COLLECTION DESIGNER
JUSTIN COUCH

Published by Dark Horse Books
A division of Dark Horse Comics, Inc.
10956 SE Main Street
Milwaukie, OR 97222

DarkHorse.com
International Licensing: (503) 905-2377

To find a comics shop in your area, call the
Comic Shop Locator Service toll-free at
(888) 266-4226.

First edition: April 2013
ISBN 978-1-61655-079-0

10 9 8 7 6 5 4 3 2 1
Printed in China

This story takes place during *Buffy the Vampire Slayer* Season 9, created by Joss Whedon.

Special thanks to Lauren Valencia at Twentieth Century Fox, Daniel Kaminsky, Shantel LaRocque, and Everett Patterson.

NEIL HANKERSON Executive Vice President • TOM WEDDLE Chief Financial Officer • RANDY STRADLEY Vice President of Publishing • MICHAEL MARTENS Vice President of Book Trade Sales • ANITA NELSON Vice President of Business Affairs • SCOTT ALLIE Editor in Chief • MATT PARKINSON Vice President of Marketing • DAVID SCROGGY Vice President of Product Development • DALE LAFOUNTAIN Vice President of Information Technology • DARLENE VOGEL Senior Director of Print, Design, and Production • KEN LIZZI General Counsel • DAVEY ESTRADA Editorial Director • CHRIS WARNER Senior Books Editor • DIANA SCHUTZ Executive Editor • CARY GRAZZINI Director of Print and Development • LIA RIBACCHI Art Director • CARA NIECE Director of Scheduling • TIM WIESCH Director of International Licensing • MARK BERNARDI Director of Digital Publishing

This volume reprints the comic-book series *Angel & Faith* #11–#15 from Dark Horse Comics.

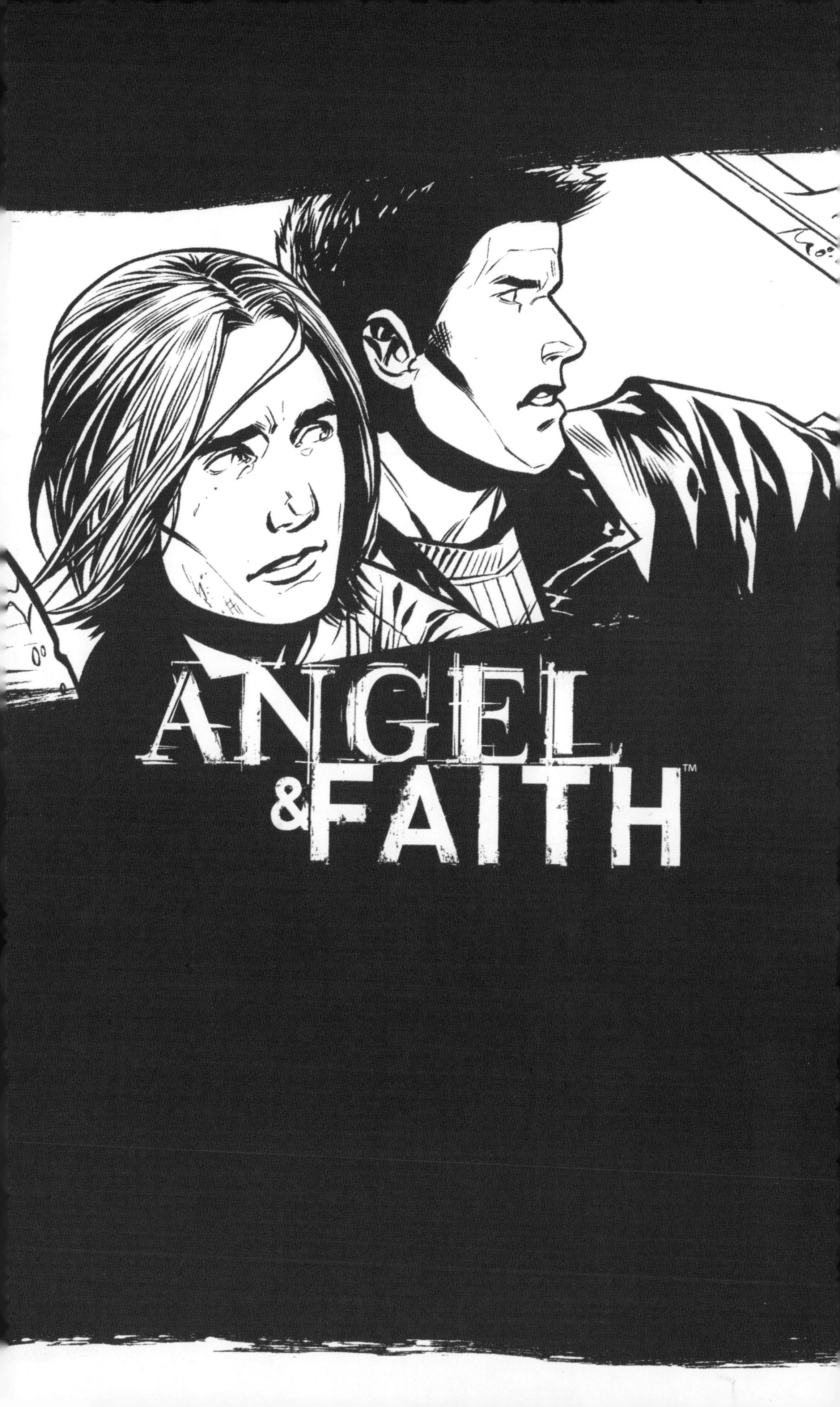
ANGEL
&FAITH™

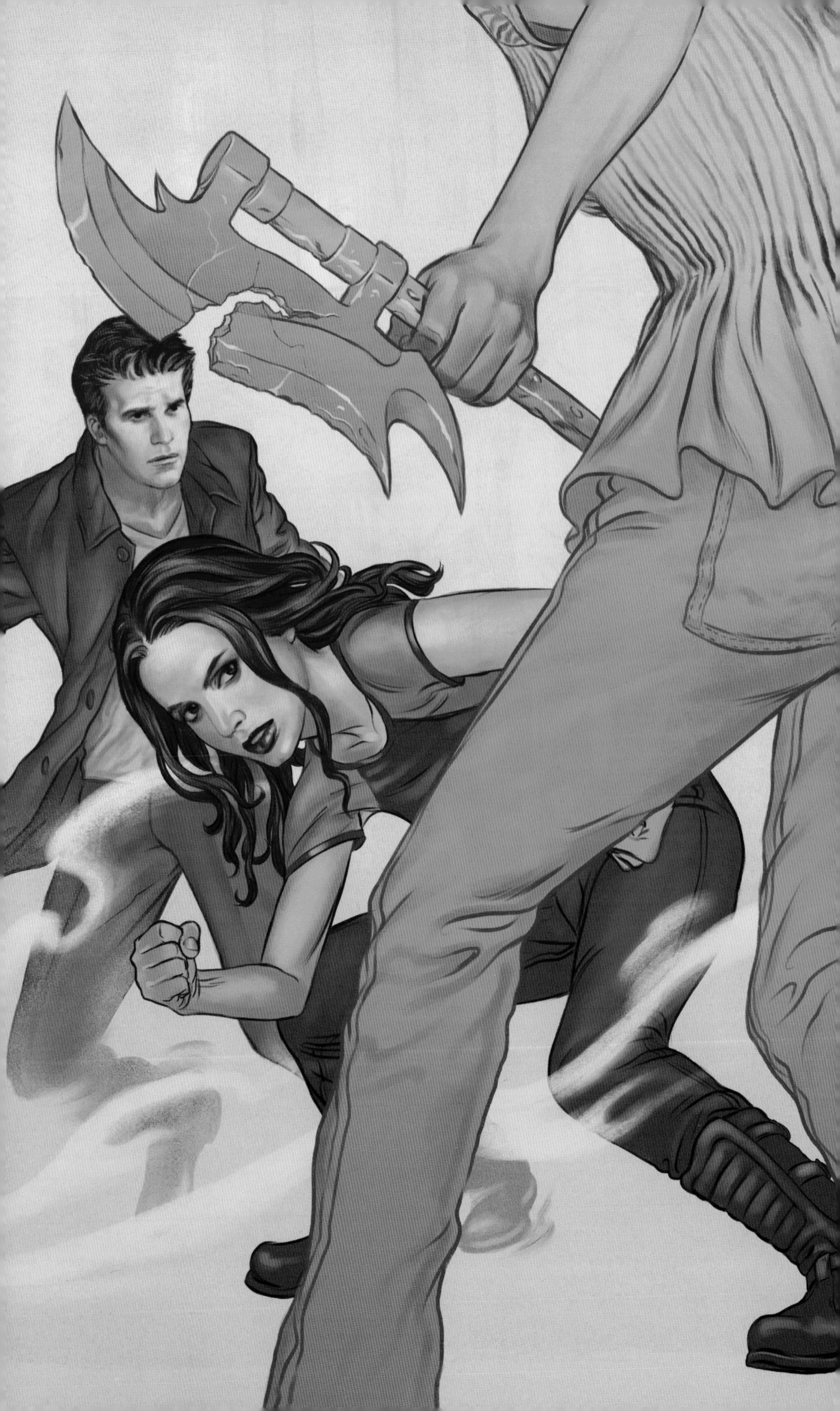

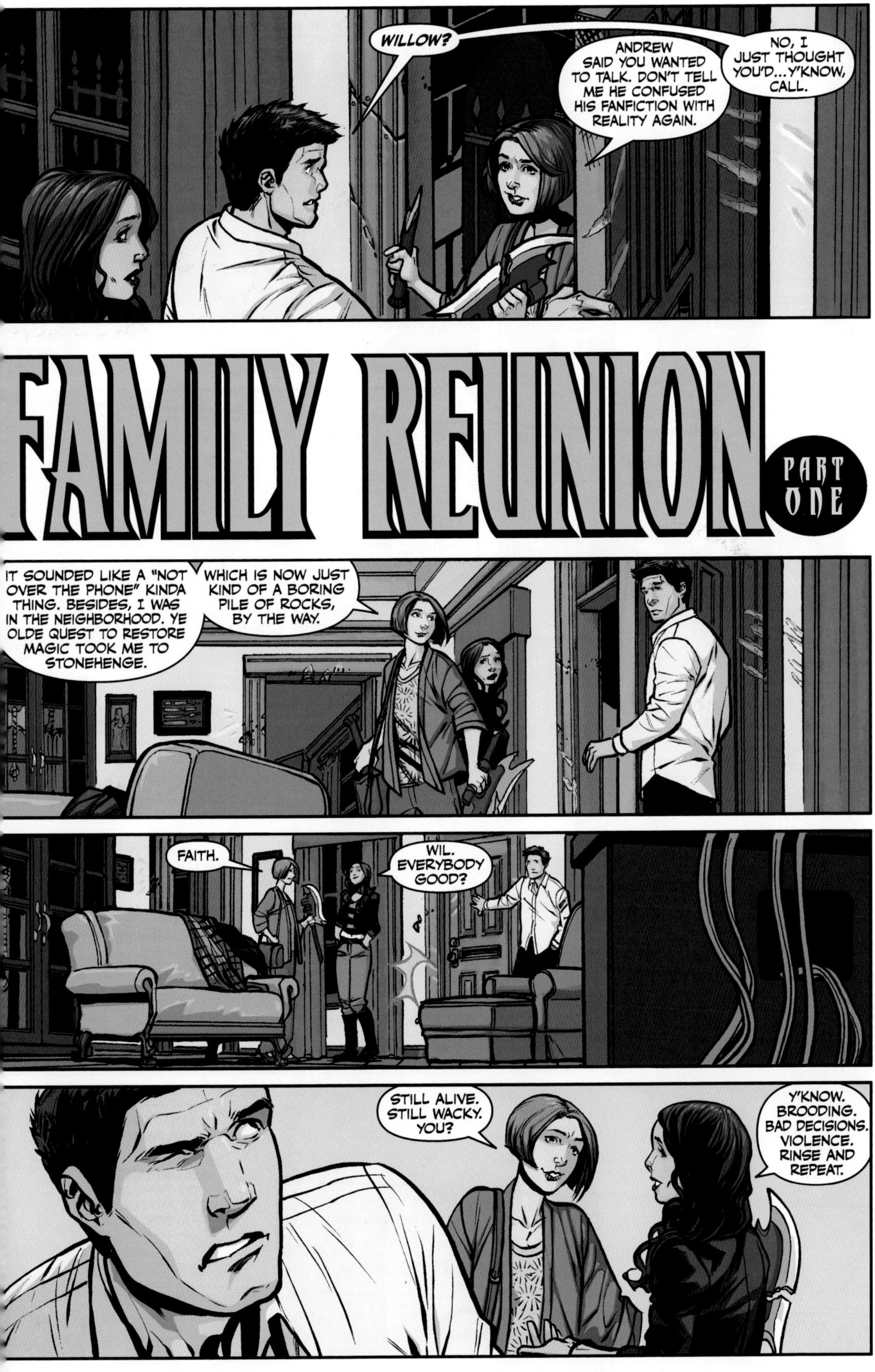
WILLOW?
ANDREW SAID YOU WANTED TO TALK. DON'T TELL ME HE CONFUSED HIS FANFICTION WITH REALITY AGAIN.
NO, I JUST THOUGHT YOU'D...Y'KNOW, CALL.
FAMILY REUNION
PART ONE
IT SOUNDED LIKE A "NOT OVER THE PHONE" KINDA THING. BESIDES, I WAS IN THE NEIGHBORHOOD. YE OLDE QUEST TO RESTORE MAGIC TOOK ME TO STONEHENGE.
WHICH IS NOW JUST KIND OF A BORING PILE OF ROCKS, BY THE WAY.
FAITH.
WIL. EVERYBODY GOOD?
STILL ALIVE. STILL WACKY. YOU?
Y'KNOW. BROODING. BAD DECISIONS. VIOLENCE. RINSE AND REPEAT.

EXCUSE ME, I THINK THERE'S A DOOR SOMEWHERE IN THIS HOUSE YOU *HAVEN'T* SLAMMED.

OH, LOOK, VIN, IT'S THAT LESBIAN WITCH FROM AMERICA. SUNFLOWER.

WILLOW. HEY, SOPHIE. LAVINIA.

YOU KNOW EACH OTHER?

FROM WHEN I WAS TRAINING WITH GILES AT HIS ESTATE IN BATH. GOTTA SAY, I'M KINDA SURPRISED THEY'RE HERE.

ALTHOUGH HAVING RECENTLY DONE A STINT IN THE WORLD OF REAL JOBS, I GUESS I CAN SEE FORGIVING MURDER IF IT MEANS THE GRAVY TRAIN KEEPS ROLLING.

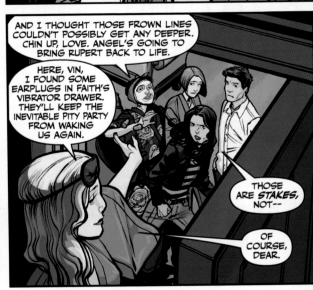

AND I THOUGHT THOSE FROWN LINES COULDN'T POSSIBLY GET ANY DEEPER. CHIN UP, LOVE. ANGEL'S GOING TO BRING RUPERT BACK TO LIFE.

HERE, VIN, I FOUND SOME EARPLUGS IN FAITH'S VIBRATOR DRAWER. THEY'LL KEEP THE INEVITABLE PITY PARTY FROM WAKING US AGAIN.

THOSE ARE *STAKES*, NOT--

OF COURSE, DEAR.

OKAY...LET ME EXPLAIN.

I'D FIGURED IT OUT. YOU CAN'T CALL HIS SOUL BACK WITH A SPELL, SO YOU'RE FINDING MAGIC ITEMS LINKED TO KEY MOMENTS IN HIS LIFE AND USING THEM TO ASSEMBLE IT PIECE BY PIECE.

THE SCYTHE'S MAGIC. AND HE WAS HOLDING IT WHEN HE DIED. I'M NOT STUPID, ANGEL.

YOU ARE. AND SELFISH. AND RECKLESS.

AND *DELUSIONAL* IF YOU THINK THIS'LL END IN ANYTHING BUT DISASTER.

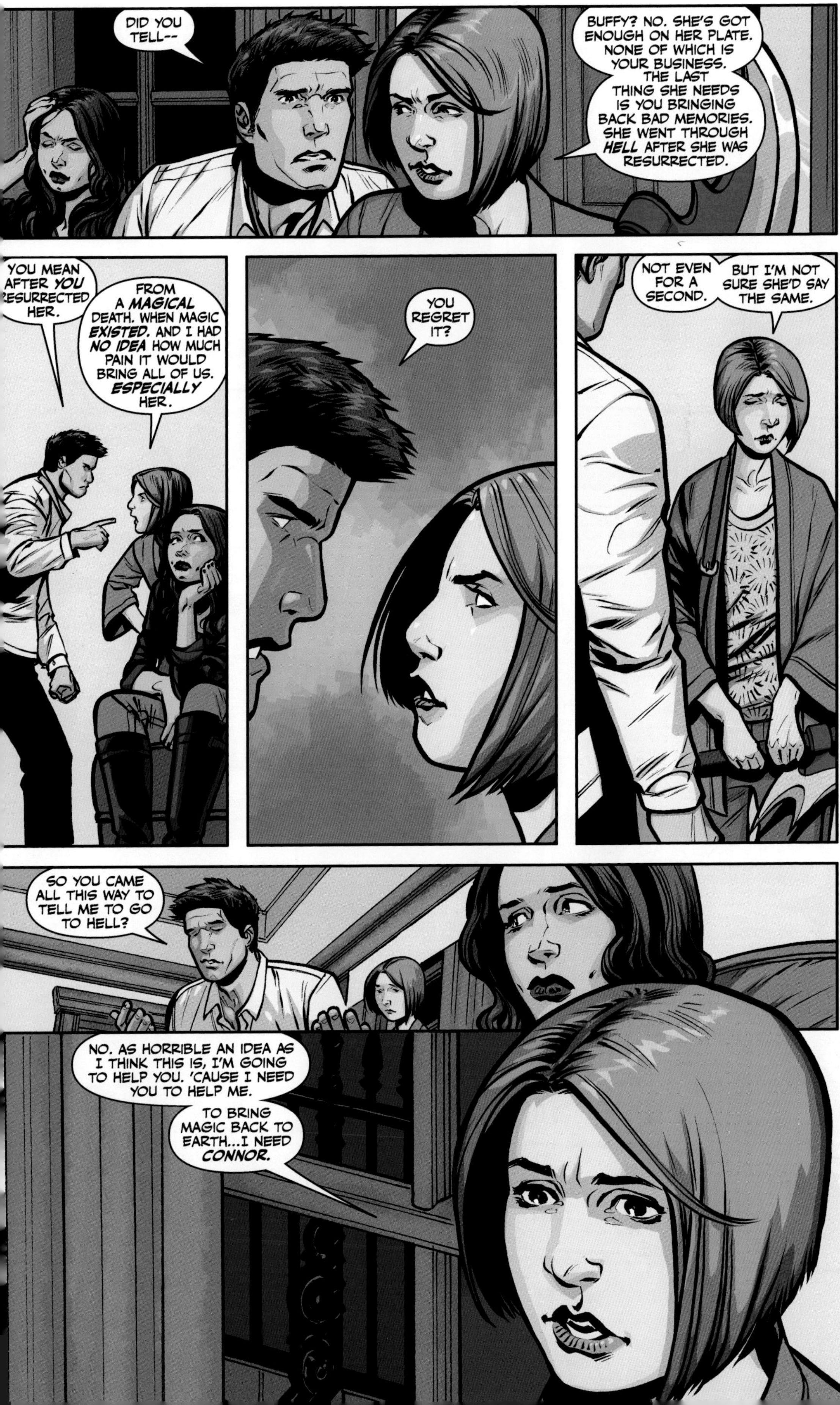

DID YOU TELL--
BUFFY? NO. SHE'S GOT ENOUGH ON HER PLATE. NONE OF WHICH IS YOUR BUSINESS.
THE LAST THING SHE NEEDS IS YOU BRINGING BACK BAD MEMORIES. SHE WENT THROUGH HELL AFTER SHE WAS RESURRECTED.
YOU MEAN AFTER YOU RESURRECTED HER.
FROM A MAGICAL DEATH. WHEN MAGIC EXISTED. AND I HAD NO IDEA HOW MUCH PAIN IT WOULD BRING ALL OF US. ESPECIALLY HER.
YOU REGRET IT?
NOT EVEN FOR A SECOND.
BUT I'M NOT SURE SHE'D SAY THE SAME.
SO YOU CAME ALL THIS WAY TO TELL ME TO GO TO HELL?
NO. AS HORRIBLE AN IDEA AS I THINK THIS IS, I'M GOING TO HELP YOU. 'CAUSE I NEED YOU TO HELP ME.
TO BRING MAGIC BACK TO EARTH...I NEED CONNOR.

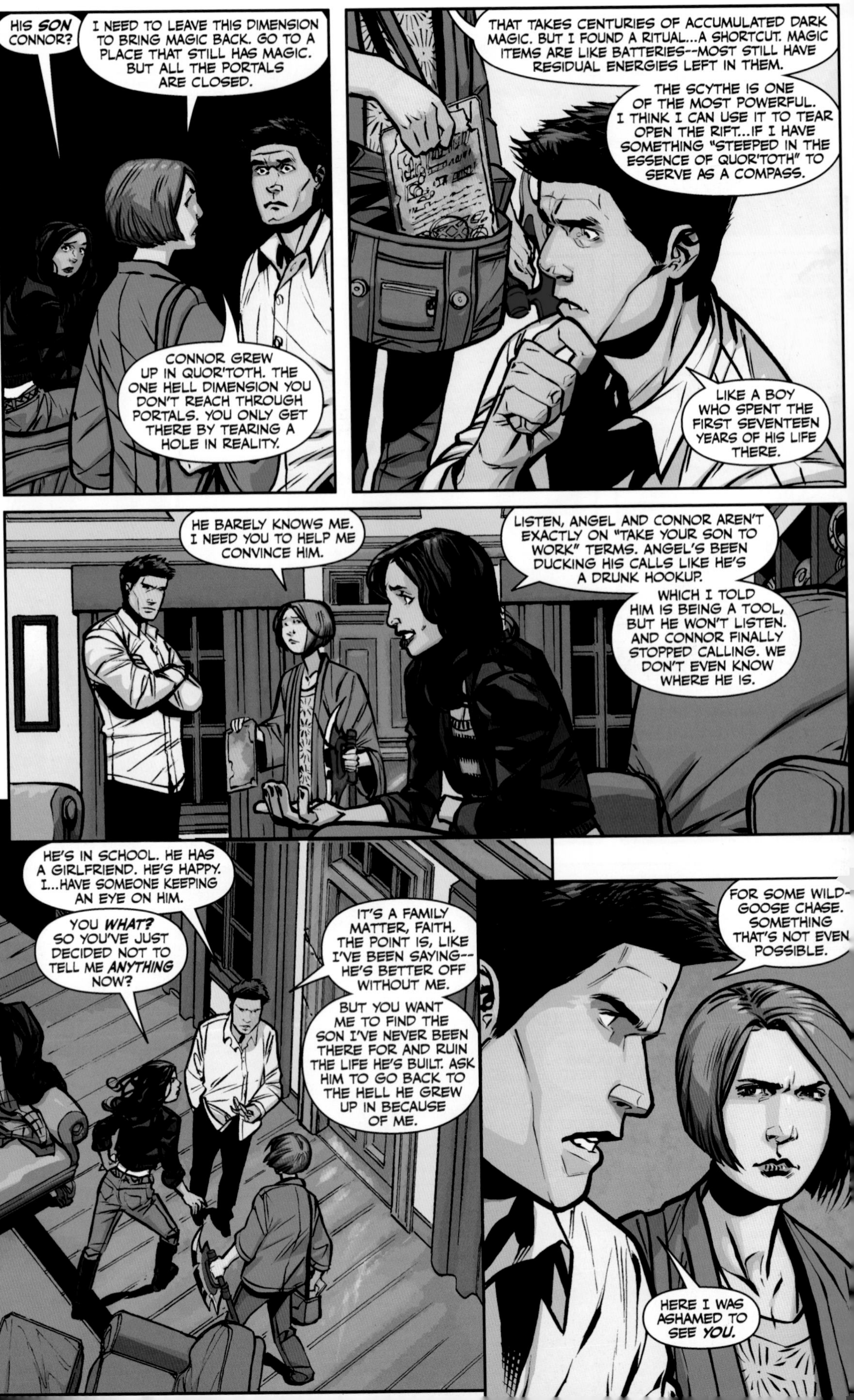
HIS SON CONNOR?
I NEED TO LEAVE THIS DIMENSION TO BRING MAGIC BACK. GO TO A PLACE THAT STILL HAS MAGIC. BUT ALL THE PORTALS ARE CLOSED.
CONNOR GREW UP IN QUOR'TOTH. THE ONE HELL DIMENSION YOU DON'T REACH THROUGH PORTALS. YOU ONLY GET THERE BY TEARING A HOLE IN REALITY.
THAT TAKES CENTURIES OF ACCUMULATED DARK MAGIC. BUT I FOUND A RITUAL...A SHORTCUT. MAGIC ITEMS ARE LIKE BATTERIES--MOST STILL HAVE RESIDUAL ENERGIES LEFT IN THEM.
THE SCYTHE IS ONE OF THE MOST POWERFUL. I THINK I CAN USE IT TO TEAR OPEN THE RIFT...IF I HAVE SOMETHING "STEEPED IN THE ESSENCE OF QUOR'TOTH" TO SERVE AS A COMPASS.
LIKE A BOY WHO SPENT THE FIRST SEVENTEEN YEARS OF HIS LIFE THERE.
HE BARELY KNOWS ME. I NEED YOU TO HELP ME CONVINCE HIM.
LISTEN, ANGEL AND CONNOR AREN'T EXACTLY ON "TAKE YOUR SON TO WORK" TERMS. ANGEL'S BEEN DUCKING HIS CALLS LIKE HE'S A DRUNK HOOKUP.
WHICH I TOLD HIM IS BEING A TOOL, BUT HE WON'T LISTEN. AND CONNOR FINALLY STOPPED CALLING. WE DON'T EVEN KNOW WHERE HE IS.
HE'S IN SCHOOL. HE HAS A GIRLFRIEND. HE'S HAPPY. I...HAVE SOMEONE KEEPING AN EYE ON HIM.
YOU WHAT? SO YOU'VE JUST DECIDED NOT TO TELL ME ANYTHING NOW?
IT'S A FAMILY MATTER, FAITH. THE POINT IS, LIKE I'VE BEEN SAYING-- HE'S BETTER OFF WITHOUT ME.
BUT YOU WANT ME TO FIND THE SON I'VE NEVER BEEN THERE FOR AND RUIN THE LIFE HE'S BUILT. ASK HIM TO GO BACK TO THE HELL HE GREW UP IN BECAUSE OF ME.
FOR SOME WILD-GOOSE CHASE. SOMETHING THAT'S NOT EVEN POSSIBLE.
HERE I WAS ASHAMED TO SEE YOU.

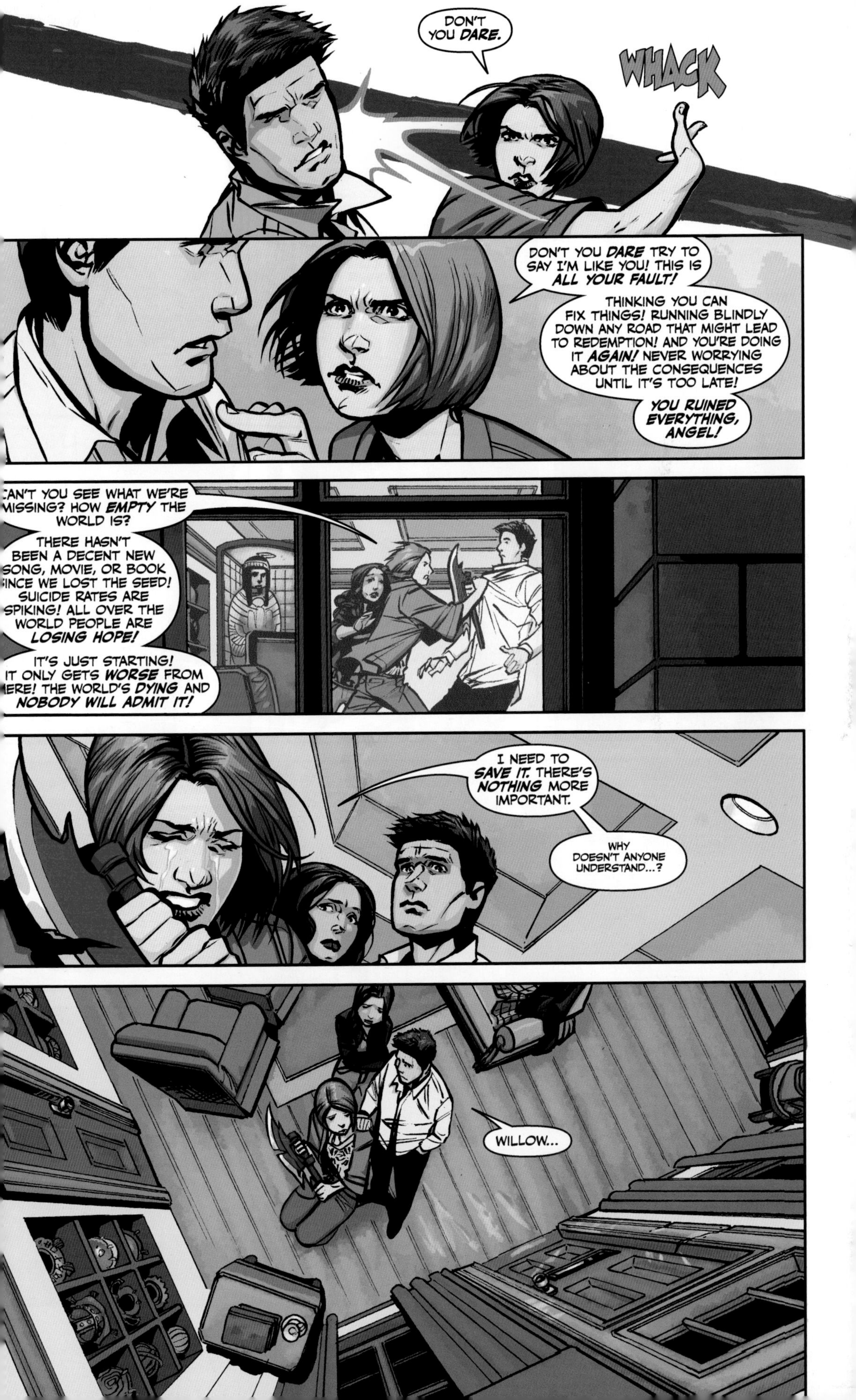
DON'T YOU DARE.
WHACK
DON'T YOU DARE TRY TO SAY I'M LIKE YOU! THIS IS ALL YOUR FAULT!
THINKING YOU CAN FIX THINGS! RUNNING BLINDLY DOWN ANY ROAD THAT MIGHT LEAD TO REDEMPTION! AND YOU'RE DOING IT AGAIN! NEVER WORRYING ABOUT THE CONSEQUENCES UNTIL IT'S TOO LATE!
YOU RUINED EVERYTHING, ANGEL!
CAN'T YOU SEE WHAT WE'RE MISSING? HOW EMPTY THE WORLD IS?
THERE HASN'T BEEN A DECENT NEW SONG, MOVIE, OR BOOK SINCE WE LOST THE SEED! SUICIDE RATES ARE SPIKING! ALL OVER THE WORLD PEOPLE ARE LOSING HOPE!
IT'S JUST STARTING! IT ONLY GETS WORSE FROM HERE! THE WORLD'S DYING AND NOBODY WILL ADMIT IT!
I NEED TO SAVE IT. THERE'S NOTHING MORE IMPORTANT.
WHY DOESN'T ANYONE UNDERSTAND...?
WILLOW...

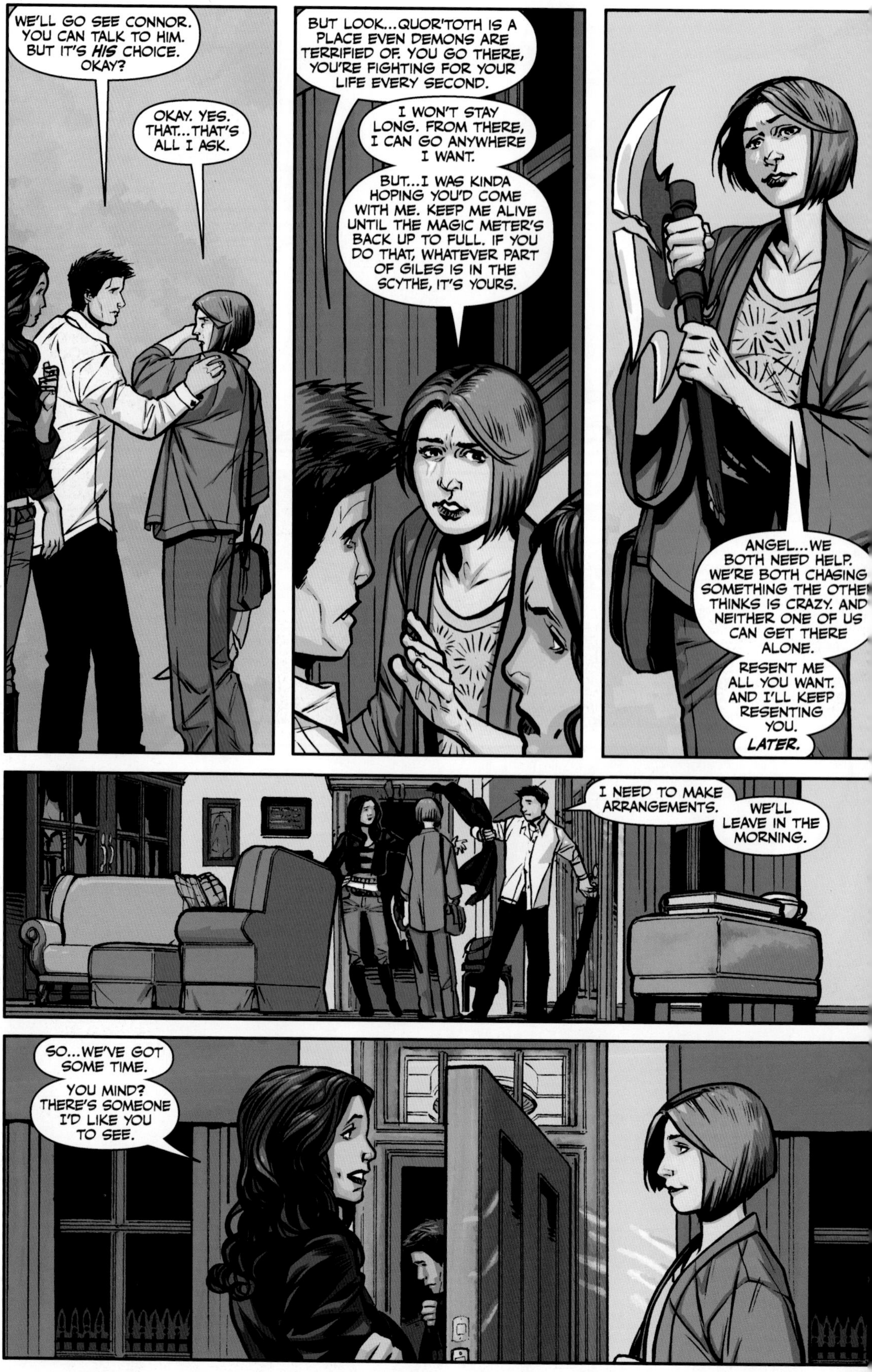
WE'LL GO SEE CONNOR. YOU CAN TALK TO HIM. BUT IT'S *HIS* CHOICE. OKAY?
OKAY. YES. THAT...THAT'S ALL I ASK.
BUT LOOK...QUOR'TOTH IS A PLACE EVEN DEMONS ARE TERRIFIED OF. YOU GO THERE, YOU'RE FIGHTING FOR YOUR LIFE EVERY SECOND.
I WON'T STAY LONG. FROM THERE, I CAN GO ANYWHERE I WANT.
BUT...I WAS KINDA HOPING YOU'D COME WITH ME. KEEP ME ALIVE UNTIL THE MAGIC METER'S BACK UP TO FULL. IF YOU DO THAT, WHATEVER PART OF GILES IS IN THE SCYTHE, IT'S YOURS.
ANGEL...WE BOTH NEED HELP. WE'RE BOTH CHASING SOMETHING THE OTHE THINKS IS CRAZY. AND NEITHER ONE OF US CAN GET THERE ALONE.
RESENT ME ALL YOU WANT. AND I'LL KEEP RESENTING YOU. *LATER.*
I NEED TO MAKE ARRANGEMENTS.
WE'LL LEAVE IN THE MORNING.
SO...WE'VE GOT SOME TIME.
YOU MIND? THERE'S SOMEONE I'D LIKE YOU TO SEE.

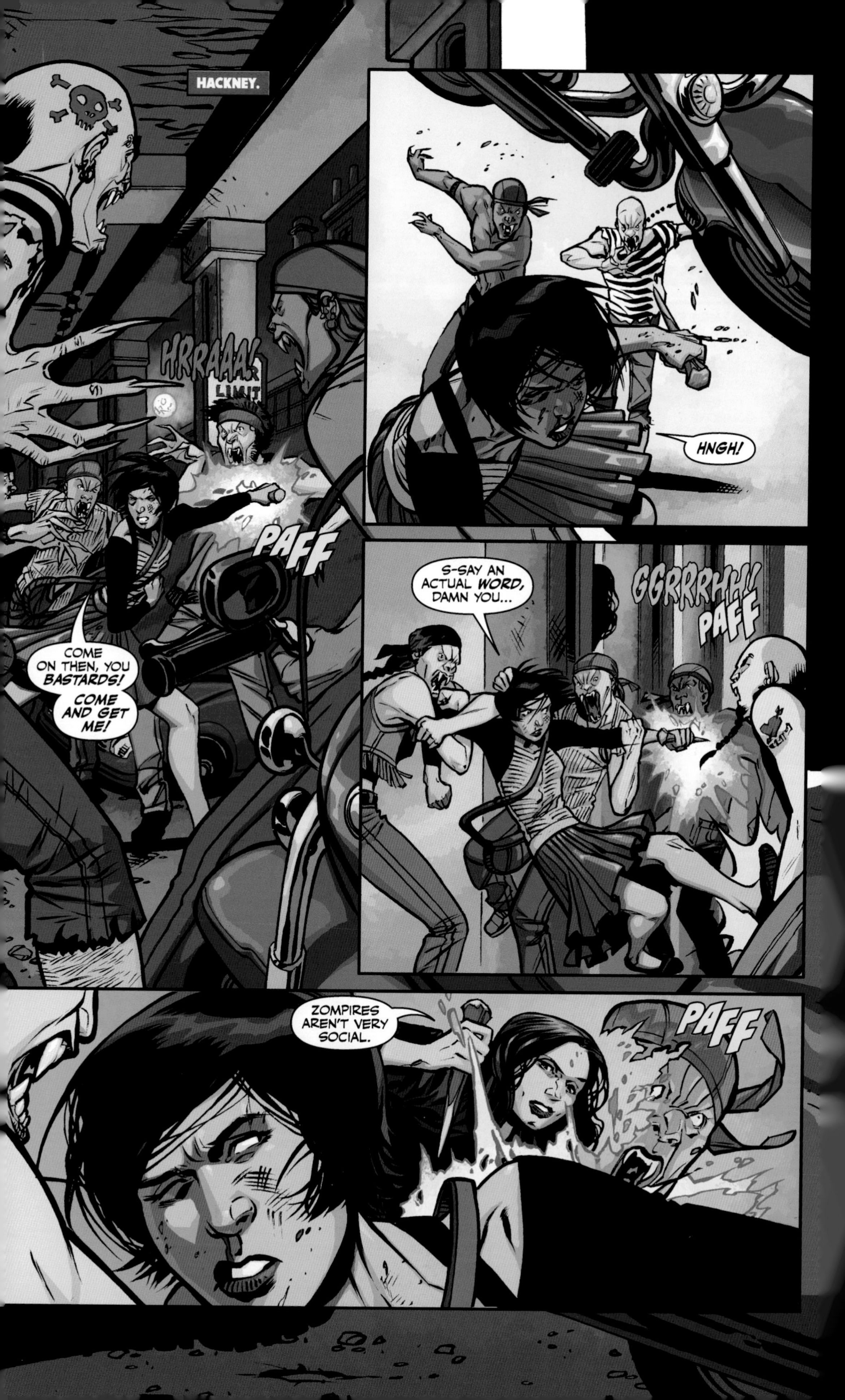
HACKNEY.
HRRAAA!
PAFF
COME ON THEN, YOU BASTARDS! COME AND GET ME!
HNGH!
S-SAY AN ACTUAL WORD, DAMN YOU...
GGRRRHH!
PAFF
ZOMPIRES AREN'T VERY SOCIAL.
PAFF

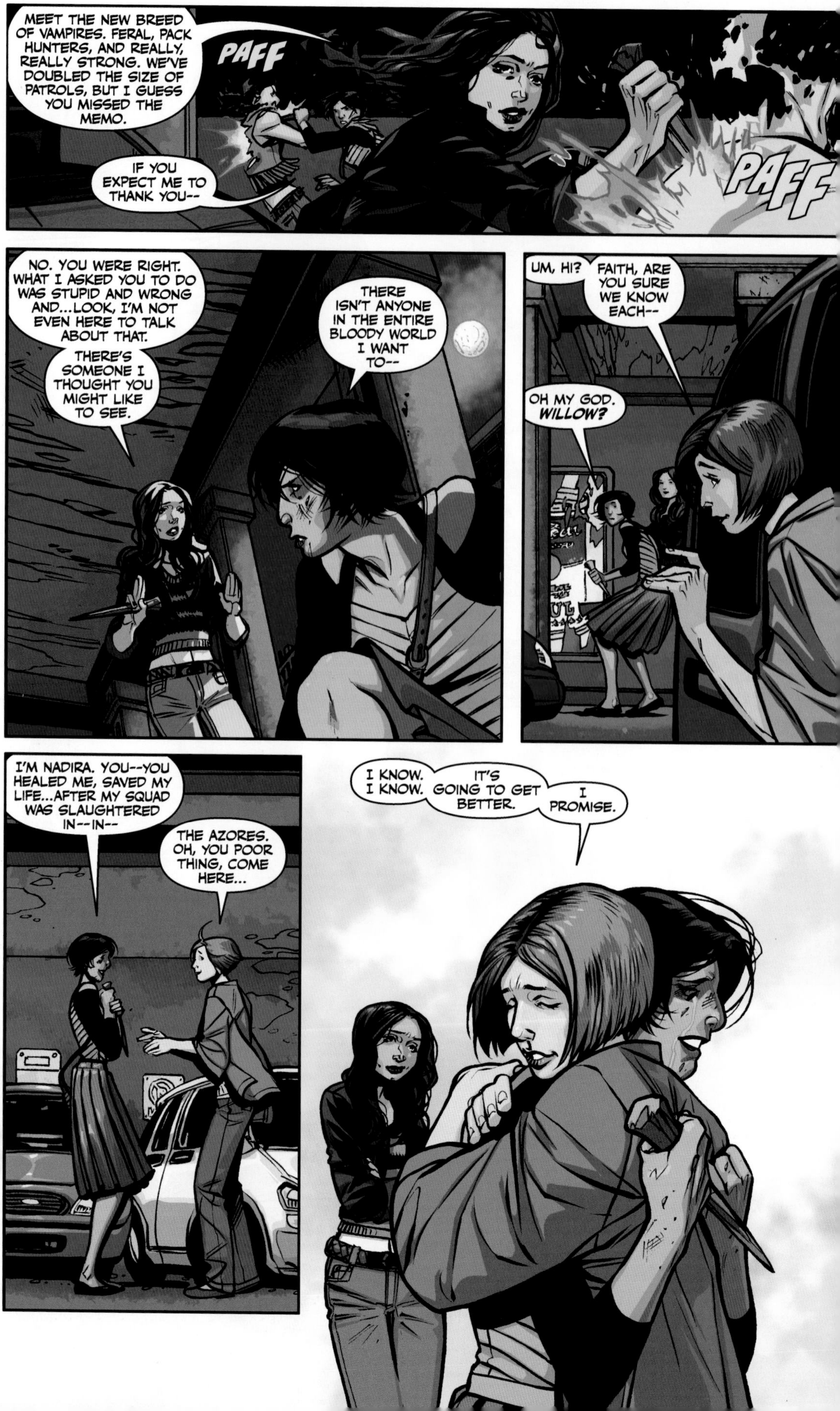
MEET THE NEW BREED OF VAMPIRES. FERAL, PACK HUNTERS, AND REALLY, REALLY STRONG. WE'VE DOUBLED THE SIZE OF PATROLS, BUT I GUESS YOU MISSED THE MEMO.
PAFF
IF YOU EXPECT ME TO THANK YOU--
PAFF
NO. YOU WERE RIGHT. WHAT I ASKED YOU TO DO WAS STUPID AND WRONG AND...LOOK, I'M NOT EVEN HERE TO TALK ABOUT THAT.
THERE'S SOMEONE I THOUGHT YOU MIGHT LIKE TO SEE.
THERE ISN'T ANYONE IN THE ENTIRE BLOODY WORLD I WANT TO--
UM, HI?
FAITH, ARE YOU SURE WE KNOW EACH--
OH MY GOD. *WILLOW?*
I'M NADIRA. YOU--YOU HEALED ME, SAVED MY LIFE...AFTER MY SQUAD WAS SLAUGHTERED IN--IN--
THE AZORES. OH, YOU POOR THING, COME HERE...
I KNOW. I KNOW.
IT'S GOING TO GET BETTER.
I PROMISE.

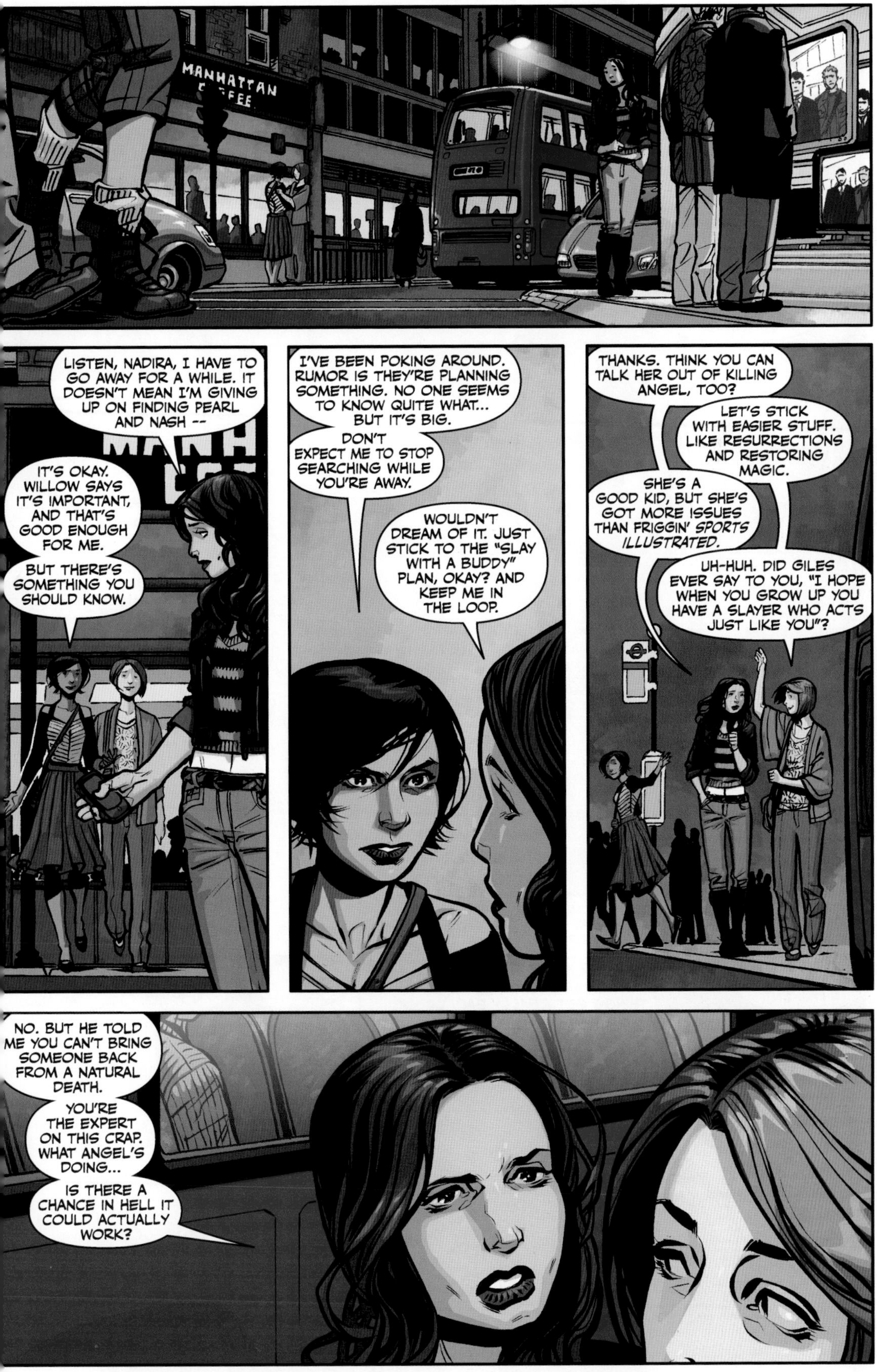
MANHATTAN COFFEE
LISTEN, NADIRA, I HAVE TO GO AWAY FOR A WHILE. IT DOESN'T MEAN I'M GIVING UP ON FINDING PEARL AND NASH --
IT'S OKAY. WILLOW SAYS IT'S IMPORTANT, AND THAT'S GOOD ENOUGH FOR ME.
BUT THERE'S SOMETHING YOU SHOULD KNOW.
I'VE BEEN POKING AROUND. RUMOR IS THEY'RE PLANNING SOMETHING. NO ONE SEEMS TO KNOW QUITE WHAT... BUT IT'S BIG.
DON'T EXPECT ME TO STOP SEARCHING WHILE YOU'RE AWAY.
WOULDN'T DREAM OF IT. JUST STICK TO THE "SLAY WITH A BUDDY" PLAN, OKAY? AND KEEP ME IN THE LOOP.
THANKS. THINK YOU CAN TALK HER OUT OF KILLING ANGEL, TOO?
LET'S STICK WITH EASIER STUFF. LIKE RESURRECTIONS AND RESTORING MAGIC.
SHE'S A GOOD KID, BUT SHE'S GOT MORE ISSUES THAN FRIGGIN' *SPORTS ILLUSTRATED.*
UH-HUH. DID GILES EVER SAY TO YOU, "I HOPE WHEN YOU GROW UP YOU HAVE A SLAYER WHO ACTS JUST LIKE YOU"?
NO. BUT HE TOLD ME YOU CAN'T BRING SOMEONE BACK FROM A NATURAL DEATH.
YOU'RE THE EXPERT ON THIS CRAP. WHAT ANGEL'S DOING...
IS THERE A CHANCE IN HELL IT COULD ACTUALLY WORK?

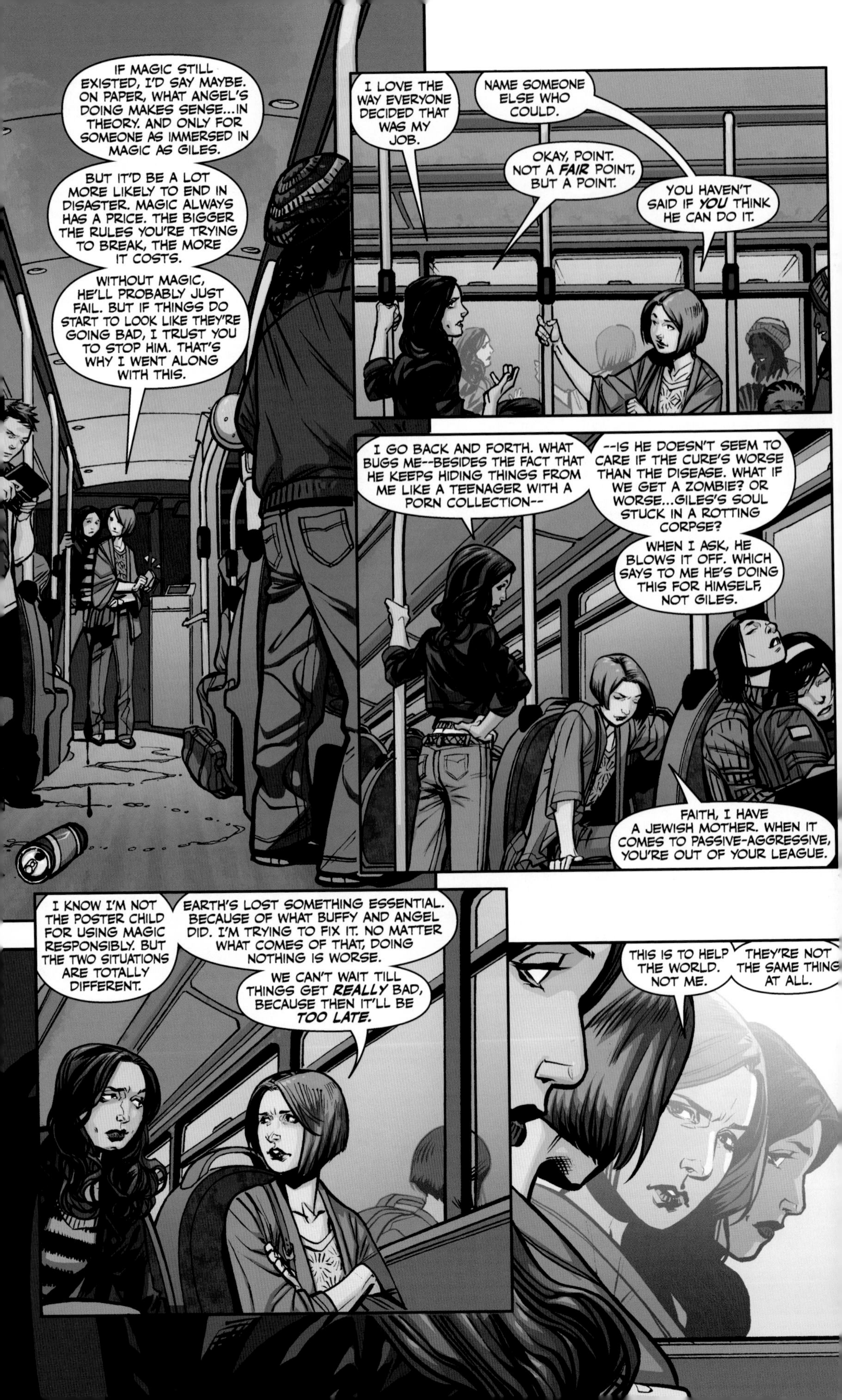

IF MAGIC STILL EXISTED, I'D SAY MAYBE. ON PAPER, WHAT ANGEL'S DOING MAKES SENSE...IN THEORY. AND ONLY FOR SOMEONE AS IMMERSED IN MAGIC AS GILES.
BUT IT'D BE A LOT MORE LIKELY TO END IN DISASTER. MAGIC ALWAYS HAS A PRICE. THE BIGGER THE RULES YOU'RE TRYING TO BREAK, THE MORE IT COSTS.
WITHOUT MAGIC, HE'LL PROBABLY JUST FAIL. BUT IF THINGS DO START TO LOOK LIKE THEY'RE GOING BAD, I TRUST YOU TO STOP HIM. THAT'S WHY I WENT ALONG WITH THIS.
I LOVE THE WAY EVERYONE DECIDED THAT WAS MY JOB.
NAME SOMEONE ELSE WHO COULD.
OKAY, POINT. NOT A *FAIR* POINT, BUT A POINT.
YOU HAVEN'T SAID IF *YOU* THINK HE CAN DO IT.
I GO BACK AND FORTH. WHAT BUGS ME--BESIDES THE FACT THAT HE KEEPS HIDING THINGS FROM ME LIKE A TEENAGER WITH A PORN COLLECTION--
--IS HE DOESN'T SEEM TO CARE IF THE CURE'S WORSE THAN THE DISEASE. WHAT IF WE GET A ZOMBIE? OR WORSE...GILES'S SOUL STUCK IN A ROTTING CORPSE?
WHEN I ASK, HE BLOWS IT OFF. WHICH SAYS TO ME HE'S DOING THIS FOR HIMSELF, NOT GILES.
FAITH, I HAVE A JEWISH MOTHER. WHEN IT COMES TO PASSIVE-AGGRESSIVE, YOU'RE OUT OF YOUR LEAGUE.
I KNOW I'M NOT THE POSTER CHILD FOR USING MAGIC RESPONSIBLY. BUT THE TWO SITUATIONS ARE TOTALLY DIFFERENT.
EARTH'S LOST SOMETHING ESSENTIAL. BECAUSE OF WHAT BUFFY AND ANGEL DID. I'M TRYING TO FIX IT. NO MATTER WHAT COMES OF THAT, DOING NOTHING IS WORSE.
WE CAN'T WAIT TILL THINGS GET *REALLY* BAD, BECAUSE THEN IT'LL BE *TOO LATE.*
THIS IS TO HELP THE WORLD. NOT ME.
THEY'RE NOT THE SAME THING AT ALL.

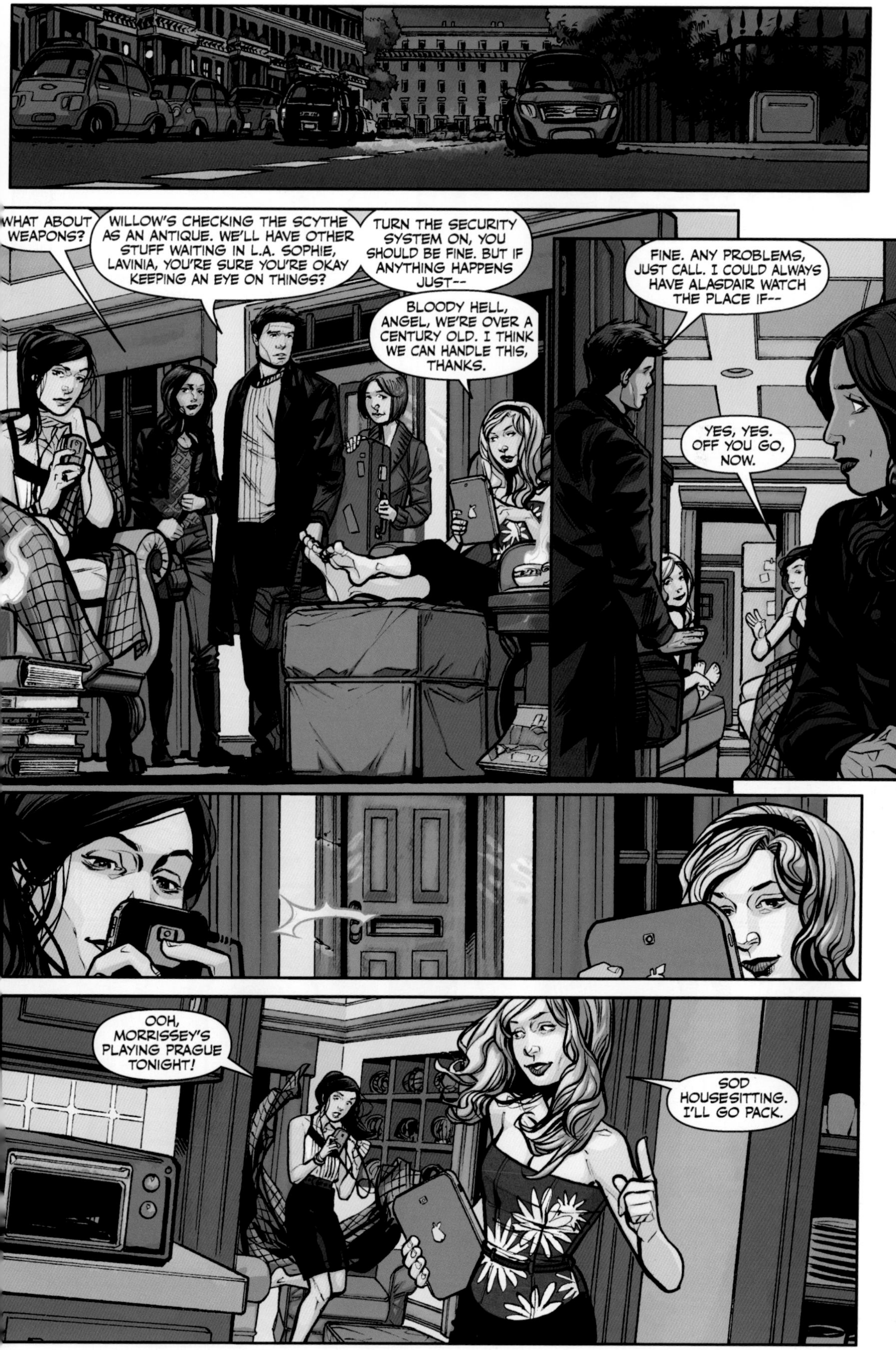
WHAT ABOUT WEAPONS?
WILLOW'S CHECKING THE SCYTHE AS AN ANTIQUE. WE'LL HAVE OTHER STUFF WAITING IN L.A. SOPHIE, LAVINIA, YOU'RE SURE YOU'RE OKAY KEEPING AN EYE ON THINGS?
TURN THE SECURITY SYSTEM ON, YOU SHOULD BE FINE. BUT IF ANYTHING HAPPENS JUST--
BLOODY HELL, ANGEL, WE'RE OVER A CENTURY OLD. I THINK WE CAN HANDLE THIS, THANKS.
FINE. ANY PROBLEMS, JUST CALL. I COULD ALWAYS HAVE ALASDAIR WATCH THE PLACE IF--
YES, YES. OFF YOU GO, NOW.
OOH, MORRISSEY'S PLAYING PRAGUE TONIGHT!
SOD HOUSESITTING. I'LL GO PACK.

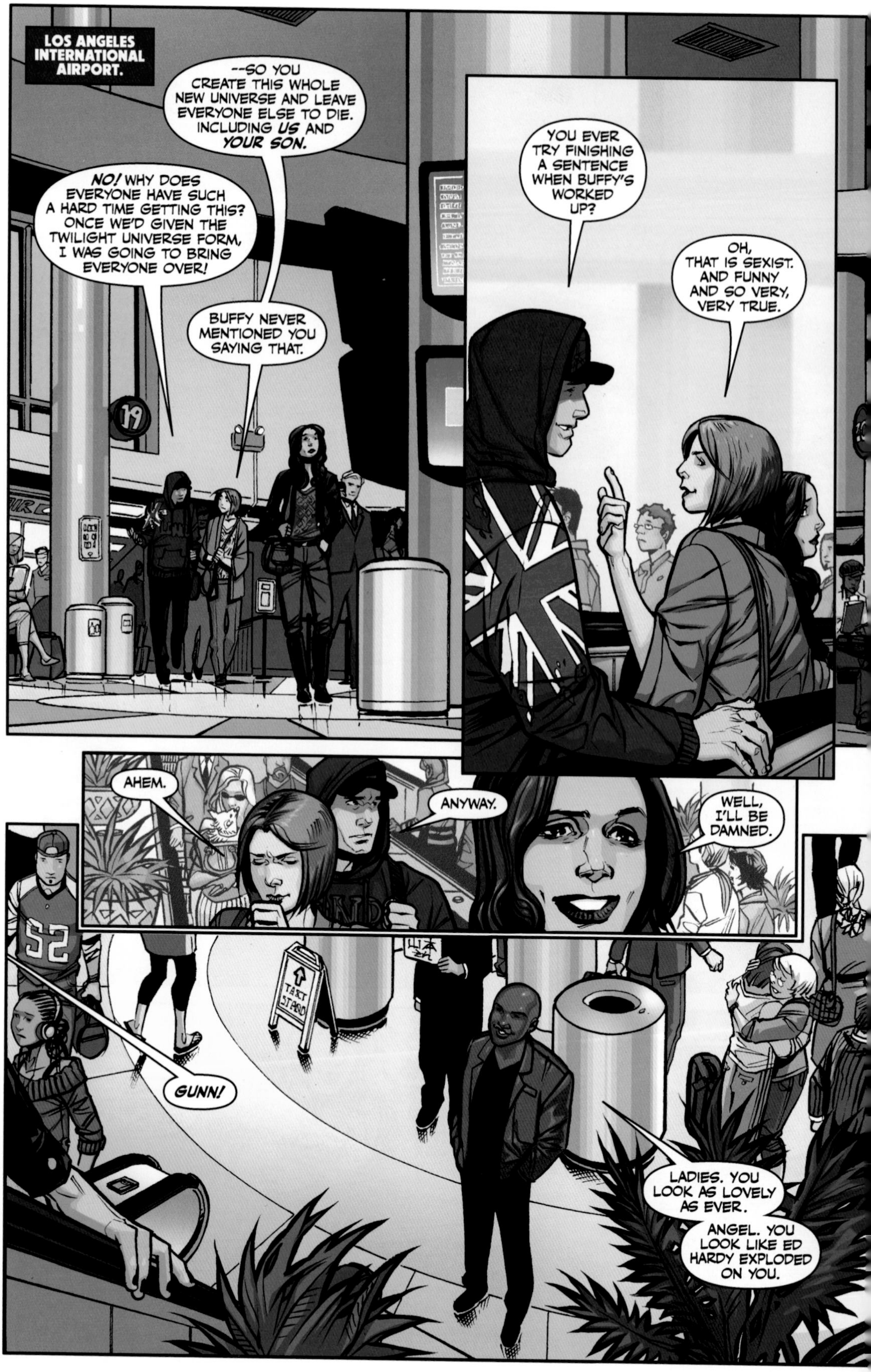
LOS ANGELES INTERNATIONAL AIRPORT.
--SO YOU CREATE THIS WHOLE NEW UNIVERSE AND LEAVE EVERYONE ELSE TO DIE. INCLUDING US AND YOUR SON.
NO! WHY DOES EVERYONE HAVE SUCH A HARD TIME GETTING THIS? ONCE WE'D GIVEN THE TWILIGHT UNIVERSE FORM, I WAS GOING TO BRING EVERYONE OVER!
BUFFY NEVER MENTIONED YOU SAYING THAT.
YOU EVER TRY FINISHING A SENTENCE WHEN BUFFY'S WORKED UP?
OH, THAT IS SEXIST. AND FUNNY AND SO VERY, VERY TRUE.
AHEM.
ANYWAY.
WELL, I'LL BE DAMNED.
GUNN!
LADIES. YOU LOOK AS LOVELY AS EVER.
ANGEL. YOU LOOK LIKE ED HARDY EXPLODED ON YOU.

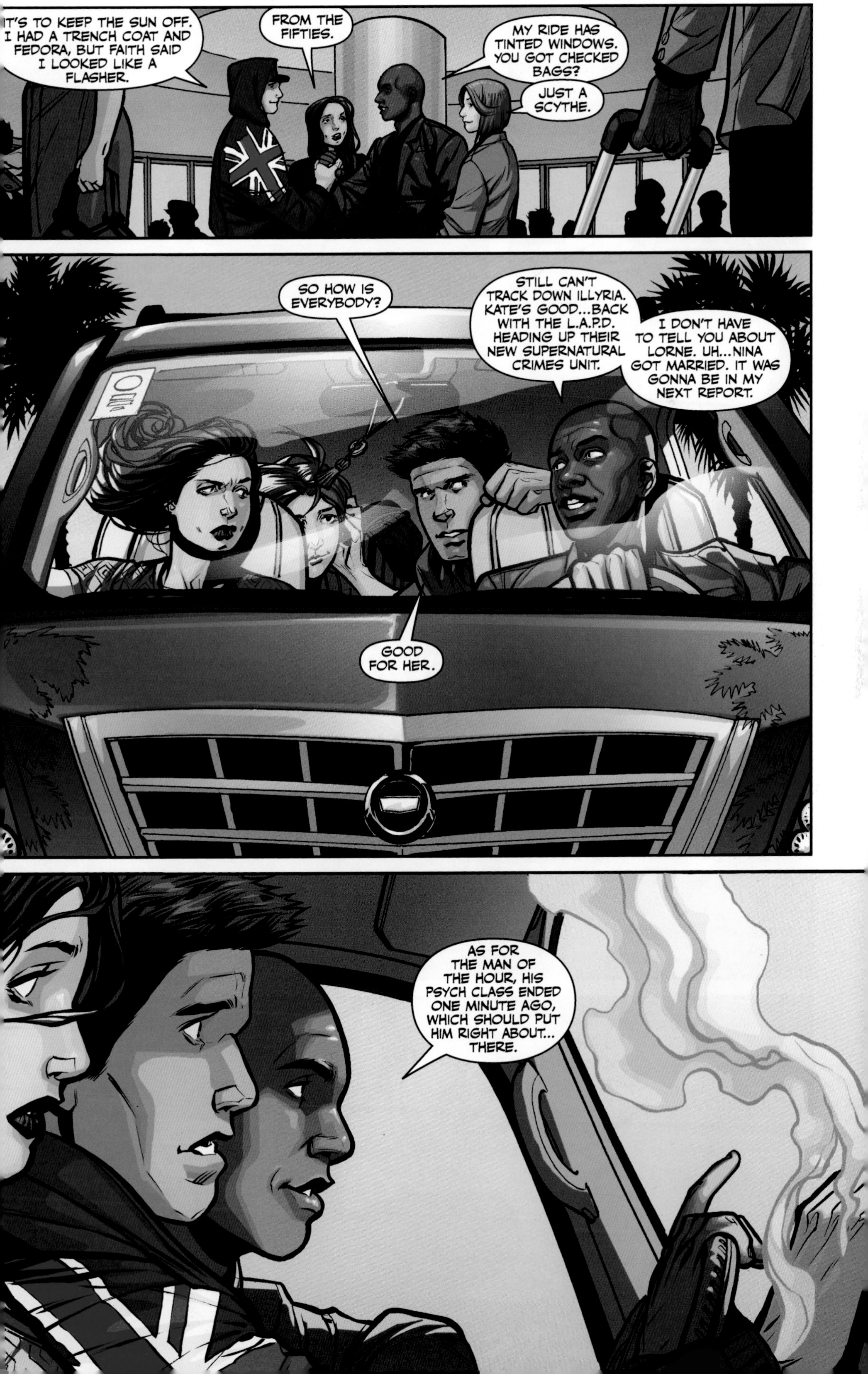
IT'S TO KEEP THE SUN OFF. I HAD A TRENCH COAT AND FEDORA, BUT FAITH SAID I LOOKED LIKE A FLASHER.
FROM THE FIFTIES.
MY RIDE HAS TINTED WINDOWS. YOU GOT CHECKED BAGS?
JUST A SCYTHE.
SO HOW IS EVERYBODY?
STILL CAN'T TRACK DOWN ILLYRIA. KATE'S GOOD...BACK WITH THE L.A.P.D. HEADING UP THEIR NEW SUPERNATURAL CRIMES UNIT.
I DON'T HAVE TO TELL YOU ABOUT LORNE. UH...NINA GOT MARRIED. IT WAS GONNA BE IN MY NEXT REPORT.
GOOD FOR HER.
AS FOR THE MAN OF THE HOUR, HIS PSYCH CLASS ENDED ONE MINUTE AGO, WHICH SHOULD PUT HIM RIGHT ABOUT... THERE.

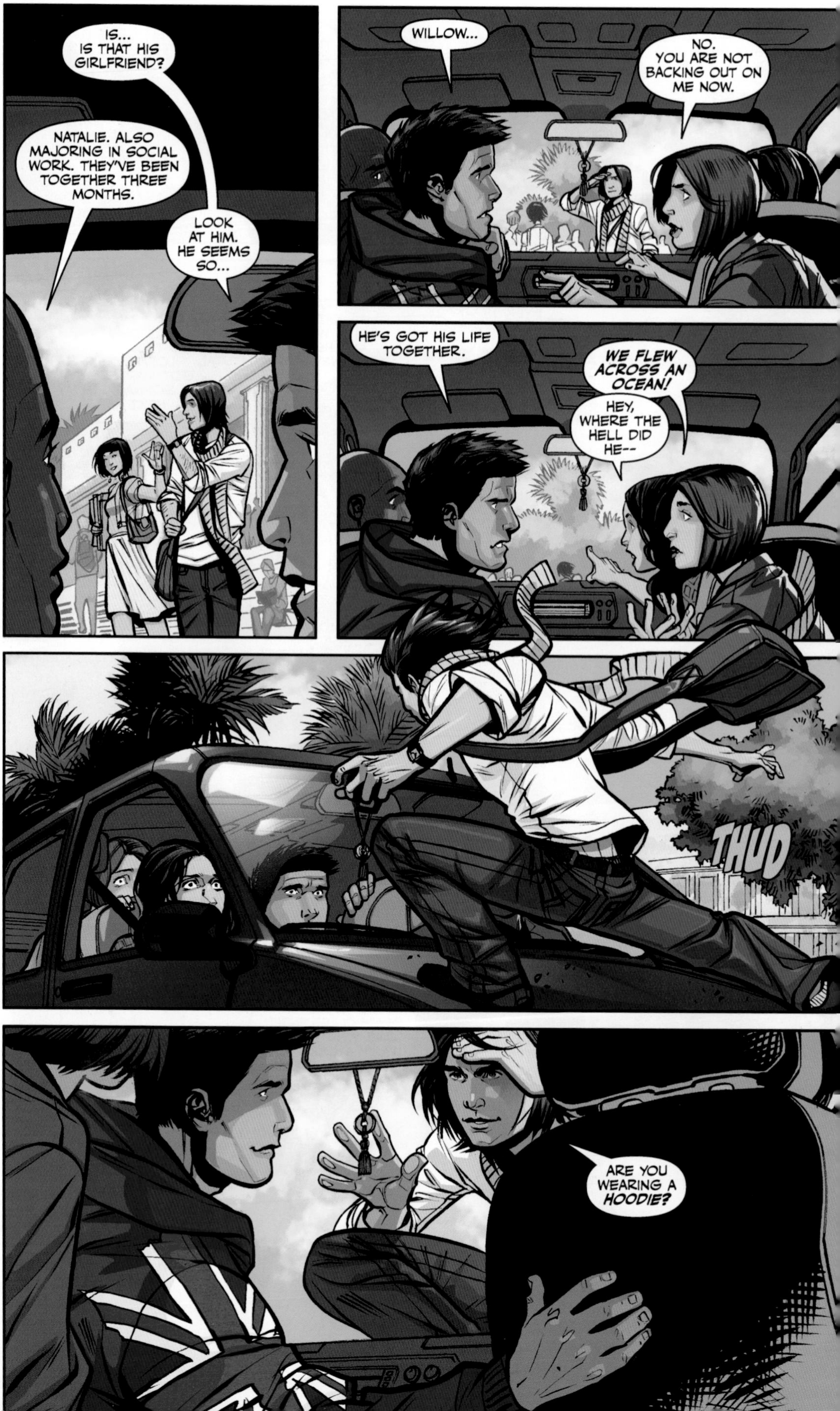
IS... IS THAT HIS GIRLFRIEND?
NATALIE. ALSO MAJORING IN SOCIAL WORK. THEY'VE BEEN TOGETHER THREE MONTHS.
LOOK AT HIM. HE SEEMS SO...
WILLOW...
NO. YOU ARE NOT BACKING OUT ON ME NOW.
HE'S GOT HIS LIFE TOGETHER.
WE FLEW ACROSS AN OCEAN!
HEY, WHERE THE HELL DID HE--
THUD
ARE YOU WEARING A HOODIE?

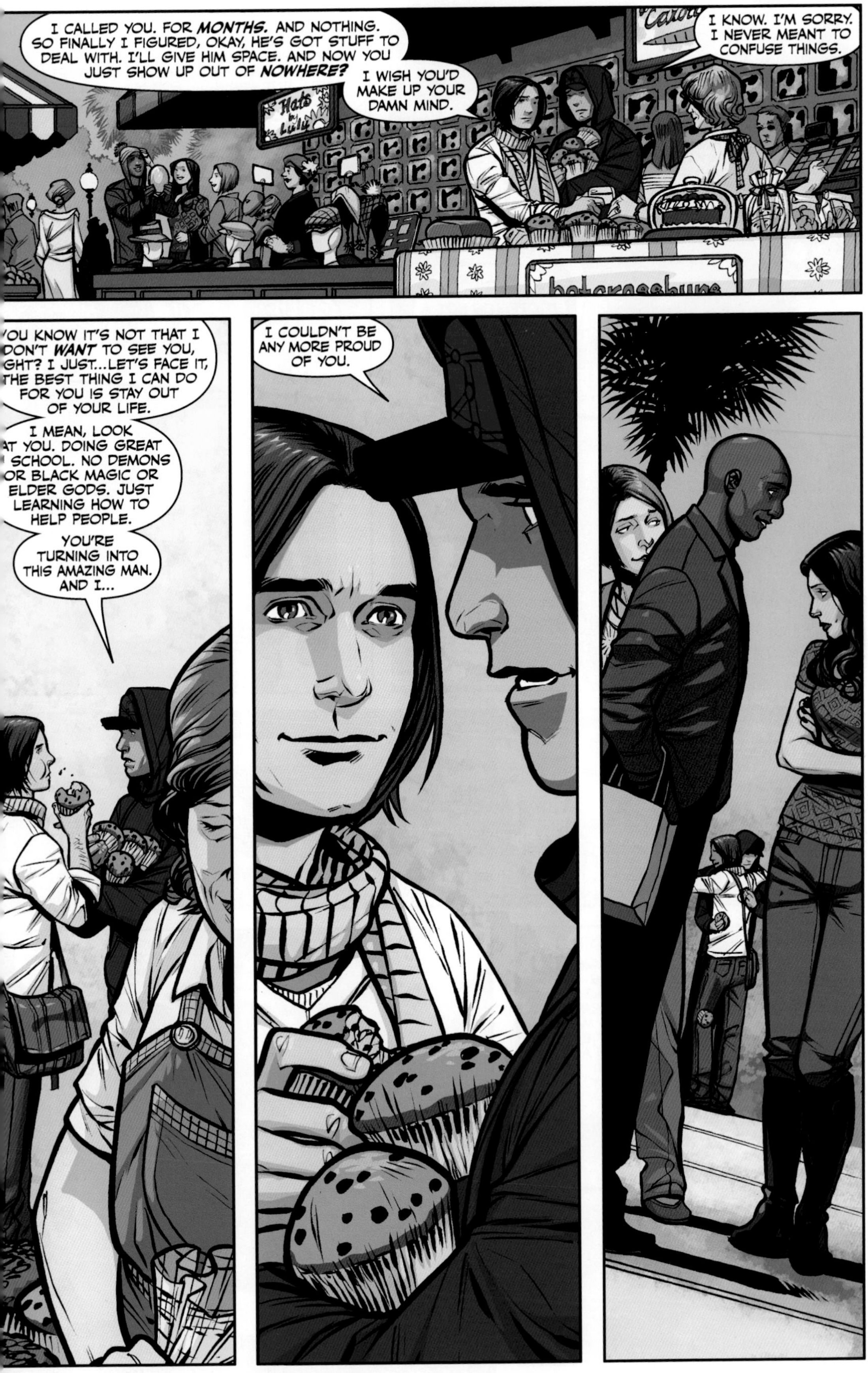
I CALLED YOU. FOR MONTHS. AND NOTHING. SO FINALLY I FIGURED, OKAY, HE'S GOT STUFF TO DEAL WITH. I'LL GIVE HIM SPACE. AND NOW YOU JUST SHOW UP OUT OF NOWHERE?
I WISH YOU'D MAKE UP YOUR DAMN MIND.
I KNOW. I'M SORRY. I NEVER MEANT TO CONFUSE THINGS.
OU KNOW IT'S NOT THAT I DON'T WANT TO SEE YOU, GHT? I JUST...LET'S FACE IT, THE BEST THING I CAN DO FOR YOU IS STAY OUT OF YOUR LIFE.
I MEAN, LOOK AT YOU. DOING GREAT SCHOOL. NO DEMONS OR BLACK MAGIC OR ELDER GODS. JUST LEARNING HOW TO HELP PEOPLE.
YOU'RE TURNING INTO THIS AMAZING MAN. AND I...
I COULDN'T BE ANY MORE PROUD OF YOU.

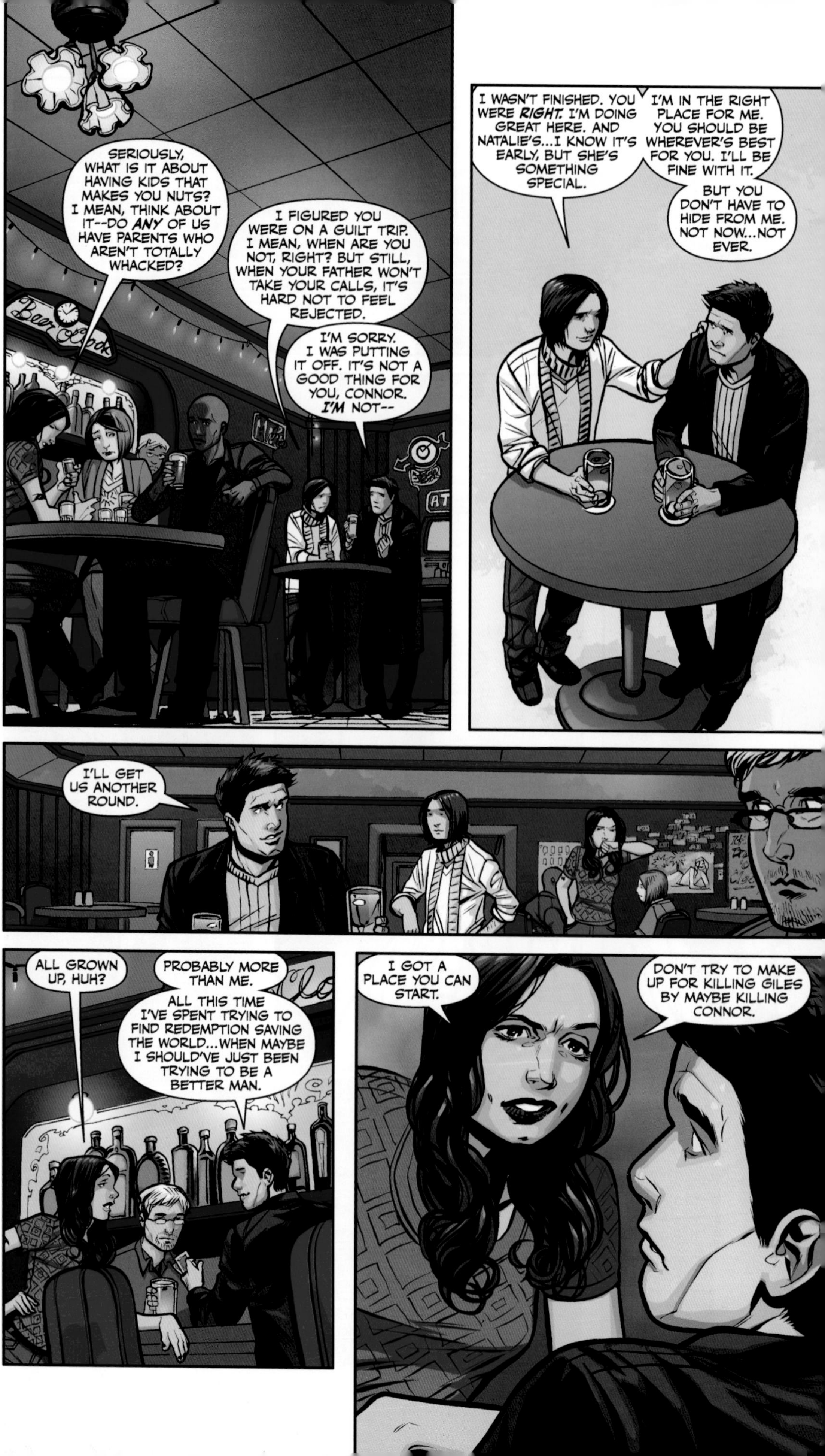

SERIOUSLY, WHAT IS IT ABOUT HAVING KIDS THAT MAKES YOU NUTS? I MEAN, THINK ABOUT IT--DO ANY OF US HAVE PARENTS WHO AREN'T TOTALLY WHACKED?
I FIGURED YOU WERE ON A GUILT TRIP. I MEAN, WHEN ARE YOU NOT, RIGHT? BUT STILL, WHEN YOUR FATHER WON'T TAKE YOUR CALLS, IT'S HARD NOT TO FEEL REJECTED.
I'M SORRY. I WAS PUTTING IT OFF. IT'S NOT A GOOD THING FOR YOU, CONNOR. I'M NOT--
I WASN'T FINISHED. YOU WERE RIGHT. I'M DOING GREAT HERE. AND NATALIE'S...I KNOW IT'S EARLY, BUT SHE'S SOMETHING SPECIAL.
I'M IN THE RIGHT PLACE FOR ME. YOU SHOULD BE WHEREVER'S BEST FOR YOU. I'LL BE FINE WITH IT.
BUT YOU DON'T HAVE TO HIDE FROM ME. NOT NOW...NOT EVER.
I'LL GET US ANOTHER ROUND.
ALL GROWN UP, HUH?
PROBABLY MORE THAN ME.
ALL THIS TIME I'VE SPENT TRYING TO FIND REDEMPTION SAVING THE WORLD...WHEN MAYBE I SHOULD'VE JUST BEEN TRYING TO BE A BETTER MAN.
I GOT A PLACE YOU CAN START.
DON'T TRY TO MAKE UP FOR KILLING GILES BY MAYBE KILLING CONNOR.

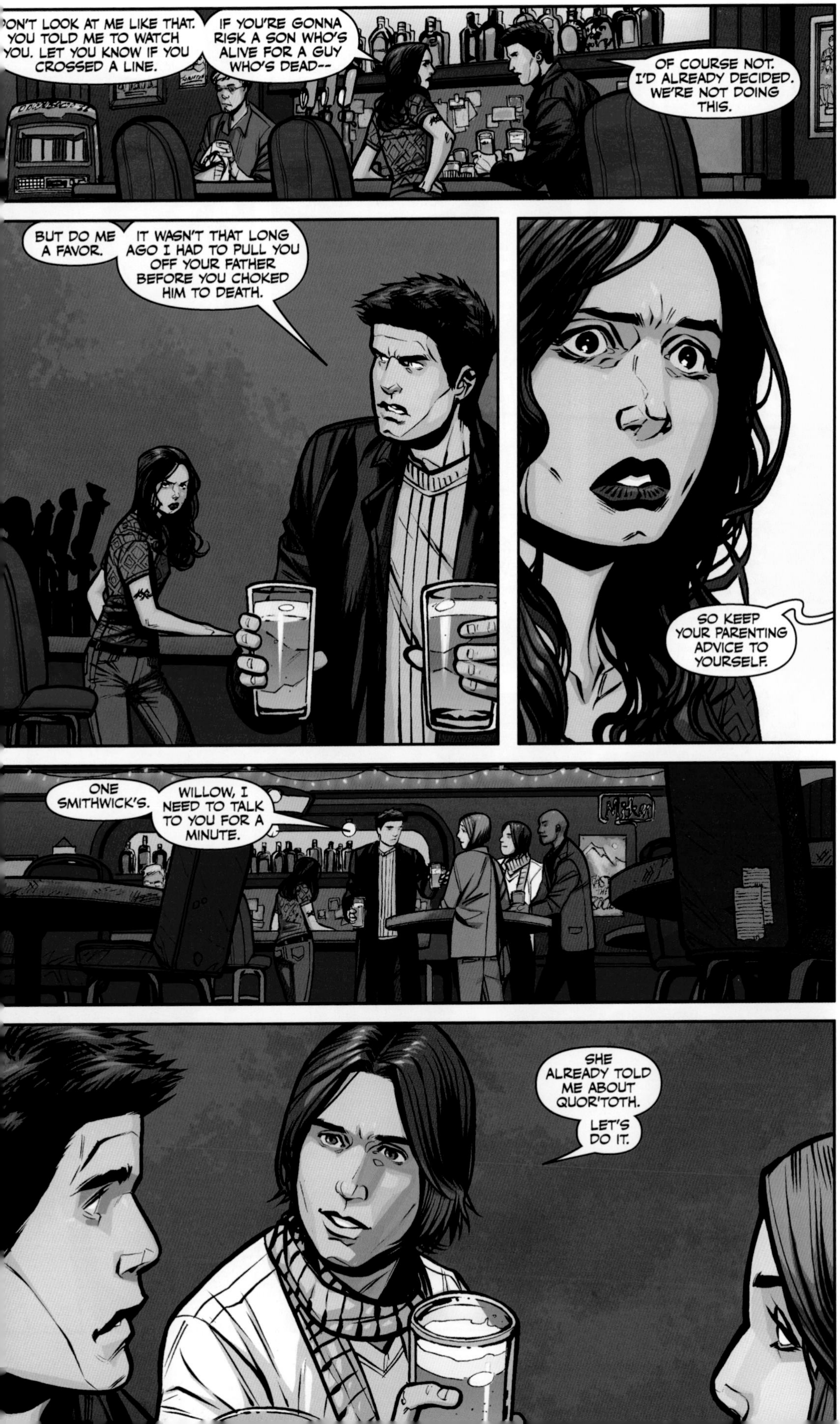
DON'T LOOK AT ME LIKE THAT. YOU TOLD ME TO WATCH YOU. LET YOU KNOW IF YOU CROSSED A LINE.
IF YOU'RE GONNA RISK A SON WHO'S ALIVE FOR A GUY WHO'S DEAD--
OF COURSE NOT. I'D ALREADY DECIDED. WE'RE NOT DOING THIS.
BUT DO ME A FAVOR.
IT WASN'T THAT LONG AGO I HAD TO PULL YOU OFF YOUR FATHER BEFORE YOU CHOKED HIM TO DEATH.
SO KEEP YOUR PARENTING ADVICE TO YOURSELF.
ONE SMITHWICK'S.
WILLOW, I NEED TO TALK TO YOU FOR A MINUTE.
SHE ALREADY TOLD ME ABOUT QUOR'TOTH.
LET'S DO IT.

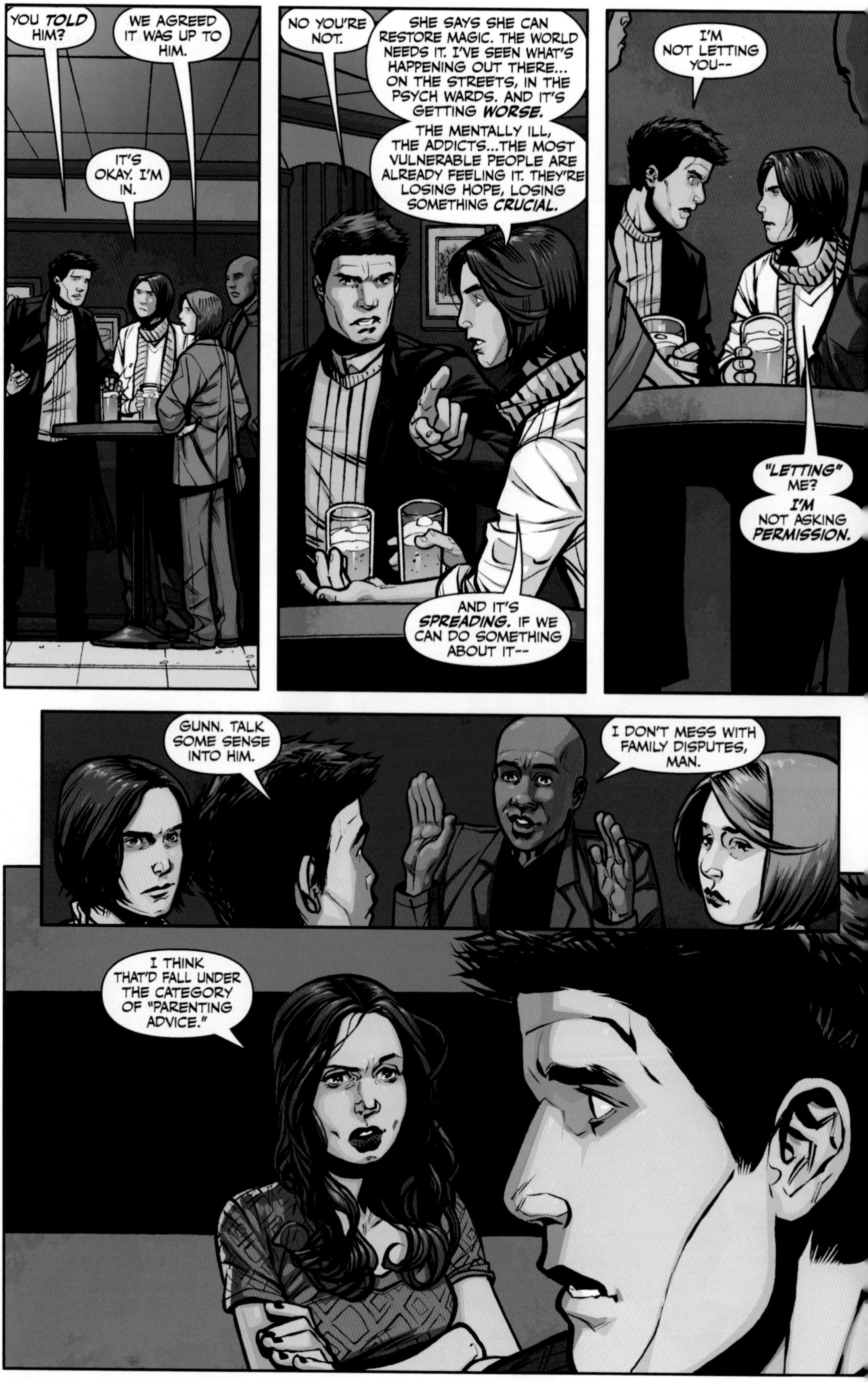
YOU TOLD HIM?
WE AGREED IT WAS UP TO HIM.
IT'S OKAY. I'M IN.
NO YOU'RE NOT.
SHE SAYS SHE CAN RESTORE MAGIC. THE WORLD NEEDS IT. I'VE SEEN WHAT'S HAPPENING OUT THERE... ON THE STREETS, IN THE PSYCH WARDS. AND IT'S GETTING WORSE.
THE MENTALLY ILL, THE ADDICTS...THE MOST VULNERABLE PEOPLE ARE ALREADY FEELING IT. THEY'RE LOSING HOPE, LOSING SOMETHING CRUCIAL.
AND IT'S SPREADING. IF WE CAN DO SOMETHING ABOUT IT--
I'M NOT LETTING YOU--
"LETTING" ME? I'M NOT ASKING PERMISSION.
GUNN. TALK SOME SENSE INTO HIM.
I DON'T MESS WITH FAMILY DISPUTES, MAN.
I THINK THAT'D FALL UNDER THE CATEGORY OF "PARENTING ADVICE."

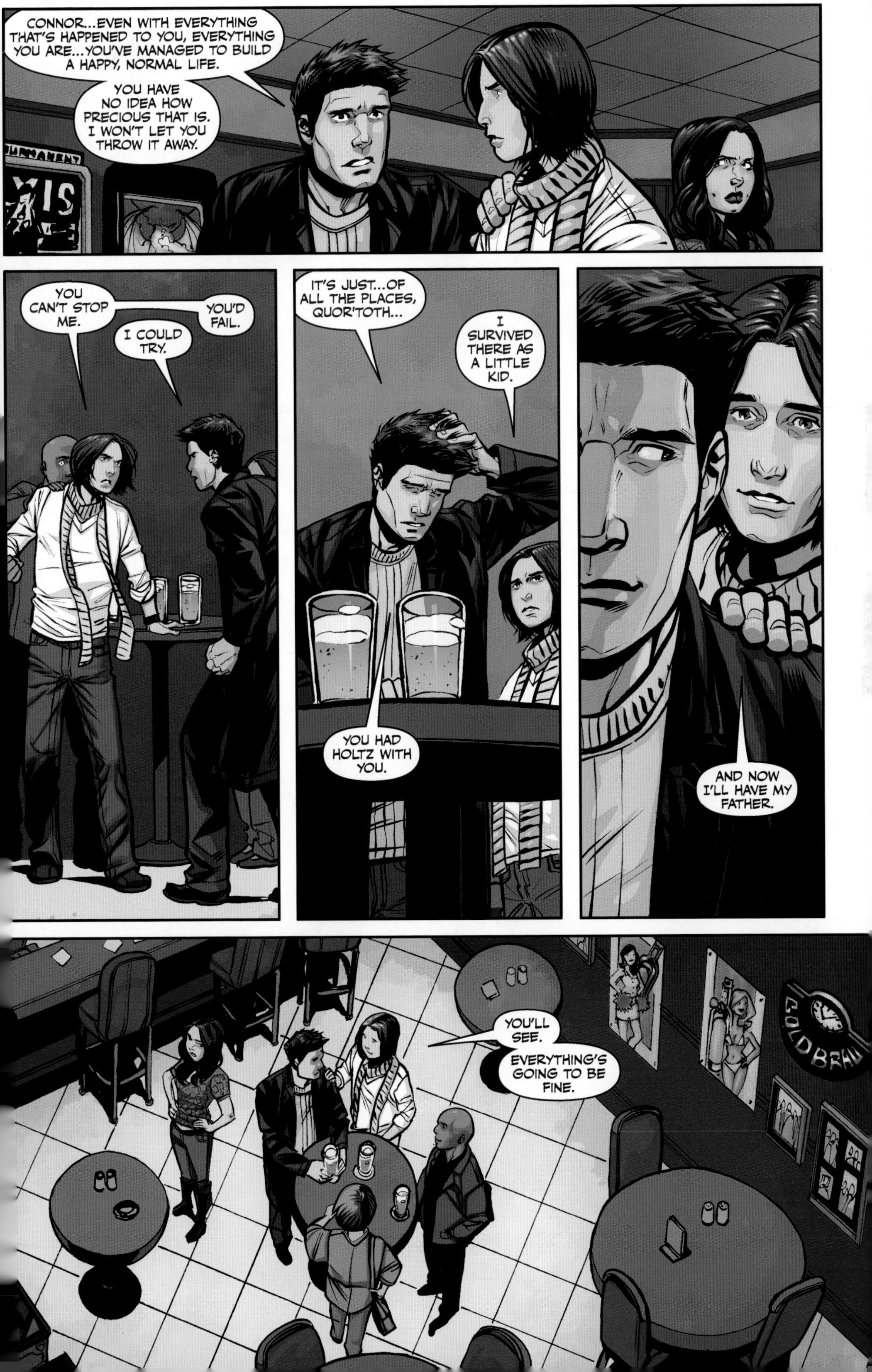
CONNOR...EVEN WITH EVERYTHING THAT'S HAPPENED TO YOU, EVERYTHING YOU ARE...YOU'VE MANAGED TO BUILD A HAPPY, NORMAL LIFE.
YOU HAVE NO IDEA HOW PRECIOUS THAT IS. I WON'T LET YOU THROW IT AWAY.
YOU CAN'T STOP ME.
YOU'D FAIL.
I COULD TRY.
IT'S JUST...OF ALL THE PLACES, QUOR'TOTH...
I SURVIVED THERE AS A LITTLE KID.
YOU HAD HOLTZ WITH YOU.
AND NOW I'LL HAVE MY FATHER.
YOU'LL SEE.
EVERYTHING'S GOING TO BE FINE.

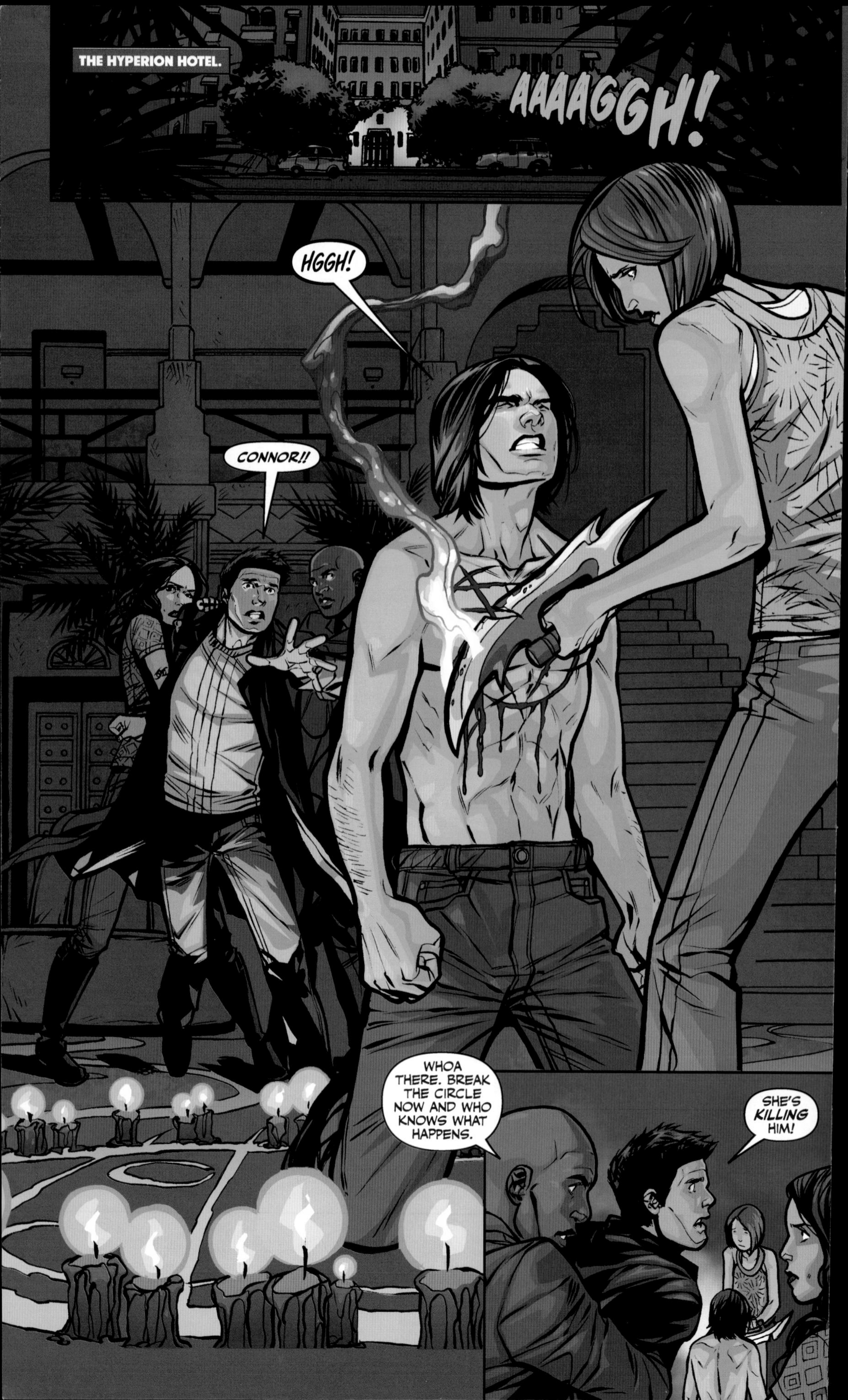
THE HYPERION HOTEL.
AAAAGGH!
HGGH!
CONNOR!!
WHOA THERE. BREAK THE CIRCLE NOW AND WHO KNOWS WHAT HAPPENS.
SHE'S *KILLING* HIM!

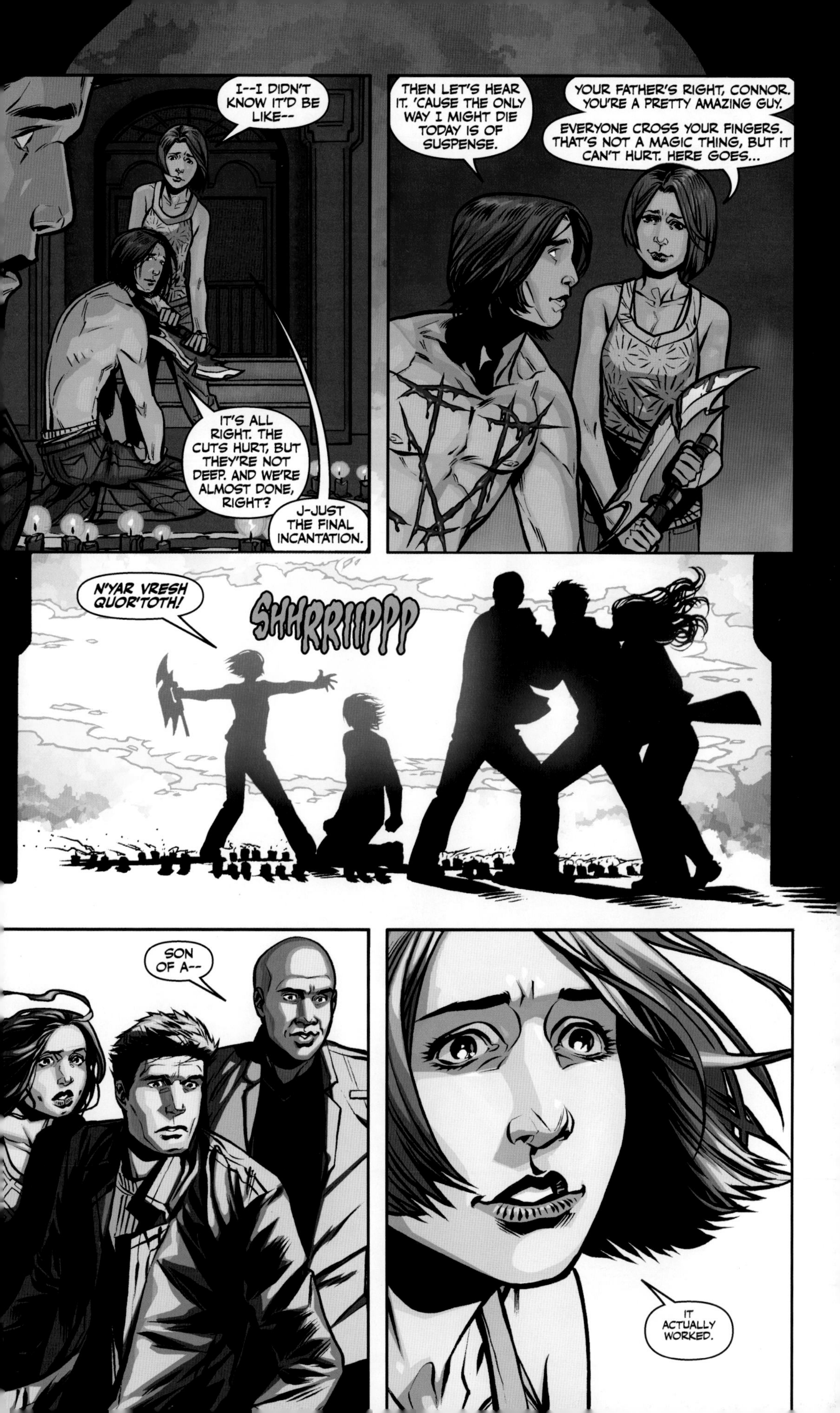
I--I DIDN'T KNOW IT'D BE LIKE--
IT'S ALL RIGHT. THE CUTS HURT, BUT THEY'RE NOT DEEP. AND WE'RE ALMOST DONE, RIGHT?
J-JUST THE FINAL INCANTATION.
THEN LET'S HEAR IT. 'CAUSE THE ONLY WAY I MIGHT DIE TODAY IS OF SUSPENSE.
YOUR FATHER'S RIGHT, CONNOR. YOU'RE A PRETTY AMAZING GUY.
EVERYONE CROSS YOUR FINGERS. THAT'S NOT A MAGIC THING, BUT IT CAN'T HURT. HERE GOES...
N'YAR VRESH QUOR'TOTH!
SHHRRIIPPP
SON OF A--
IT ACTUALLY WORKED.

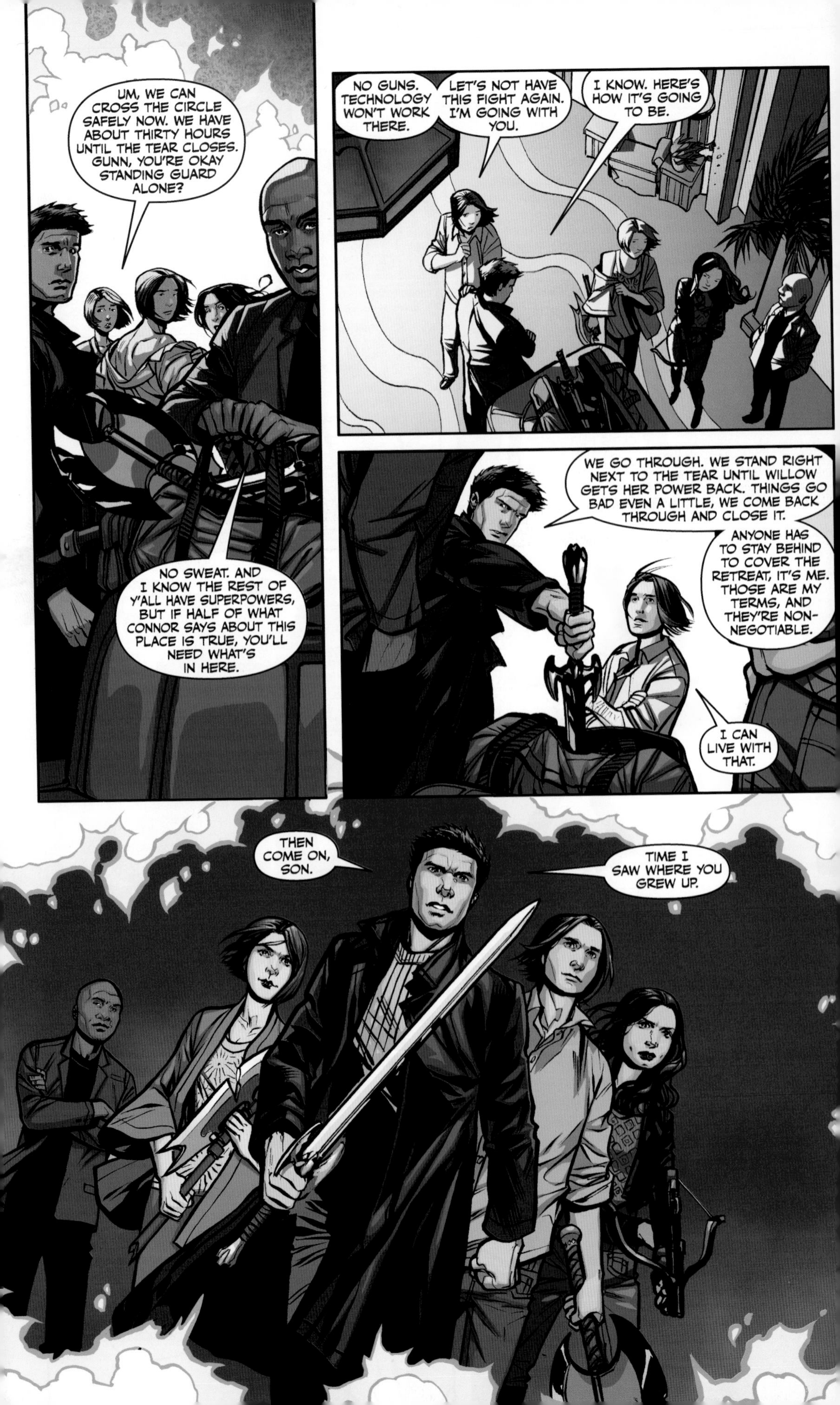
UM, WE CAN CROSS THE CIRCLE SAFELY NOW. WE HAVE ABOUT THIRTY HOURS UNTIL THE TEAR CLOSES. GUNN, YOU'RE OKAY STANDING GUARD ALONE?
NO SWEAT. AND I KNOW THE REST OF Y'ALL HAVE SUPERPOWERS, BUT IF HALF OF WHAT CONNOR SAYS ABOUT THIS PLACE IS TRUE, YOU'LL NEED WHAT'S IN HERE.
NO GUNS. TECHNOLOGY WON'T WORK THERE.
LET'S NOT HAVE THIS FIGHT AGAIN. I'M GOING WITH YOU.
I KNOW. HERE'S HOW IT'S GOING TO BE.
WE GO THROUGH. WE STAND RIGHT NEXT TO THE TEAR UNTIL WILLOW GETS HER POWER BACK. THINGS GO BAD EVEN A LITTLE, WE COME BACK THROUGH AND CLOSE IT.
ANYONE HAS TO STAY BEHIND TO COVER THE RETREAT, IT'S ME. THOSE ARE MY TERMS, AND THEY'RE NON-NEGOTIABLE.
I CAN LIVE WITH THAT.
THEN COME ON, SON.
TIME I SAW WHERE YOU GREW UP.

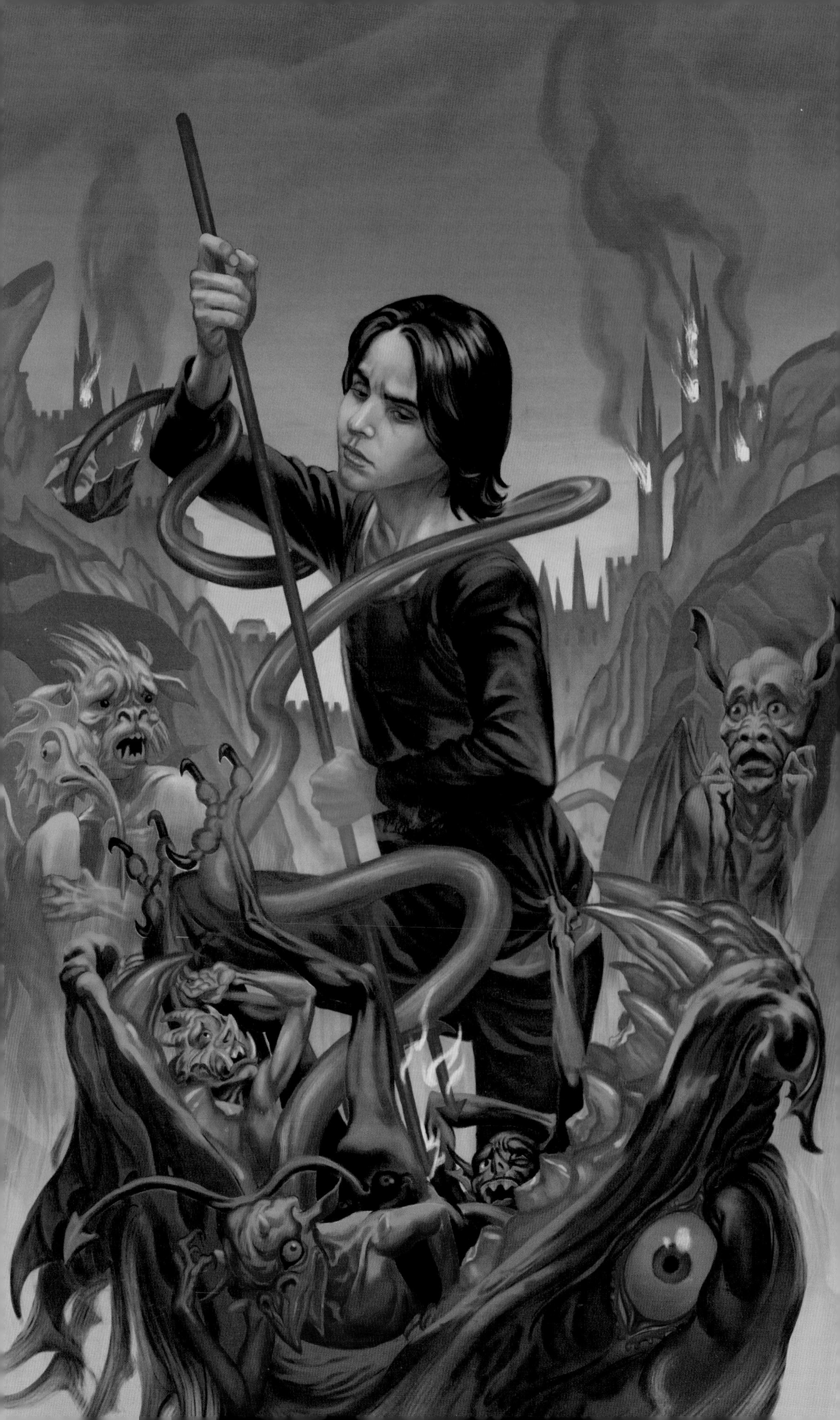

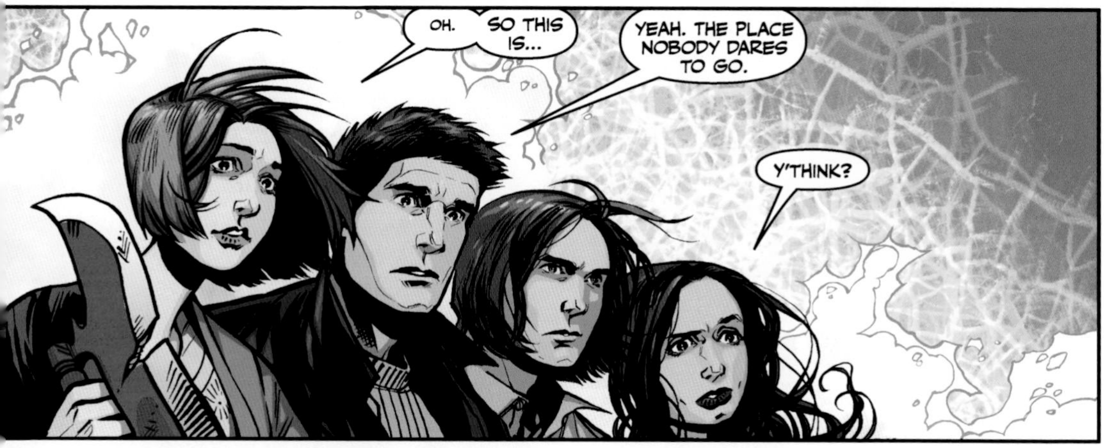
OH.
SO THIS IS...
YEAH. THE PLACE NOBODY DARES TO GO.
Y'THINK?

FAMILY REUNION

PART TWO

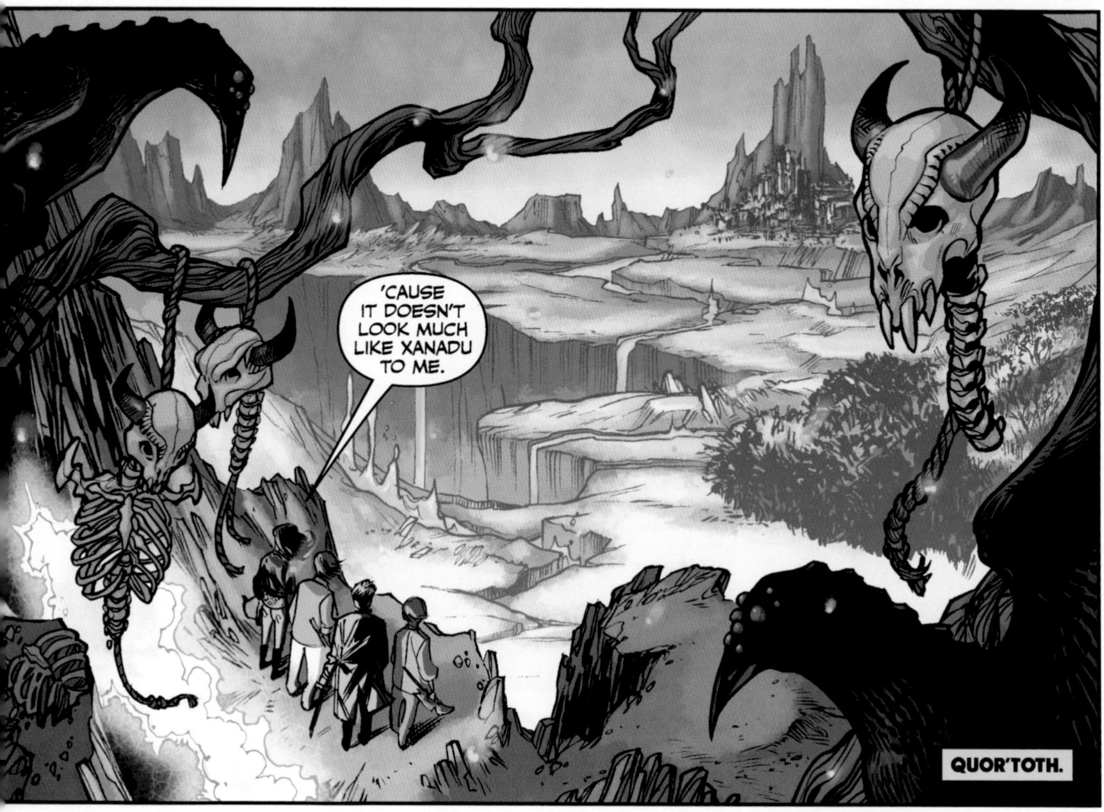
'CAUSE IT DOESN'T LOOK MUCH LIKE XANADU TO ME.
QUOR'TOTH.

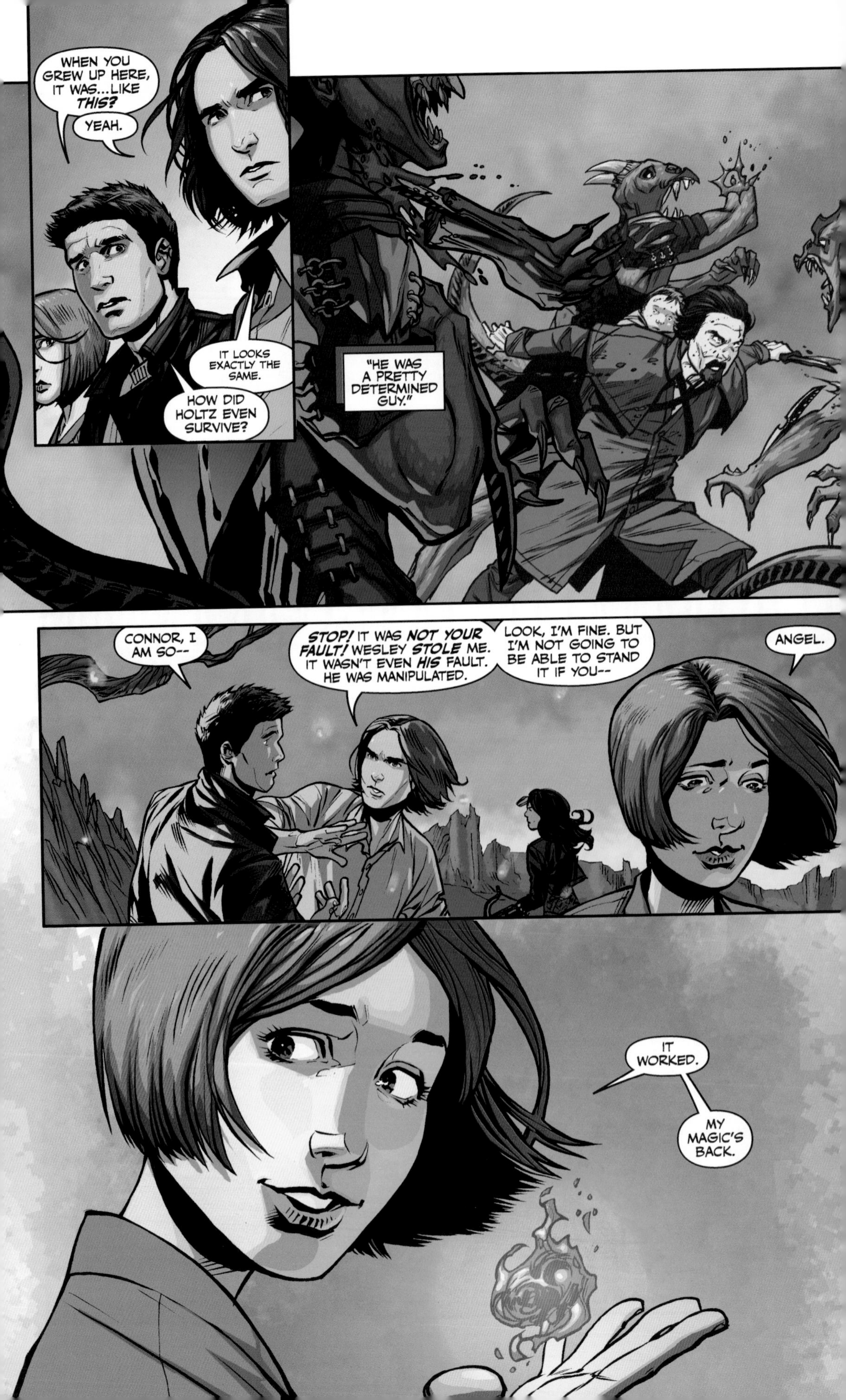
WHEN YOU GREW UP HERE, IT WAS...LIKE *THIS?*
YEAH.
IT LOOKS EXACTLY THE SAME.
HOW DID HOLTZ EVEN SURVIVE?
"HE WAS A PRETTY DETERMINED GUY."
CONNOR, I AM SO--
STOP! IT WAS *NOT YOUR FAULT!* WESLEY *STOLE* ME. IT WASN'T EVEN *HIS* FAULT. HE WAS MANIPULATED.
LOOK, I'M FINE. BUT I'M NOT GOING TO BE ABLE TO STAND IT IF YOU--
ANGEL.
IT WORKED.
MY MAGIC'S BACK.

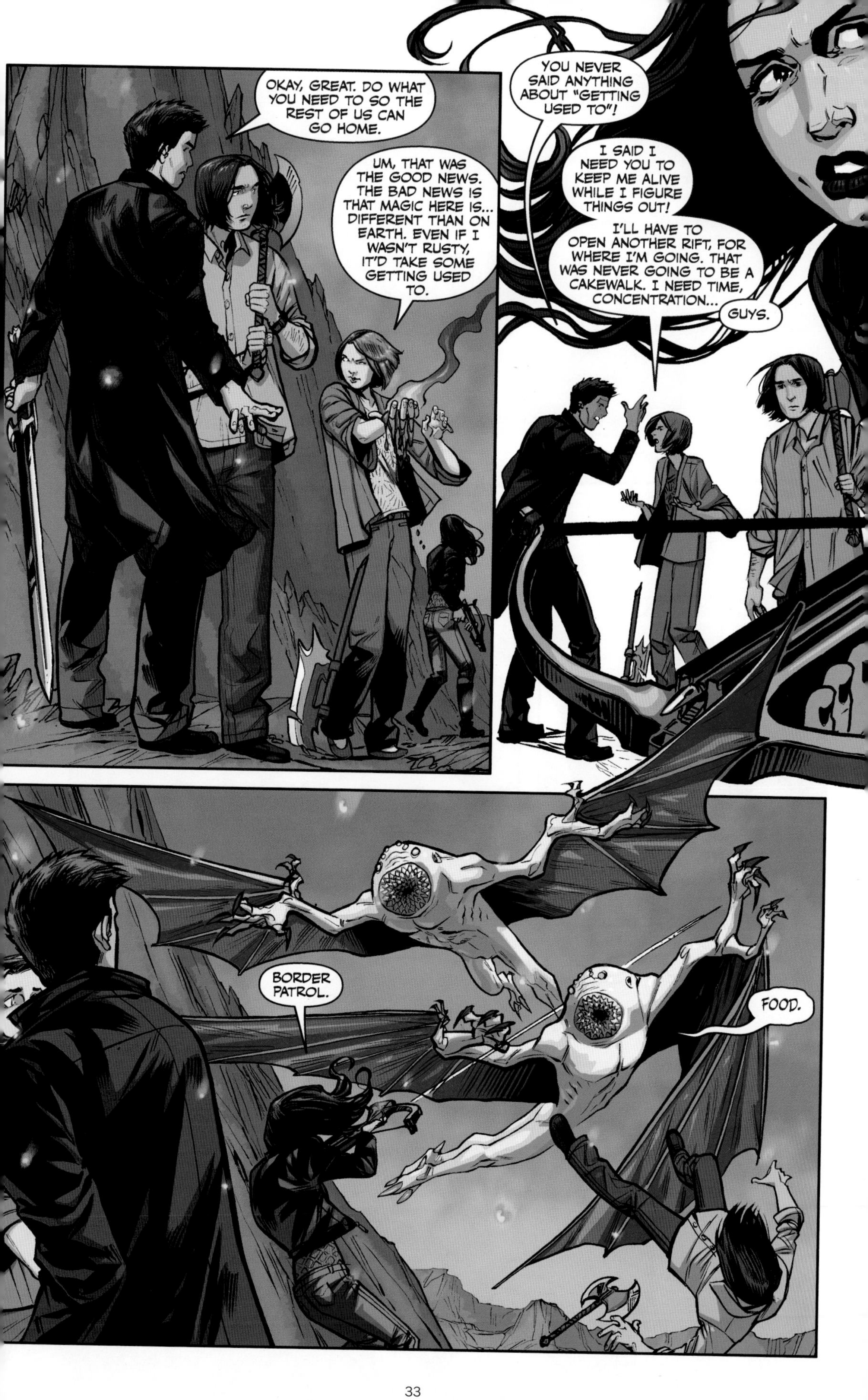
OKAY, GREAT. DO WHAT YOU NEED TO SO THE REST OF US CAN GO HOME.
UM, THAT WAS THE GOOD NEWS. THE BAD NEWS IS THAT MAGIC HERE IS... DIFFERENT THAN ON EARTH. EVEN IF I WASN'T RUSTY, IT'D TAKE SOME GETTING USED TO.
YOU NEVER SAID ANYTHING ABOUT "GETTING USED TO"!
I SAID I NEED YOU TO KEEP ME ALIVE WHILE I FIGURE THINGS OUT!
I'LL HAVE TO OPEN ANOTHER RIFT, FOR WHERE I'M GOING. THAT WAS NEVER GOING TO BE A CAKEWALK. I NEED TIME, CONCENTRATION...
GUYS.
BORDER PATROL.
FOOD.

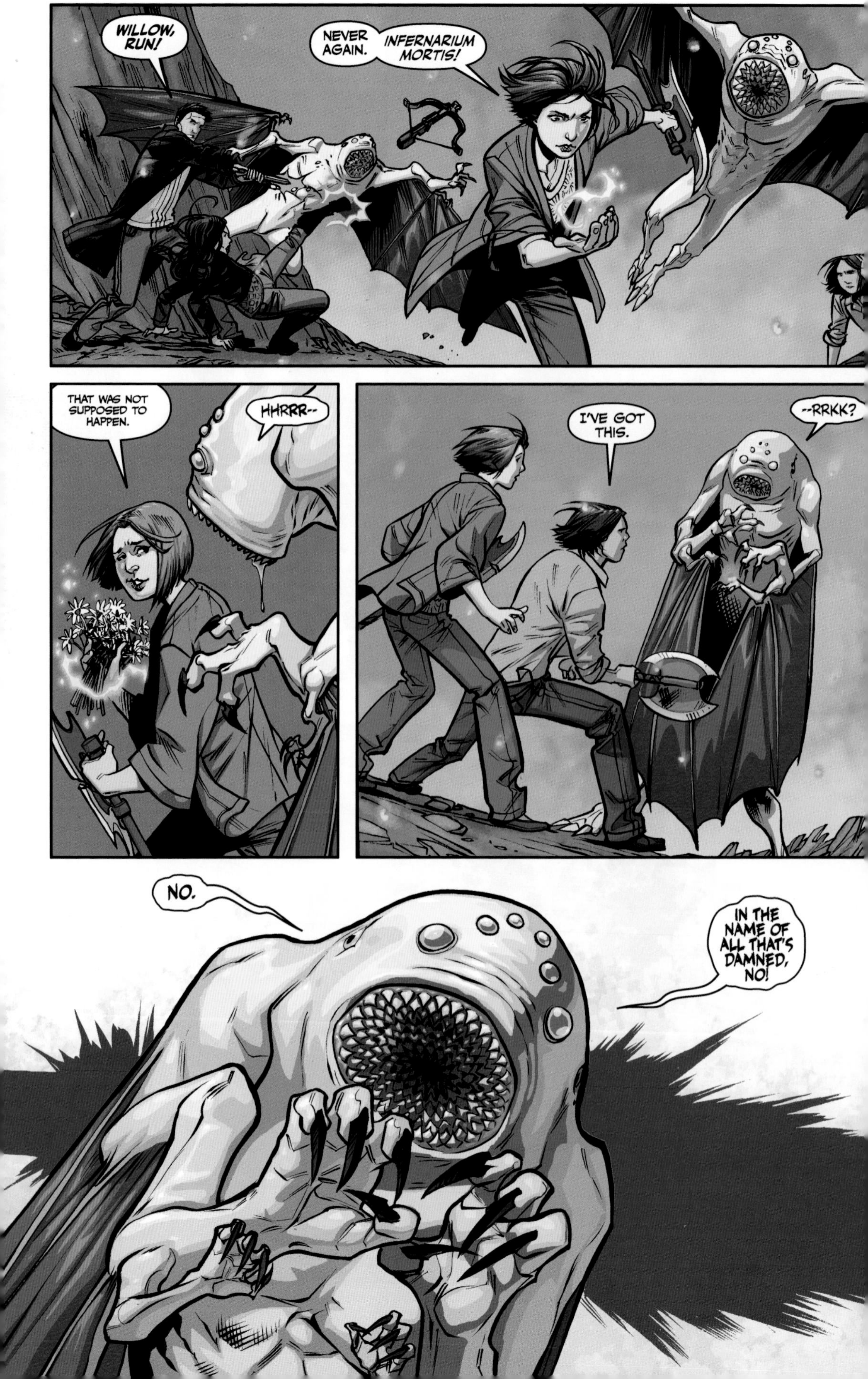
WILLOW, RUN!
NEVER AGAIN.
INFERNARIUM MORTIS!
THAT WAS NOT SUPPOSED TO HAPPEN.
HHRRR--
I'VE GOT THIS.
--RRKK?
NO.
IN THE NAME OF ALL THAT'S DAMNED, NO!

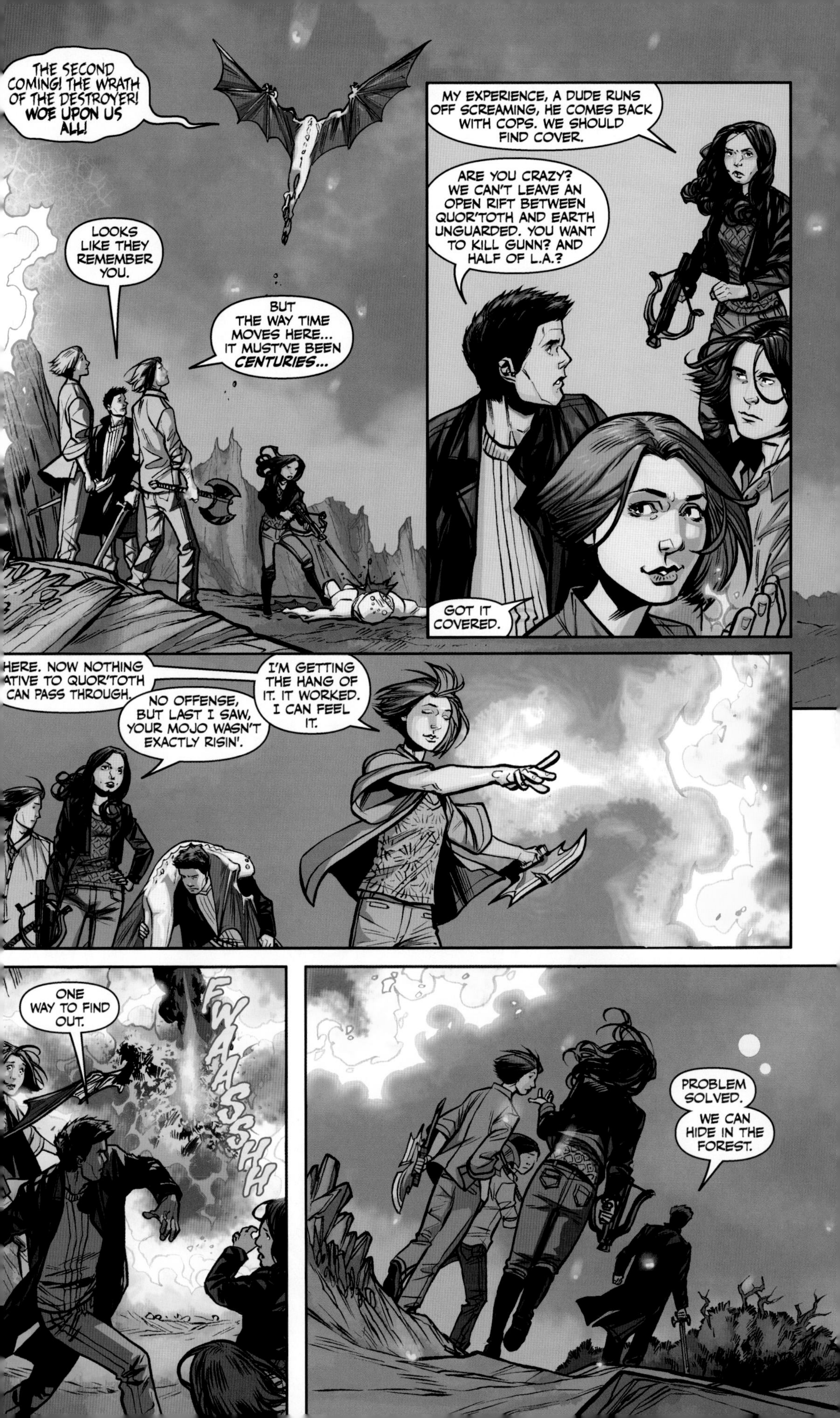
THE SECOND COMING! THE WRATH OF THE DESTROYER! WOE UPON US ALL!
LOOKS LIKE THEY REMEMBER YOU.
BUT THE WAY TIME MOVES HERE... IT MUST'VE BEEN CENTURIES...
MY EXPERIENCE, A DUDE RUNS OFF SCREAMING, HE COMES BACK WITH COPS. WE SHOULD FIND COVER.
ARE YOU CRAZY? WE CAN'T LEAVE AN OPEN RIFT BETWEEN QUOR'TOTH AND EARTH UNGUARDED. YOU WANT TO KILL GUNN? AND HALF OF L.A.?
GOT IT COVERED.
HERE. NOW NOTHING ATIVE TO QUOR'TOTH CAN PASS THROUGH.
NO OFFENSE, BUT LAST I SAW, YOUR MOJO WASN'T EXACTLY RISIN'.
I'M GETTING THE HANG OF IT. IT WORKED. I CAN FEEL IT.
ONE WAY TO FIND OUT.
FWAASSHH
PROBLEM SOLVED.
WE CAN HIDE IN THE FOREST.

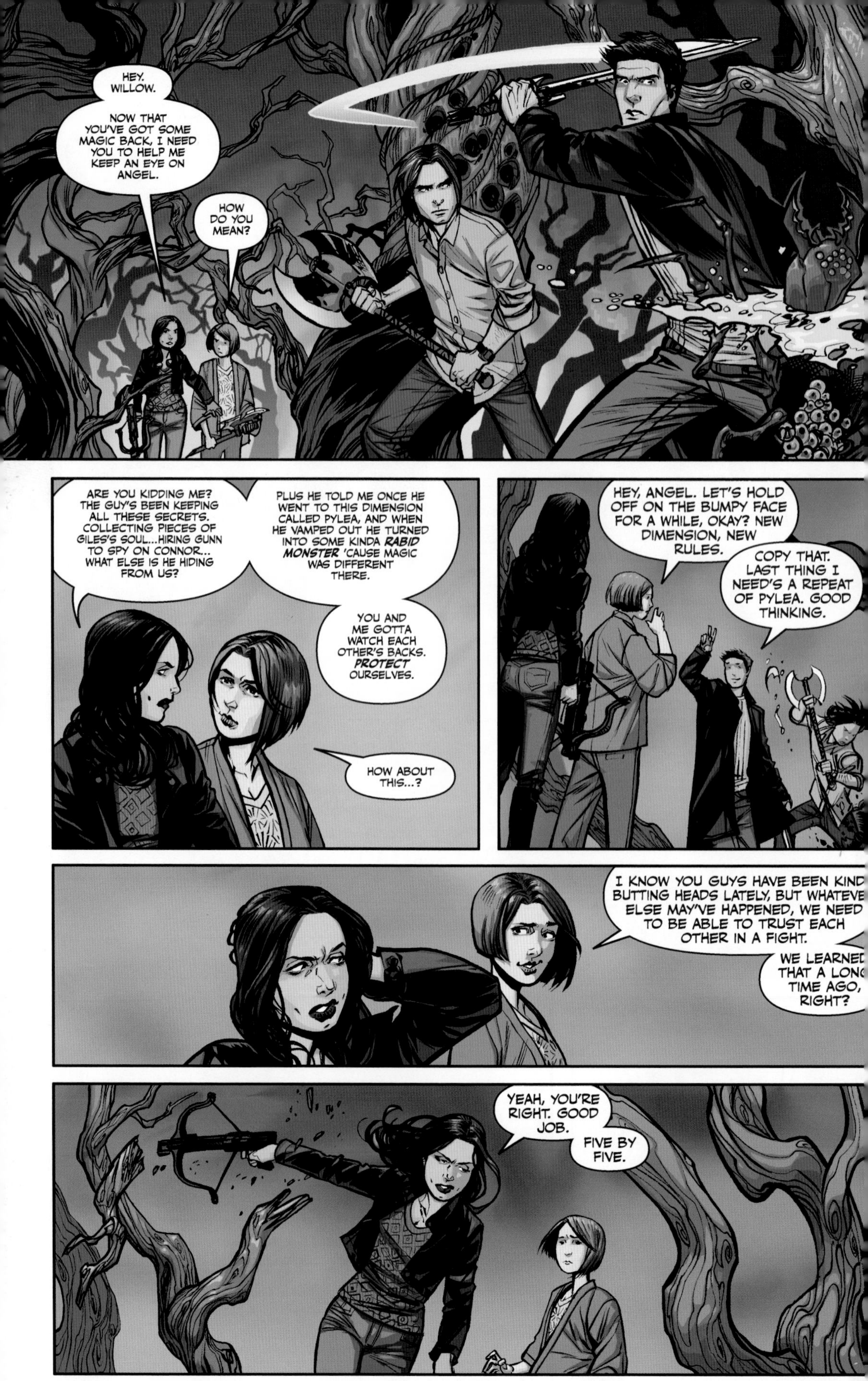
HEY. WILLOW.
NOW THAT YOU'VE GOT SOME MAGIC BACK, I NEED YOU TO HELP ME KEEP AN EYE ON ANGEL.
HOW DO YOU MEAN?
ARE YOU KIDDING ME? THE GUY'S BEEN KEEPING ALL THESE SECRETS. COLLECTING PIECES OF GILES'S SOUL...HIRING GUNN TO SPY ON CONNOR... WHAT ELSE IS HE HIDING FROM US?
PLUS HE TOLD ME ONCE HE WENT TO THIS DIMENSION CALLED PYLEA, AND WHEN HE VAMPED OUT HE TURNED INTO SOME KINDA *RABID MONSTER* 'CAUSE MAGIC WAS DIFFERENT THERE.
YOU AND ME GOTTA WATCH EACH OTHER'S BACKS. *PROTECT* OURSELVES.
HOW ABOUT THIS...?
HEY, ANGEL. LET'S HOLD OFF ON THE BUMPY FACE FOR A WHILE, OKAY? NEW DIMENSION, NEW RULES.
COPY THAT. LAST THING I NEED'S A REPEAT OF PYLEA. GOOD THINKING.
I KNOW YOU GUYS HAVE BEEN KIND BUTTING HEADS LATELY, BUT WHATEVE ELSE MAY'VE HAPPENED, WE NEED TO BE ABLE TO TRUST EACH OTHER IN A FIGHT.
WE LEARNED THAT A LONG TIME AGO, RIGHT?
YEAH, YOU'RE RIGHT. GOOD JOB.
FIVE BY FIVE.

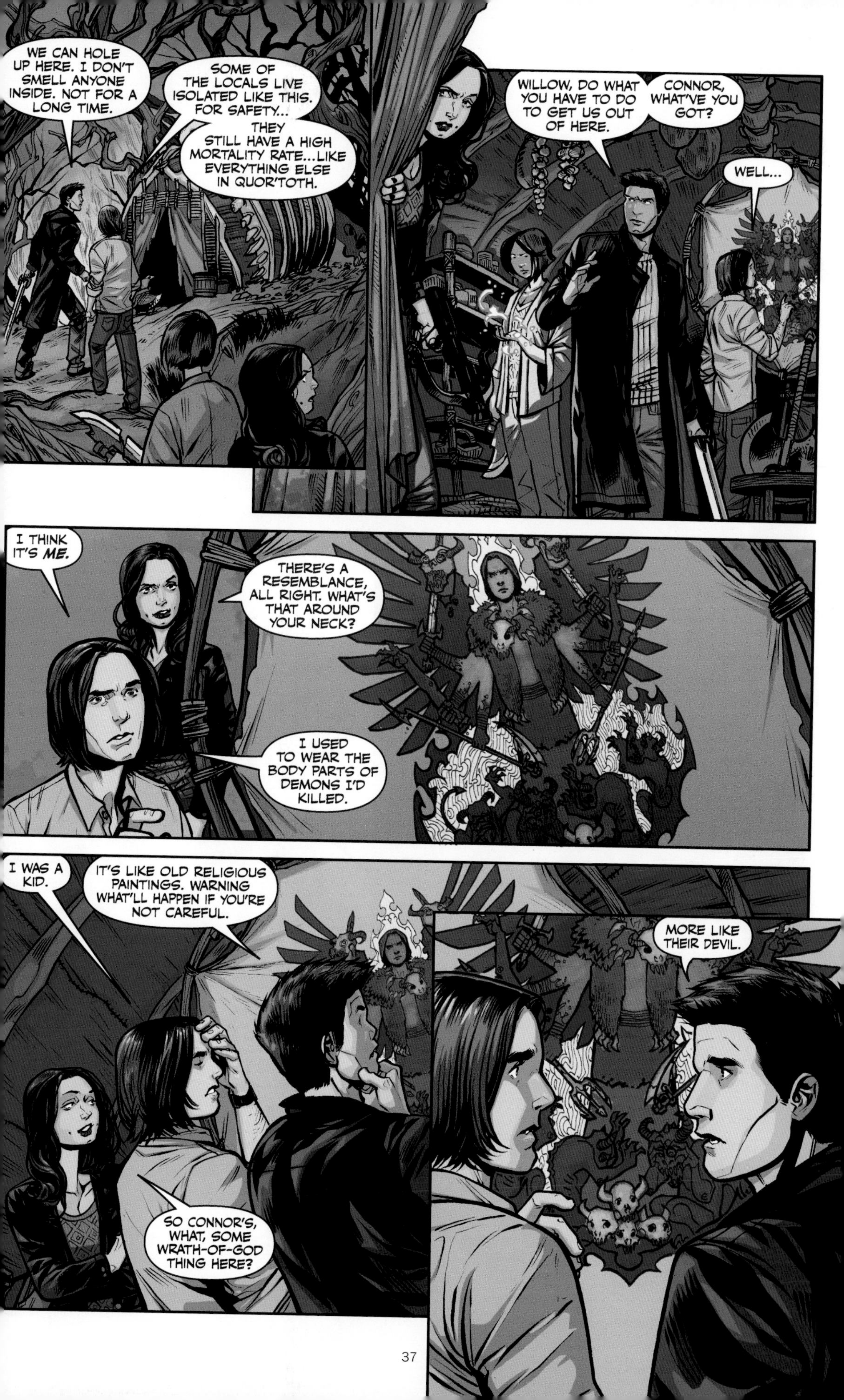
WE CAN HOLE UP HERE. I DON'T SMELL ANYONE INSIDE. NOT FOR A LONG TIME.
SOME OF THE LOCALS LIVE ISOLATED LIKE THIS. FOR SAFETY...
THEY STILL HAVE A HIGH MORTALITY RATE...LIKE EVERYTHING ELSE IN QUOR'TOTH.
WILLOW, DO WHAT YOU HAVE TO DO TO GET US OUT OF HERE.
CONNOR, WHAT'VE YOU GOT?
WELL...
I THINK IT'S *ME.*
THERE'S A RESEMBLANCE, ALL RIGHT. WHAT'S THAT AROUND YOUR NECK?
I USED TO WEAR THE BODY PARTS OF DEMONS I'D KILLED.
I WAS A KID.
IT'S LIKE OLD RELIGIOUS PAINTINGS. WARNING WHAT'LL HAPPEN IF YOU'RE NOT CAREFUL.
SO CONNOR'S, WHAT, SOME WRATH-OF-GOD THING HERE?
MORE LIKE THEIR DEVIL.

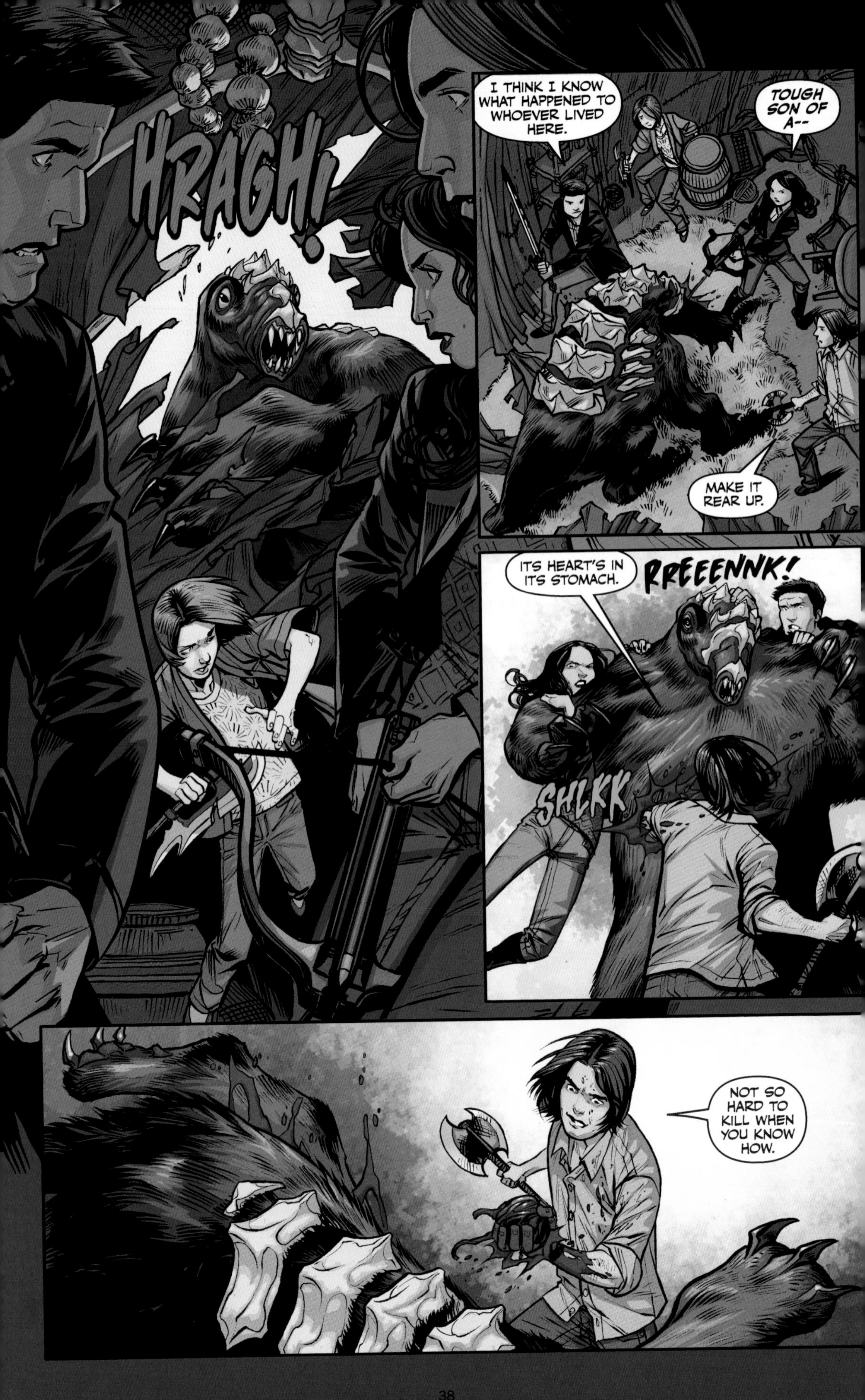
HRAGH!
I THINK I KNOW WHAT HAPPENED TO WHOEVER LIVED HERE.
TOUGH SON OF A--
MAKE IT REAR UP.
ITS HEART'S IN ITS STOMACH.
RREEENNK!
SHLKK
NOT SO HARD TO KILL WHEN YOU KNOW HOW.

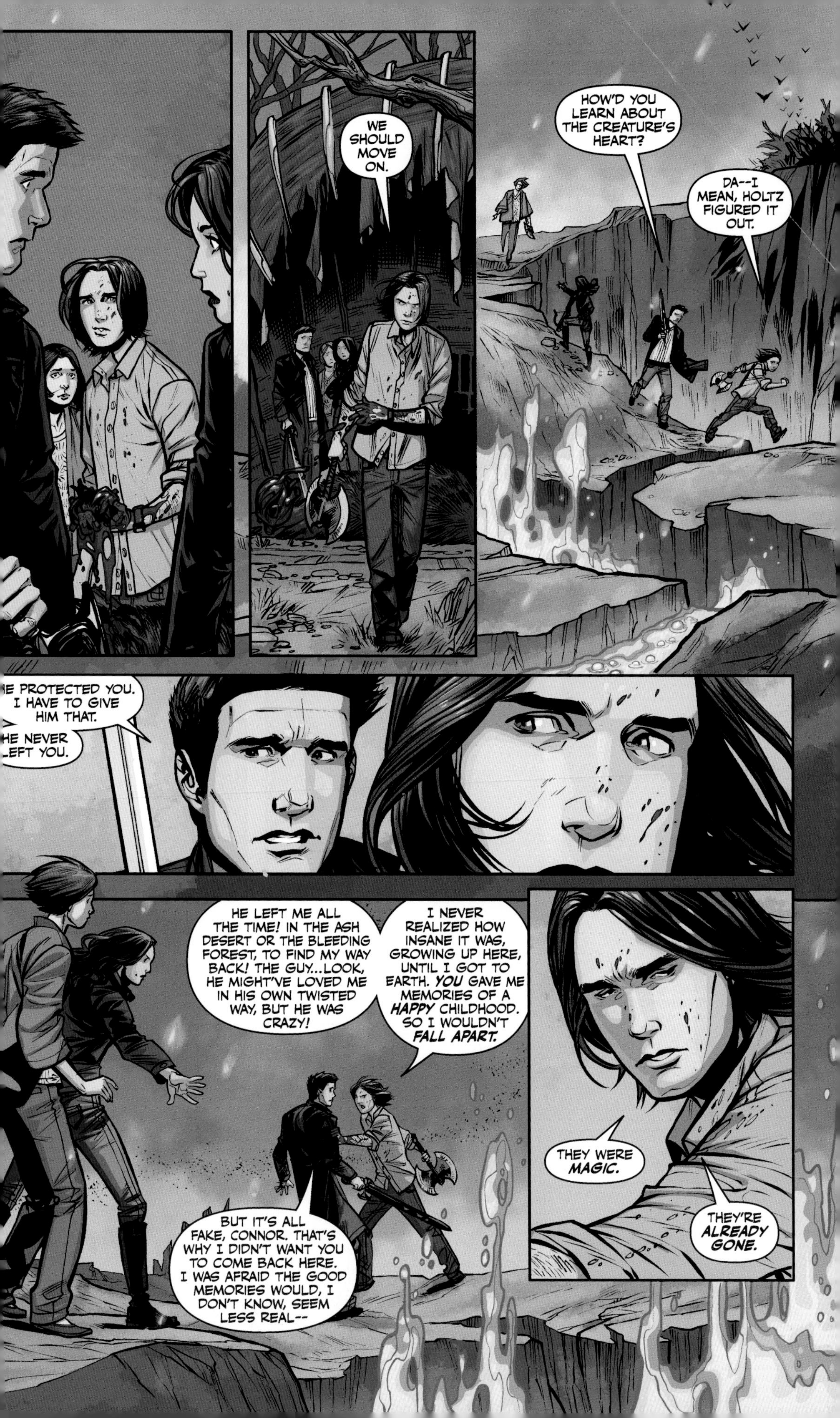
WE SHOULD MOVE ON.
HOW'D YOU LEARN ABOUT THE CREATURE'S HEART?
DA--I MEAN, HOLTZ FIGURED IT OUT.
HE PROTECTED YOU. I HAVE TO GIVE HIM THAT.
HE NEVER LEFT YOU.
HE LEFT ME ALL THE TIME! IN THE ASH DESERT OR THE BLEEDING FOREST, TO FIND MY WAY BACK! THE GUY...LOOK, HE MIGHT'VE LOVED ME IN HIS OWN TWISTED WAY, BUT HE WAS CRAZY!
I NEVER REALIZED HOW INSANE IT WAS, GROWING UP HERE, UNTIL I GOT TO EARTH. *YOU* GAVE ME MEMORIES OF A *HAPPY* CHILDHOOD. SO I WOULDN'T *FALL APART.*
BUT IT'S ALL FAKE, CONNOR. THAT'S WHY I DIDN'T WANT YOU TO COME BACK HERE. I WAS AFRAID THE GOOD MEMORIES WOULD, I DON'T KNOW, SEEM LESS REAL--
THEY WERE *MAGIC.*
THEY'RE *ALREADY GONE.*

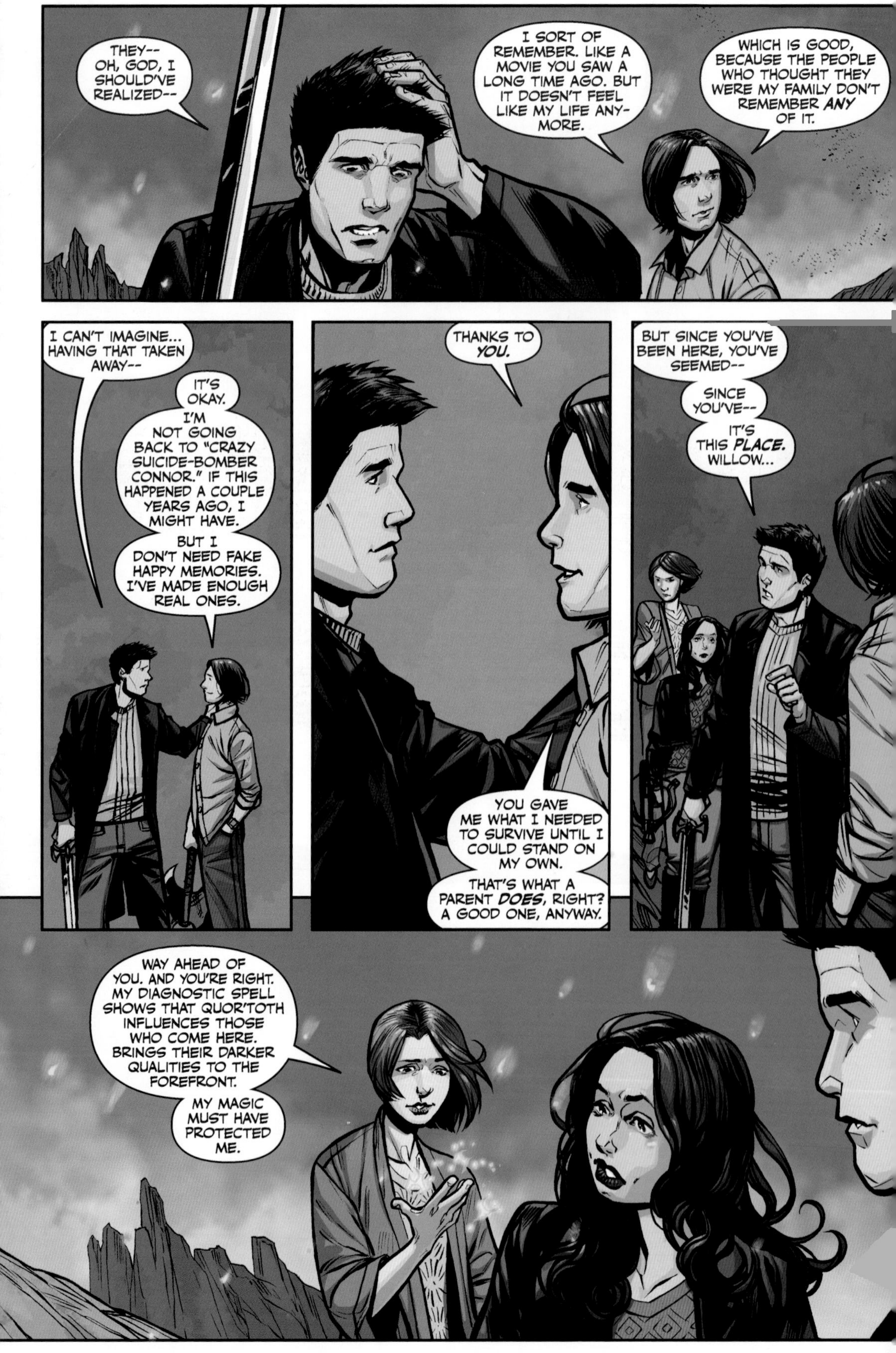
THEY-- OH, GOD, I SHOULD'VE REALIZED--
I SORT OF REMEMBER. LIKE A MOVIE YOU SAW A LONG TIME AGO. BUT IT DOESN'T FEEL LIKE MY LIFE ANY-MORE.
WHICH IS GOOD, BECAUSE THE PEOPLE WHO THOUGHT THEY WERE MY FAMILY DON'T REMEMBER ANY OF IT.
I CAN'T IMAGINE... HAVING THAT TAKEN AWAY--
IT'S OKAY.
I'M NOT GOING BACK TO "CRAZY SUICIDE-BOMBER CONNOR." IF THIS HAPPENED A COUPLE YEARS AGO, I MIGHT HAVE.
BUT I DON'T NEED FAKE HAPPY MEMORIES. I'VE MADE ENOUGH REAL ONES.
THANKS TO YOU.
YOU GAVE ME WHAT I NEEDED TO SURVIVE UNTIL I COULD STAND ON MY OWN.
THAT'S WHAT A PARENT DOES, RIGHT? A GOOD ONE, ANYWAY.
BUT SINCE YOU'VE BEEN HERE, YOU'VE SEEMED--
SINCE YOU'VE--
IT'S THIS PLACE. WILLOW...
WAY AHEAD OF YOU. AND YOU'RE RIGHT. MY DIAGNOSTIC SPELL SHOWS THAT QUOR'TOTH INFLUENCES THOSE WHO COME HERE. BRINGS THEIR DARKER QUALITIES TO THE FOREFRONT.
MY MAGIC MUST HAVE PROTECTED ME.

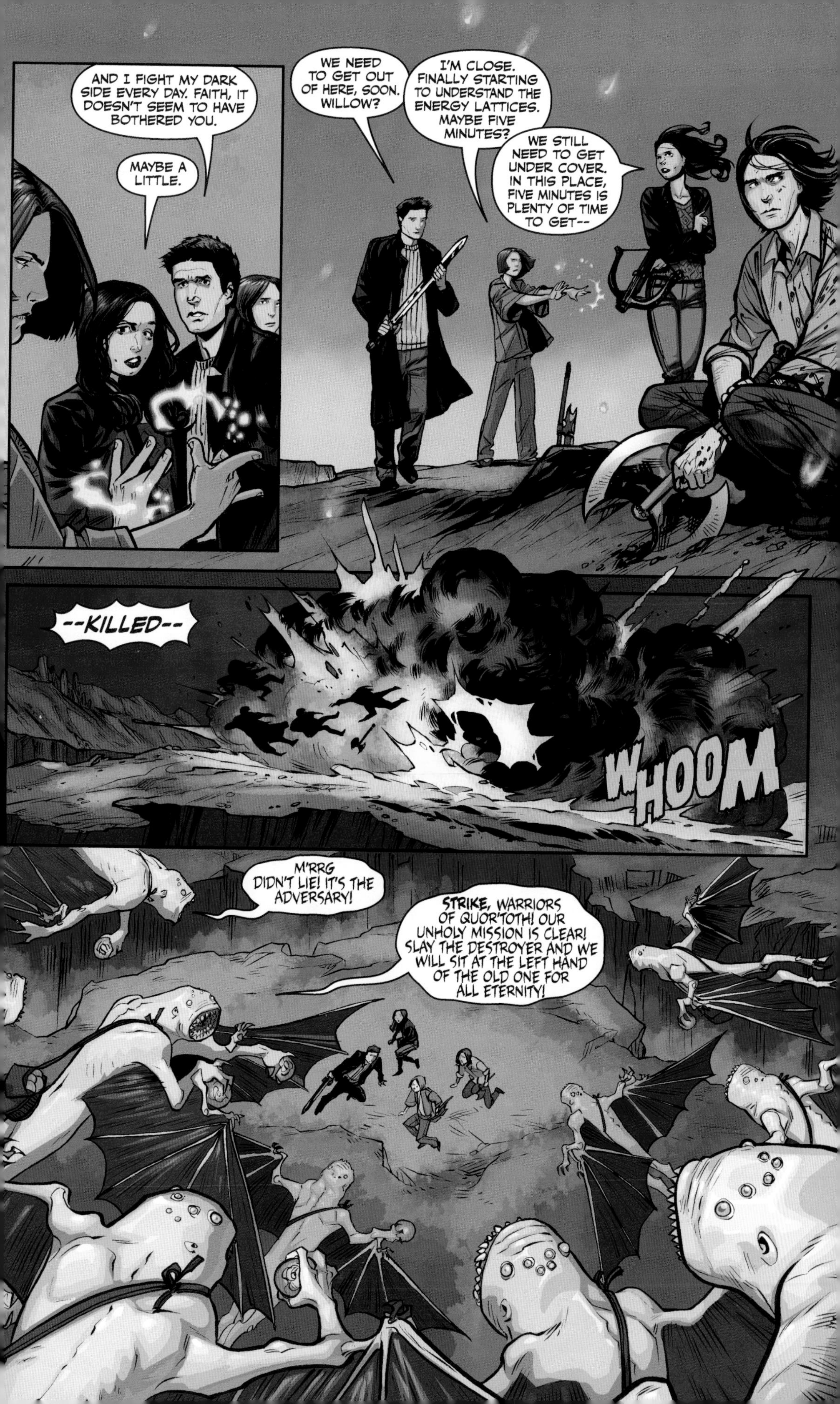
AND I FIGHT MY DARK SIDE EVERY DAY. FAITH, IT DOESN'T SEEM TO HAVE BOTHERED YOU.
MAYBE A LITTLE.
WE NEED TO GET OUT OF HERE, SOON. WILLOW?
I'M CLOSE. FINALLY STARTING TO UNDERSTAND THE ENERGY LATTICES. MAYBE FIVE MINUTES?
WE STILL NEED TO GET UNDER COVER. IN THIS PLACE, FIVE MINUTES IS PLENTY OF TIME TO GET--
--KILLED--
WHOOM
M'RRG DIDN'T LIE! IT'S THE ADVERSARY!
STRIKE, WARRIORS OF QUOR'TOTH! OUR UNHOLY MISSION IS CLEAR! SLAY THE DESTROYER AND WE WILL SIT AT THE LEFT HAND OF THE OLD ONE FOR ALL ETERNITY!

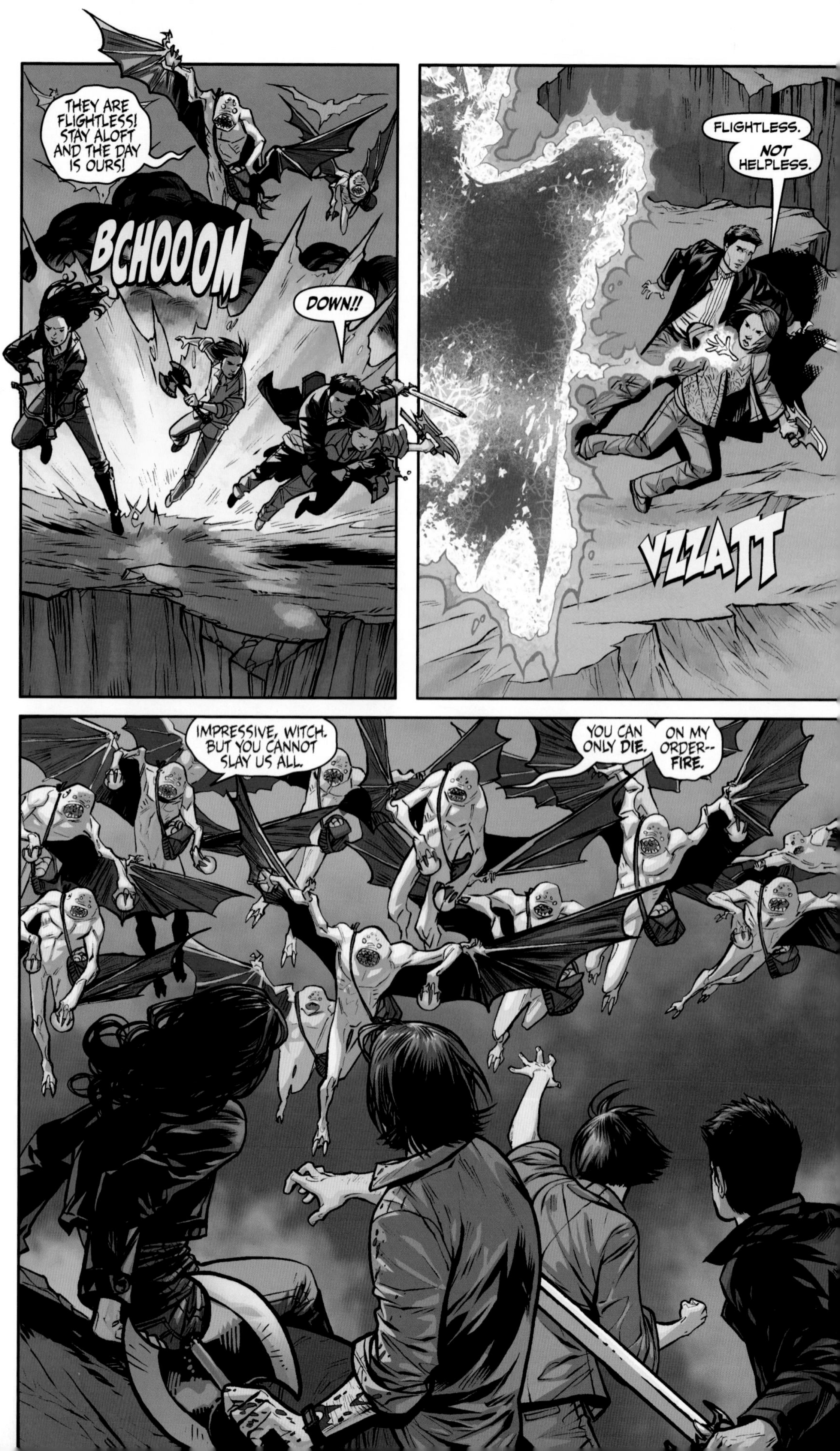
THEY ARE FLIGHTLESS! STAY ALOFT AND THE DAY IS OURS!
BCHOOOM
DOWN!!
FLIGHTLESS. NOT HELPLESS.
VZZATT
IMPRESSIVE, WITCH. BUT YOU CANNOT SLAY US ALL.
YOU CAN ONLY DIE.
ON MY ORDER-- FIRE.

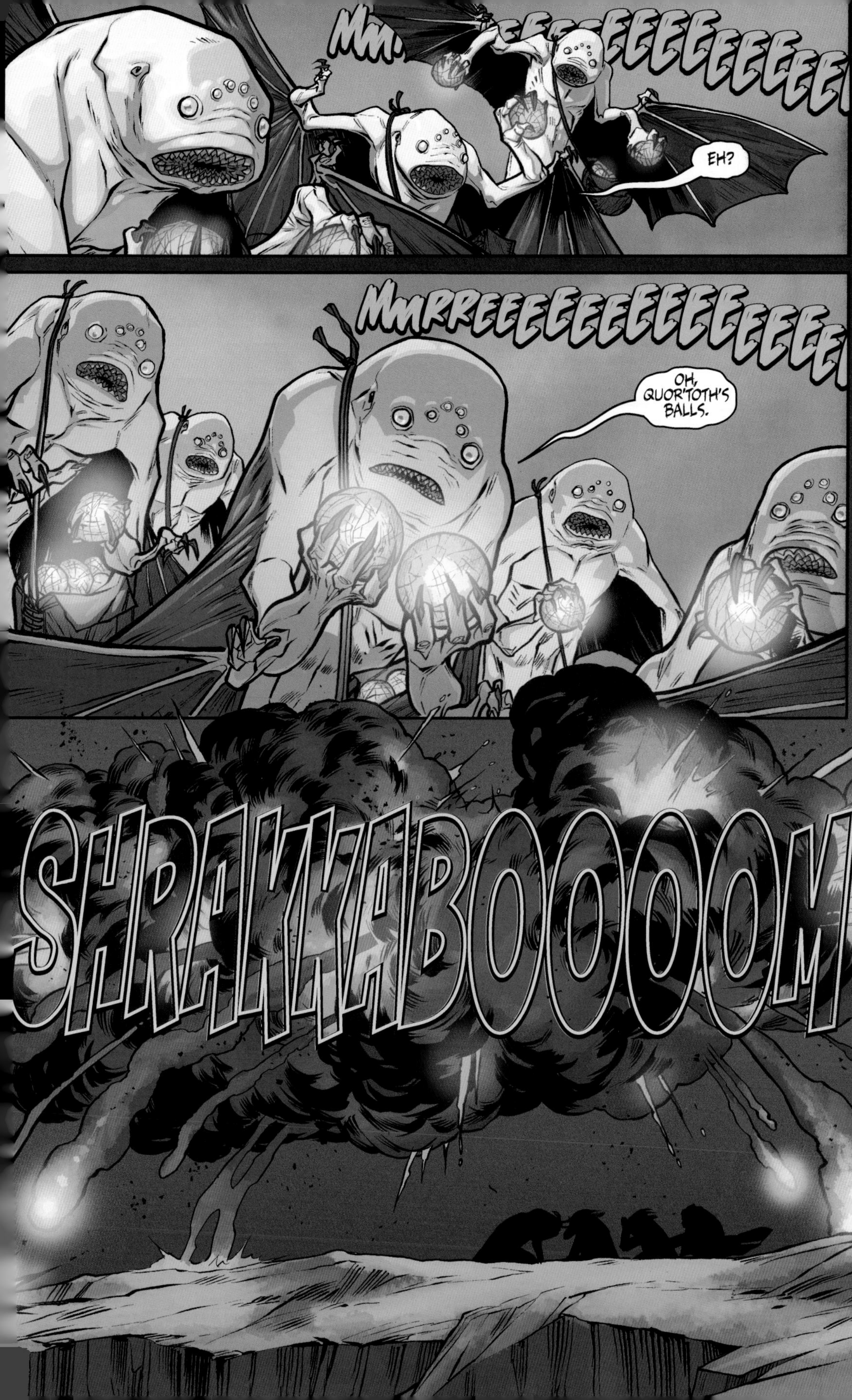
MMREEEEEEEEEEEE
EH?
MMRREEEEEEEEEEEEEEE
OH, QUOR'TOTH'S BALLS.
SHRAKKABOOOOOM

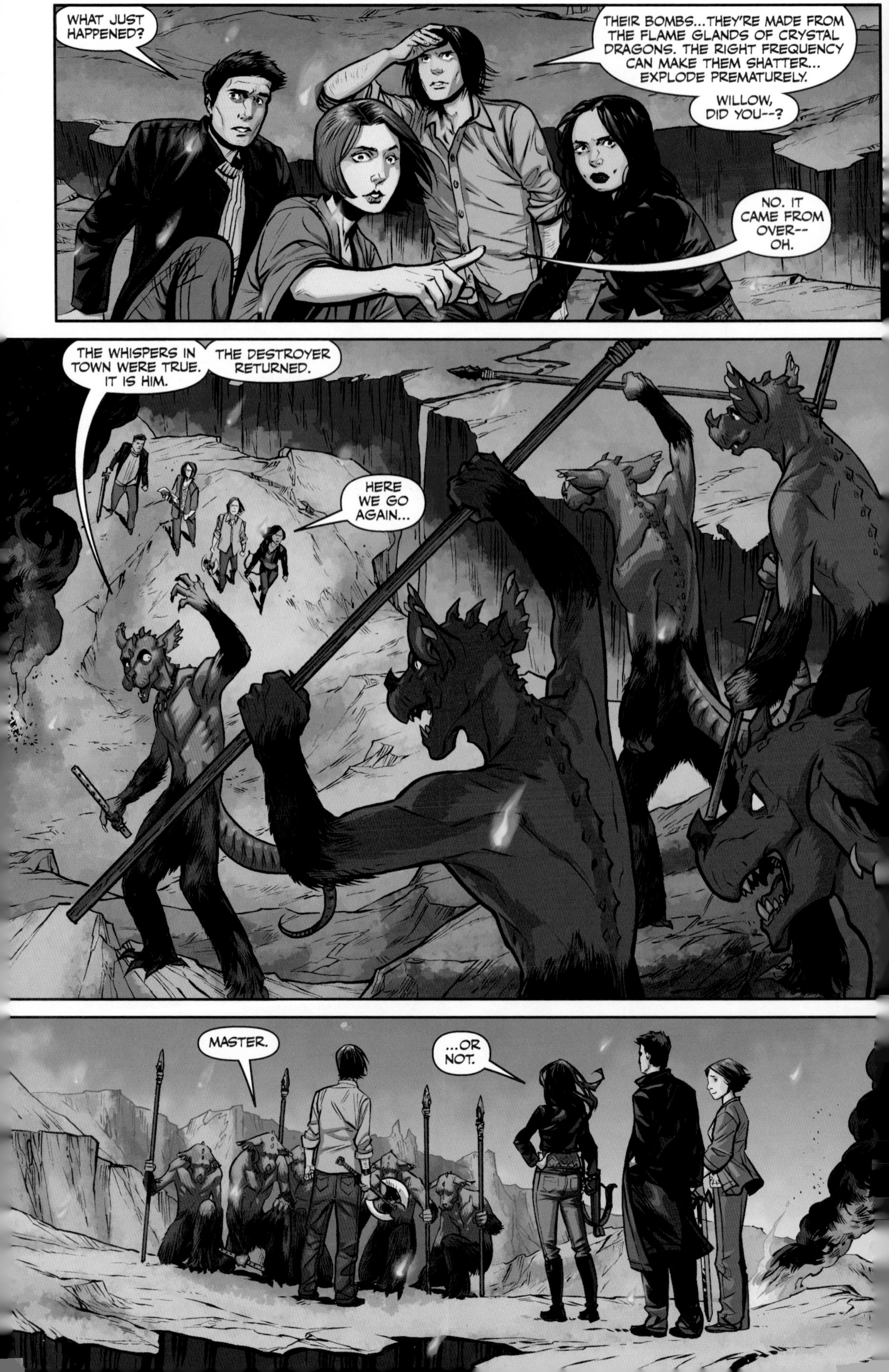
WHAT JUST HAPPENED?
THEIR BOMBS...THEY'RE MADE FROM THE FLAME GLANDS OF CRYSTAL DRAGONS. THE RIGHT FREQUENCY CAN MAKE THEM SHATTER... EXPLODE PREMATURELY.
WILLOW, DID YOU--?
NO. IT CAME FROM OVER-- OH.
THE WHISPERS IN TOWN WERE TRUE. IT IS HIM.
THE DESTROYER RETURNED.
HERE WE GO AGAIN...
MASTER.
...OR NOT.

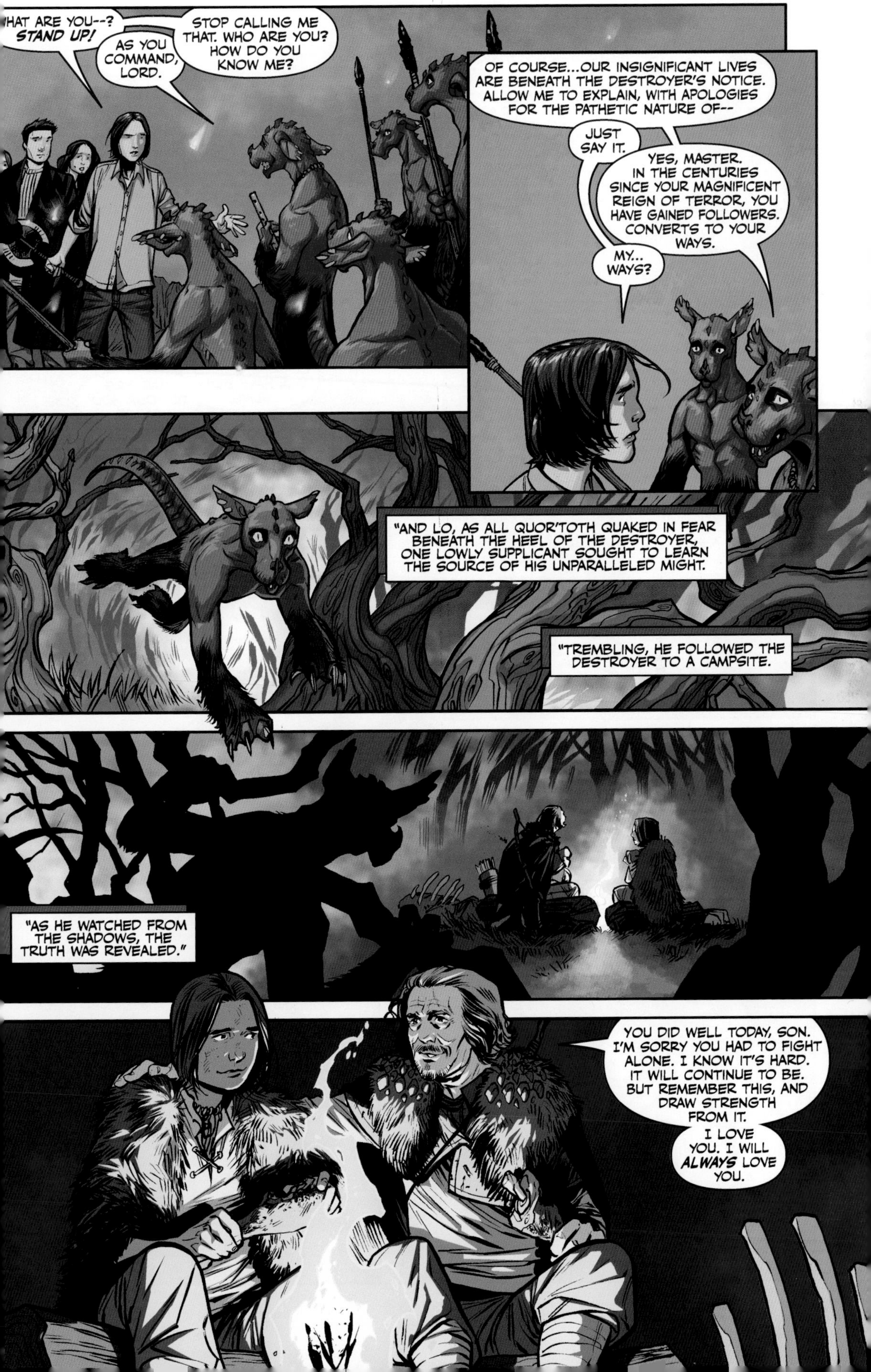
WHAT ARE YOU--? STAND UP!
AS YOU COMMAND, LORD.
STOP CALLING ME THAT. WHO ARE YOU? HOW DO YOU KNOW ME?
OF COURSE...OUR INSIGNIFICANT LIVES ARE BENEATH THE DESTROYER'S NOTICE. ALLOW ME TO EXPLAIN, WITH APOLOGIES FOR THE PATHETIC NATURE OF--
JUST SAY IT.
YES, MASTER. IN THE CENTURIES SINCE YOUR MAGNIFICENT REIGN OF TERROR, YOU HAVE GAINED FOLLOWERS. CONVERTS TO YOUR WAYS.
MY... WAYS?
"AND LO, AS ALL QUOR'TOTH QUAKED IN FEAR BENEATH THE HEEL OF THE DESTROYER, ONE LOWLY SUPPLICANT SOUGHT TO LEARN THE SOURCE OF HIS UNPARALLELED MIGHT.
"TREMBLING, HE FOLLOWED THE DESTROYER TO A CAMPSITE.
"AS HE WATCHED FROM THE SHADOWS, THE TRUTH WAS REVEALED."
YOU DID WELL TODAY, SON. I'M SORRY YOU HAD TO FIGHT ALONE. I KNOW IT'S HARD. IT WILL CONTINUE TO BE. BUT REMEMBER THIS, AND DRAW STRENGTH FROM IT.
I LOVE YOU. I WILL ALWAYS LOVE YOU.

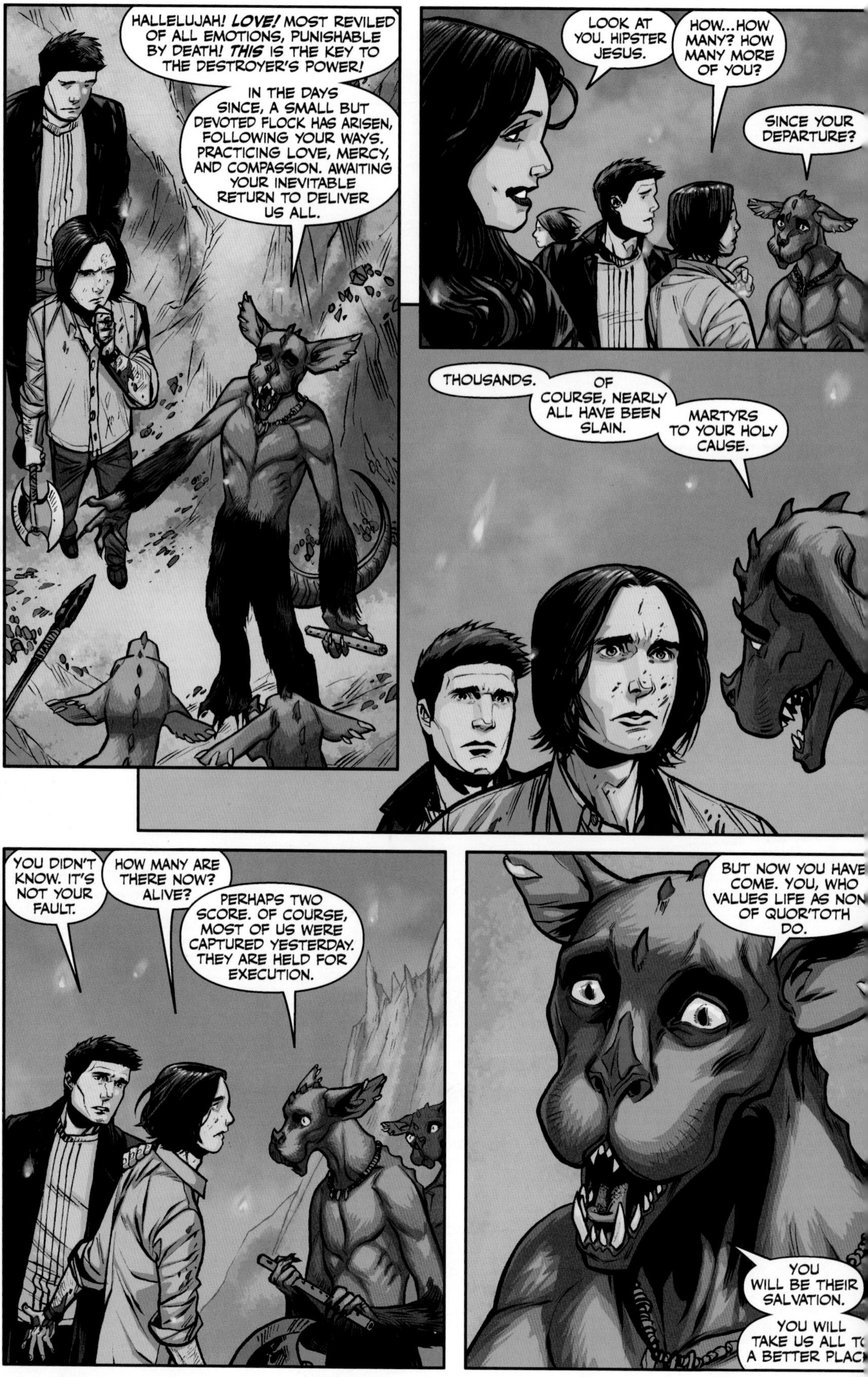
HALLELUJAH! *LOVE!* MOST REVILED OF ALL EMOTIONS, PUNISHABLE BY DEATH! *THIS* IS THE KEY TO THE DESTROYER'S POWER!
IN THE DAYS SINCE, A SMALL BUT DEVOTED FLOCK HAS ARISEN, FOLLOWING YOUR WAYS. PRACTICING LOVE, MERCY, AND COMPASSION. AWAITING YOUR INEVITABLE RETURN TO DELIVER US ALL.
LOOK AT YOU. HIPSTER JESUS.
HOW...HOW MANY? HOW MANY MORE OF YOU?
SINCE YOUR DEPARTURE?
THOUSANDS.
OF COURSE, NEARLY ALL HAVE BEEN SLAIN.
MARTYRS TO YOUR HOLY CAUSE.
YOU DIDN'T KNOW. IT'S NOT YOUR FAULT.
HOW MANY ARE THERE NOW? ALIVE?
PERHAPS TWO SCORE. OF COURSE, MOST OF US WERE CAPTURED YESTERDAY. THEY ARE HELD FOR EXECUTION.
BUT NOW YOU HAVE COME. YOU, WHO VALUES LIFE AS NON OF QUOR'TOTH DO.
YOU WILL BE THEIR SALVATION.
YOU WILL TAKE US ALL T A BETTER PLAC

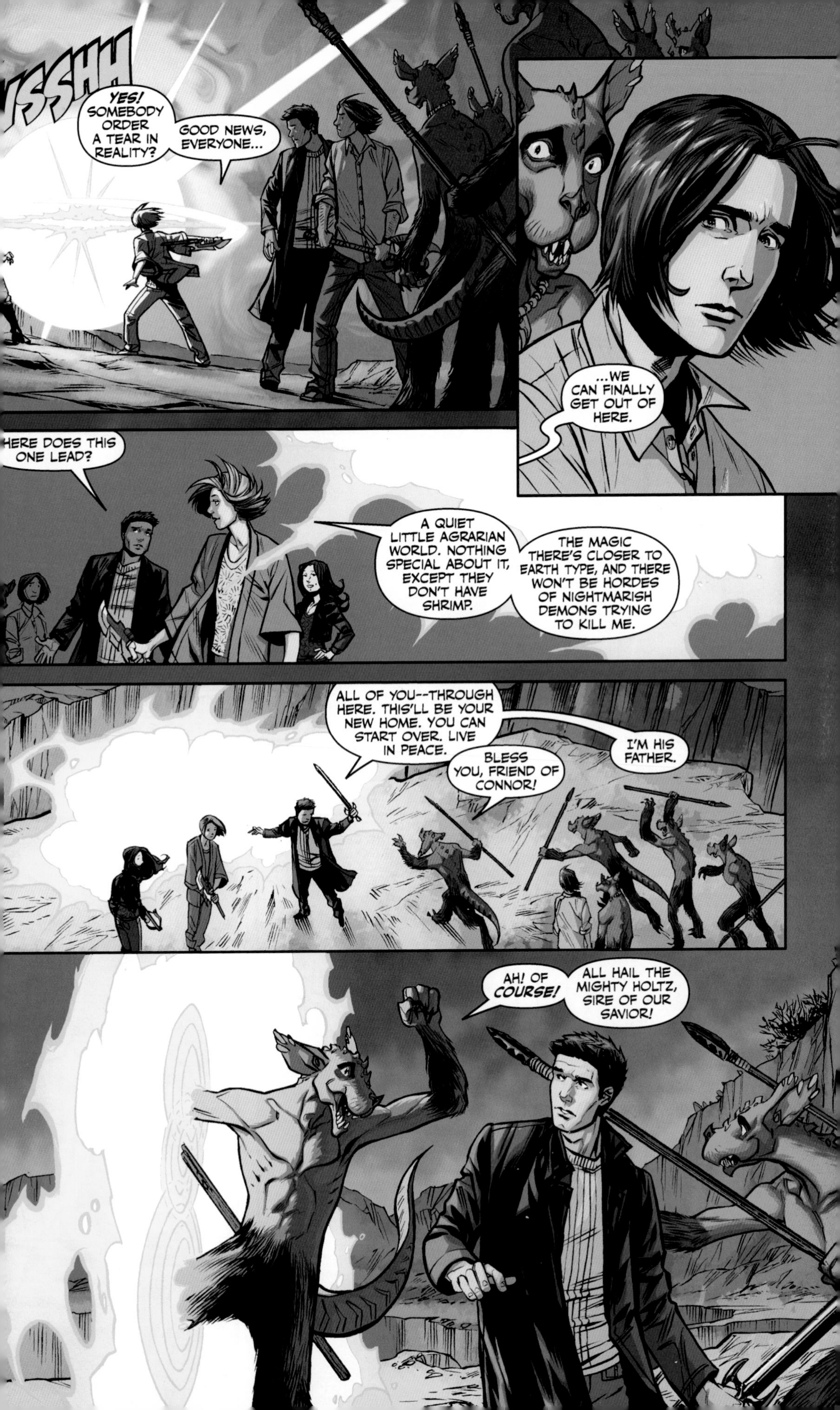

ISSHH
YES! SOMEBODY ORDER A TEAR IN REALITY?
GOOD NEWS, EVERYONE...
...WE CAN FINALLY GET OUT OF HERE.
HERE DOES THIS ONE LEAD?
A QUIET LITTLE AGRARIAN WORLD. NOTHING SPECIAL ABOUT IT, EXCEPT THEY DON'T HAVE SHRIMP.
THE MAGIC THERE'S CLOSER TO EARTH TYPE, AND THERE WON'T BE HORDES OF NIGHTMARISH DEMONS TRYING TO KILL ME.
ALL OF YOU--THROUGH HERE. THIS'LL BE YOUR NEW HOME. YOU CAN START OVER. LIVE IN PEACE.
BLESS YOU, FRIEND OF CONNOR!
I'M HIS FATHER.
AH! OF COURSE!
ALL HAIL THE MIGHTY HOLTZ, SIRE OF OUR SAVIOR!

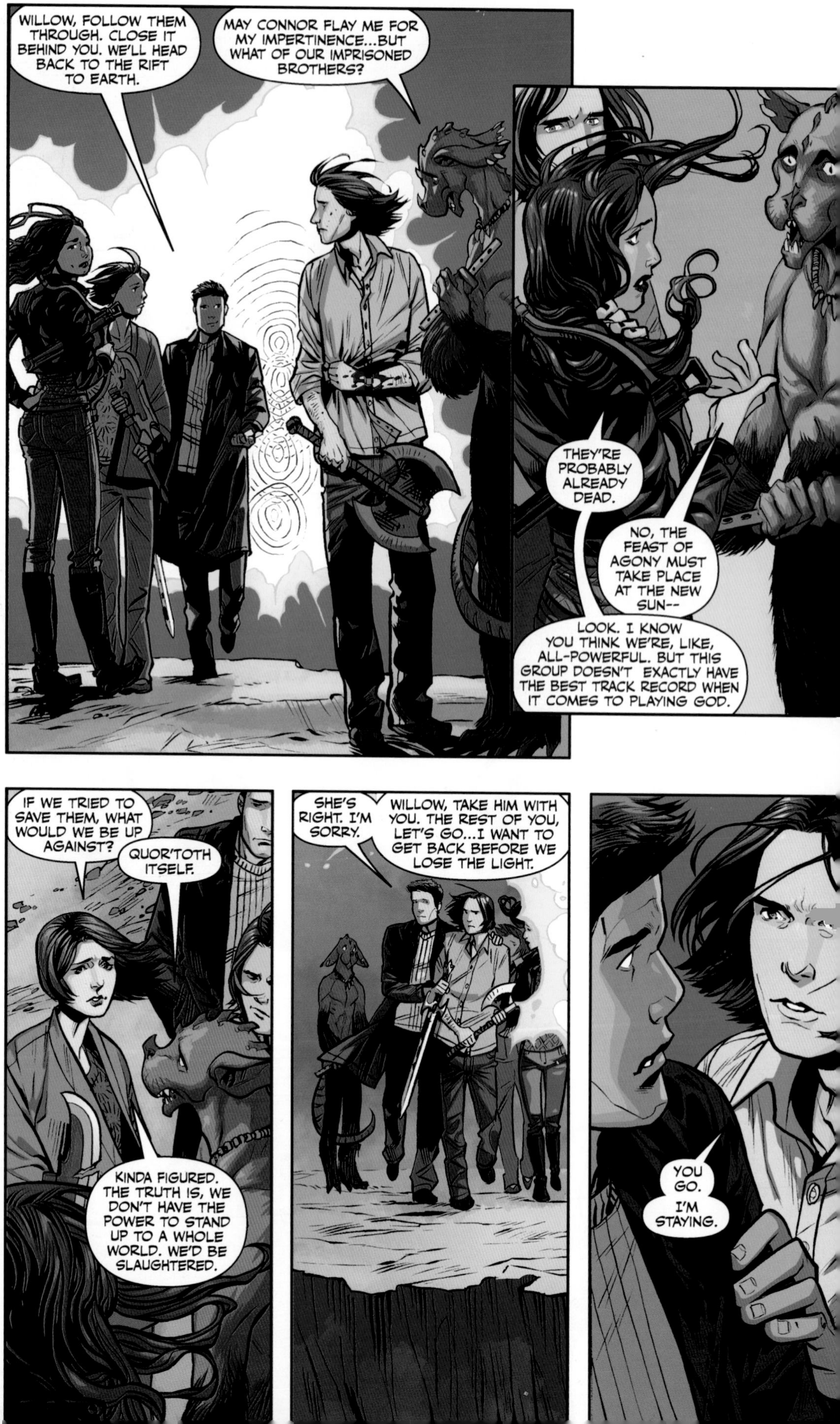
WILLOW, FOLLOW THEM THROUGH. CLOSE IT BEHIND YOU. WE'LL HEAD BACK TO THE RIFT TO EARTH.
MAY CONNOR FLAY ME FOR MY IMPERTINENCE...BUT WHAT OF OUR IMPRISONED BROTHERS?
THEY'RE PROBABLY ALREADY DEAD.
NO, THE FEAST OF AGONY MUST TAKE PLACE AT THE NEW SUN--
LOOK. I KNOW YOU THINK WE'RE, LIKE, ALL-POWERFUL. BUT THIS GROUP DOESN'T EXACTLY HAVE THE BEST TRACK RECORD WHEN IT COMES TO PLAYING GOD.
IF WE TRIED TO SAVE THEM, WHAT WOULD WE BE UP AGAINST?
QUOR'TOTH ITSELF.
KINDA FIGURED. THE TRUTH IS, WE DON'T HAVE THE POWER TO STAND UP TO A WHOLE WORLD. WE'D BE SLAUGHTERED.
SHE'S RIGHT. I'M SORRY.
WILLOW, TAKE HIM WITH YOU. THE REST OF YOU, LET'S GO...I WANT TO GET BACK BEFORE WE LOSE THE LIGHT.
YOU GO.
I'M STAYING.

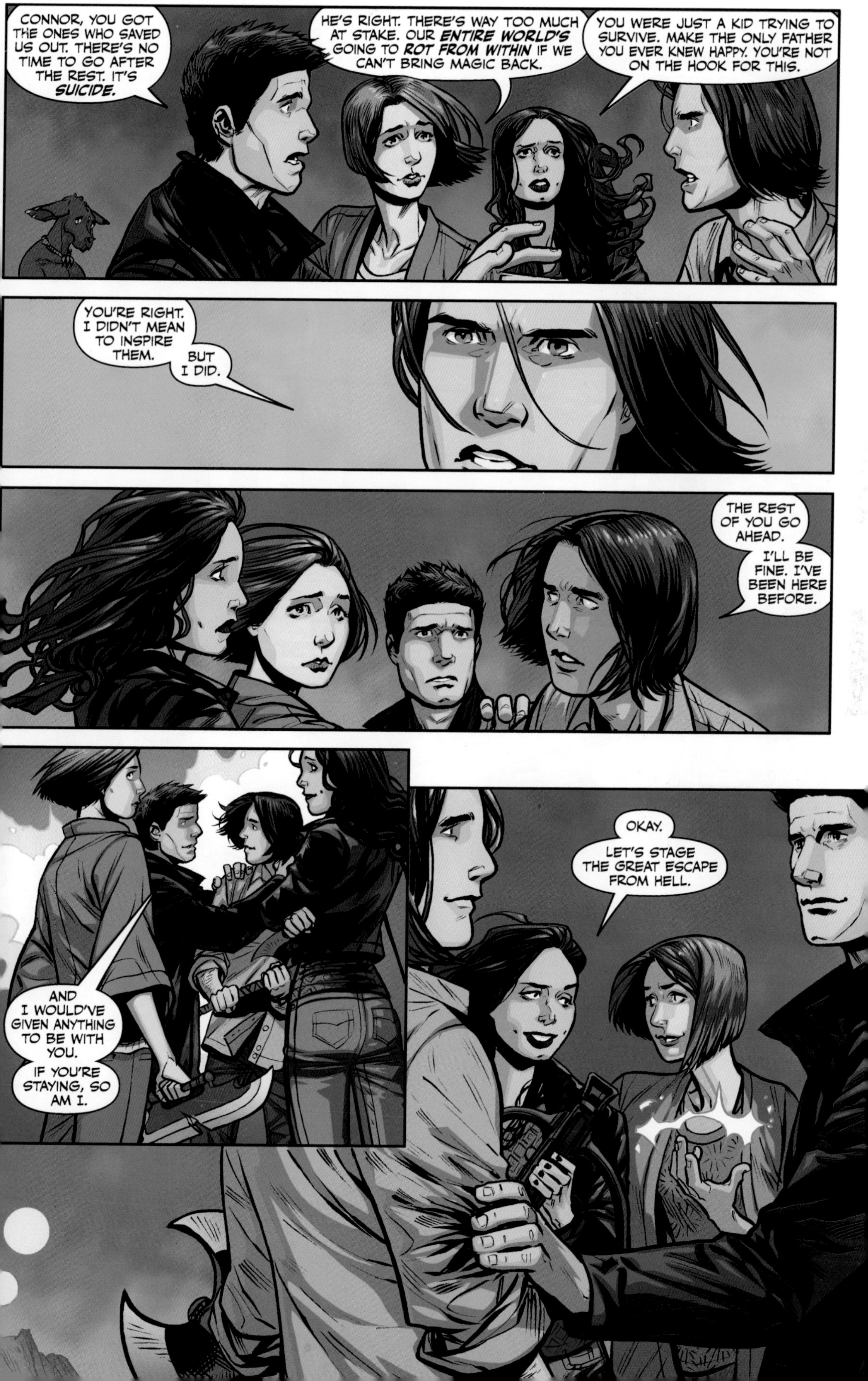

CONNOR, YOU GOT THE ONES WHO SAVED US OUT. THERE'S NO TIME TO GO AFTER THE REST. IT'S SUICIDE.
HE'S RIGHT. THERE'S WAY TOO MUCH AT STAKE. OUR ENTIRE WORLD'S GOING TO ROT FROM WITHIN IF WE CAN'T BRING MAGIC BACK.
YOU WERE JUST A KID TRYING TO SURVIVE. MAKE THE ONLY FATHER YOU EVER KNEW HAPPY. YOU'RE NOT ON THE HOOK FOR THIS.
YOU'RE RIGHT. I DIDN'T MEAN TO INSPIRE THEM.
BUT I DID.
THE REST OF YOU GO AHEAD.
I'LL BE FINE. I'VE BEEN HERE BEFORE.
AND I WOULD'VE GIVEN ANYTHING TO BE WITH YOU.
IF YOU'RE STAYING, SO AM I.
OKAY.
LET'S STAGE THE GREAT ESCAPE FROM HELL.

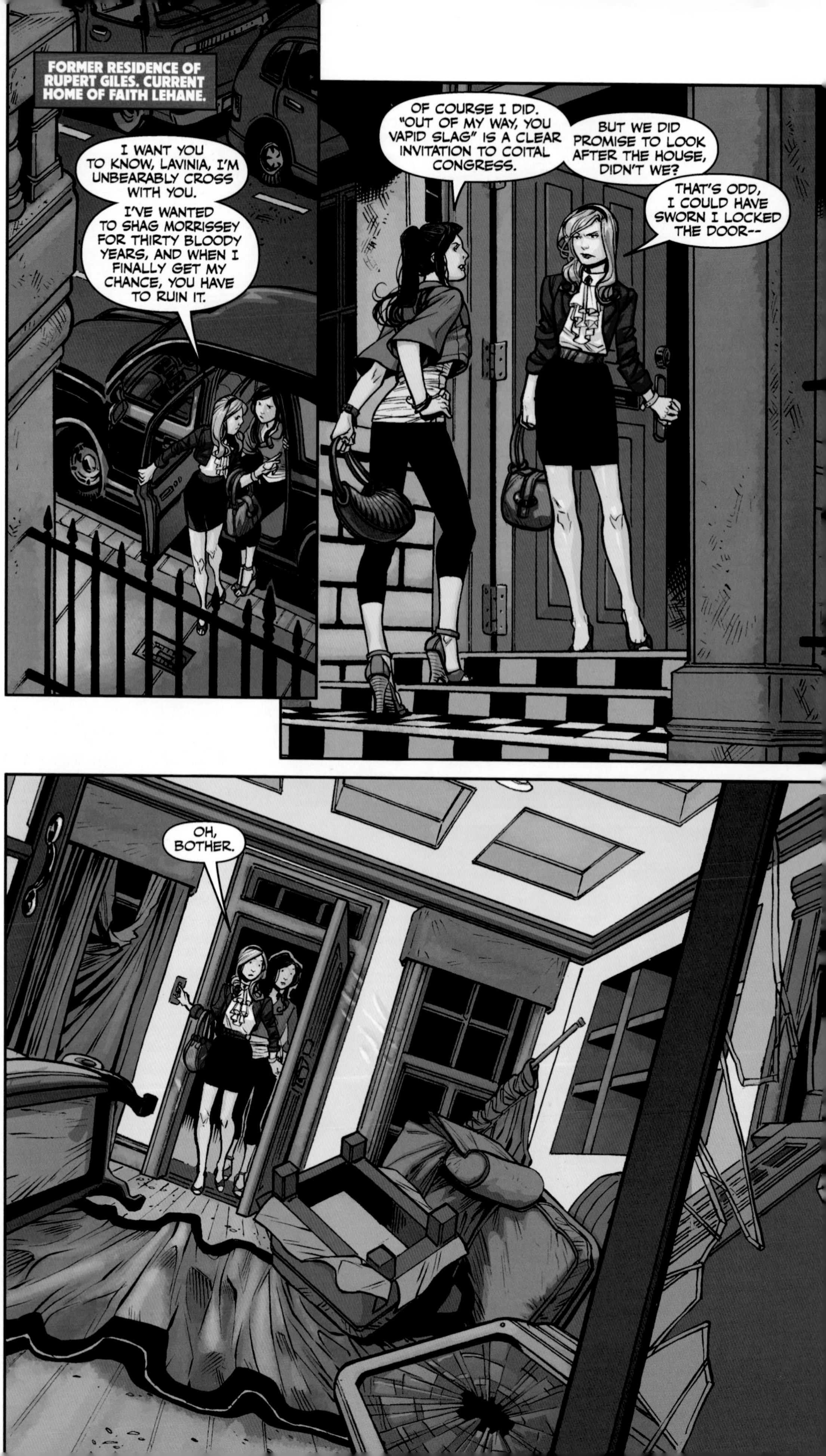
FORMER RESIDENCE OF RUPERT GILES. CURRENT HOME OF FAITH LEHANE.
I WANT YOU TO KNOW, LAVINIA, I'M UNBEARABLY CROSS WITH YOU.
I'VE WANTED TO SHAG MORRISSEY FOR THIRTY BLOODY YEARS, AND WHEN I FINALLY GET MY CHANCE, YOU HAVE TO RUIN IT.
OF COURSE I DID. "OUT OF MY WAY, YOU VAPID SLAG" IS A CLEAR INVITATION TO COITAL CONGRESS.
BUT WE DID PROMISE TO LOOK AFTER THE HOUSE, DIDN'T WE?
THAT'S ODD, I COULD HAVE SWORN I LOCKED THE DOOR--
OH, BOTHER.

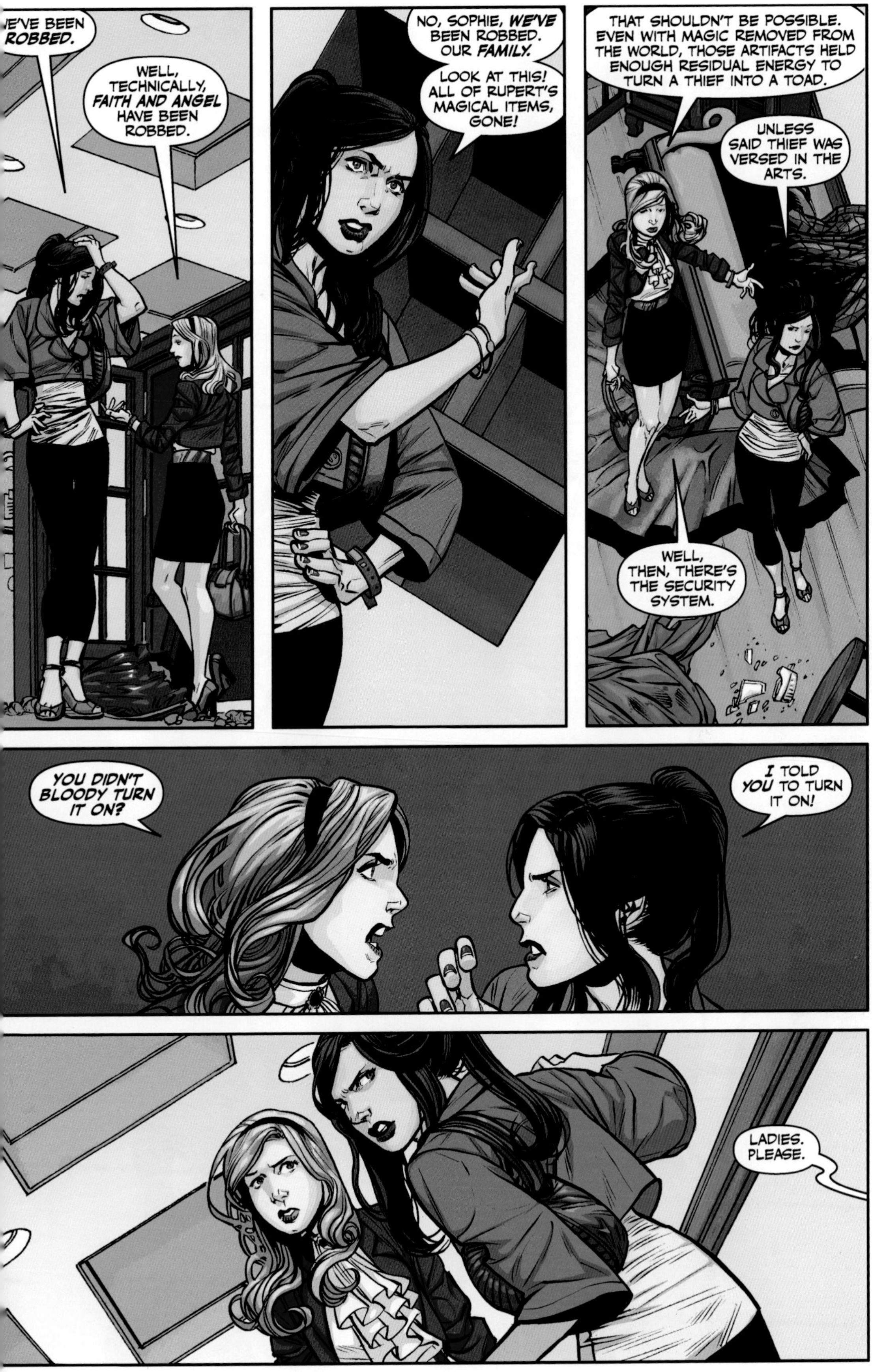
E'VE BEEN ROBBED.
WELL, TECHNICALLY, FAITH AND ANGEL HAVE BEEN ROBBED.
NO, SOPHIE, WE'VE BEEN ROBBED. OUR FAMILY.
LOOK AT THIS! ALL OF RUPERT'S MAGICAL ITEMS, GONE!
THAT SHOULDN'T BE POSSIBLE. EVEN WITH MAGIC REMOVED FROM THE WORLD, THOSE ARTIFACTS HELD ENOUGH RESIDUAL ENERGY TO TURN A THIEF INTO A TOAD.
UNLESS SAID THIEF WAS VERSED IN THE ARTS.
WELL, THEN, THERE'S THE SECURITY SYSTEM.
YOU DIDN'T BLOODY TURN IT ON?
I TOLD YOU TO TURN IT ON!
LADIES. PLEASE.

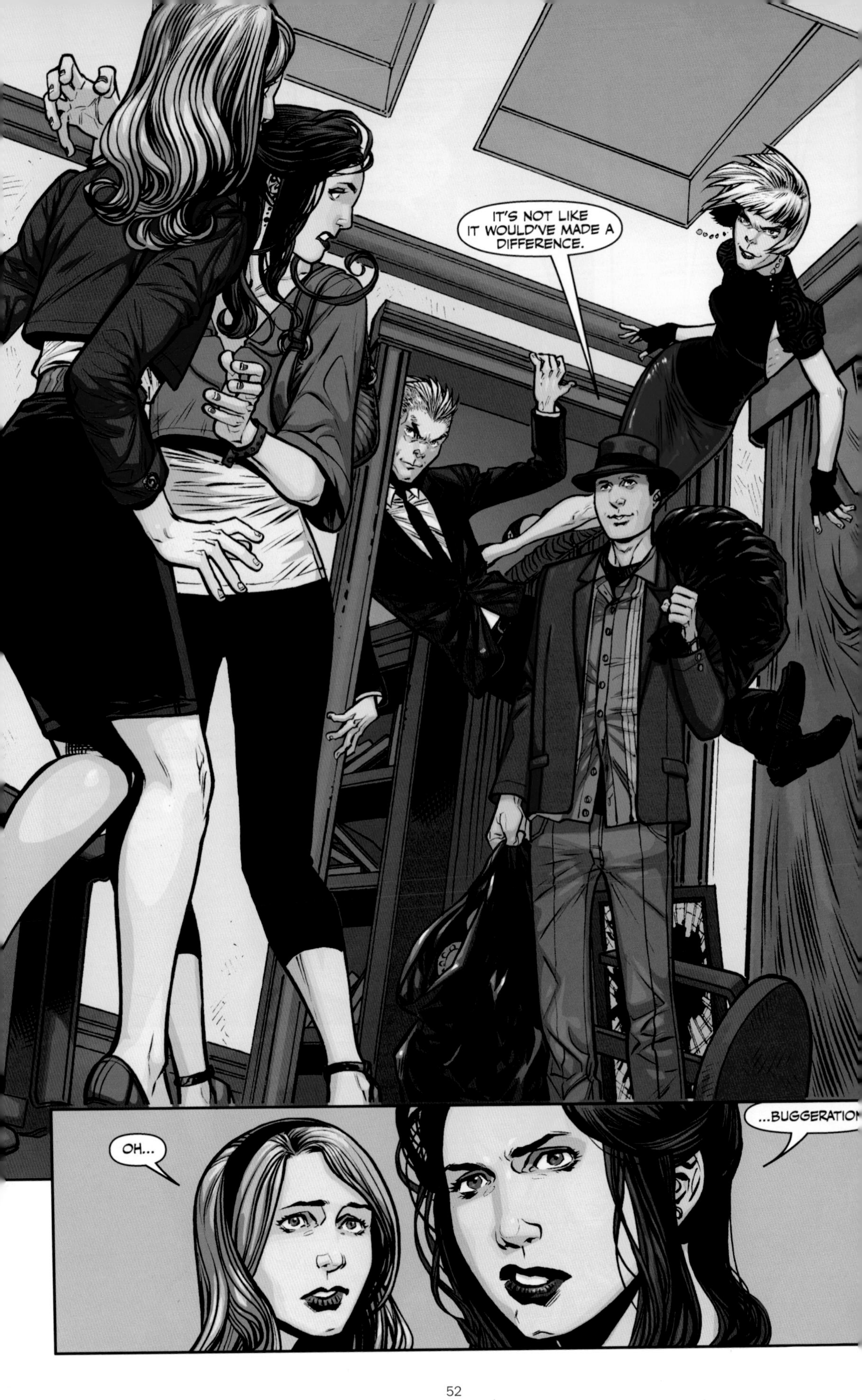
IT'S NOT LIKE IT WOULD'VE MADE A DIFFERENCE.
OH...
...BUGGERATIO

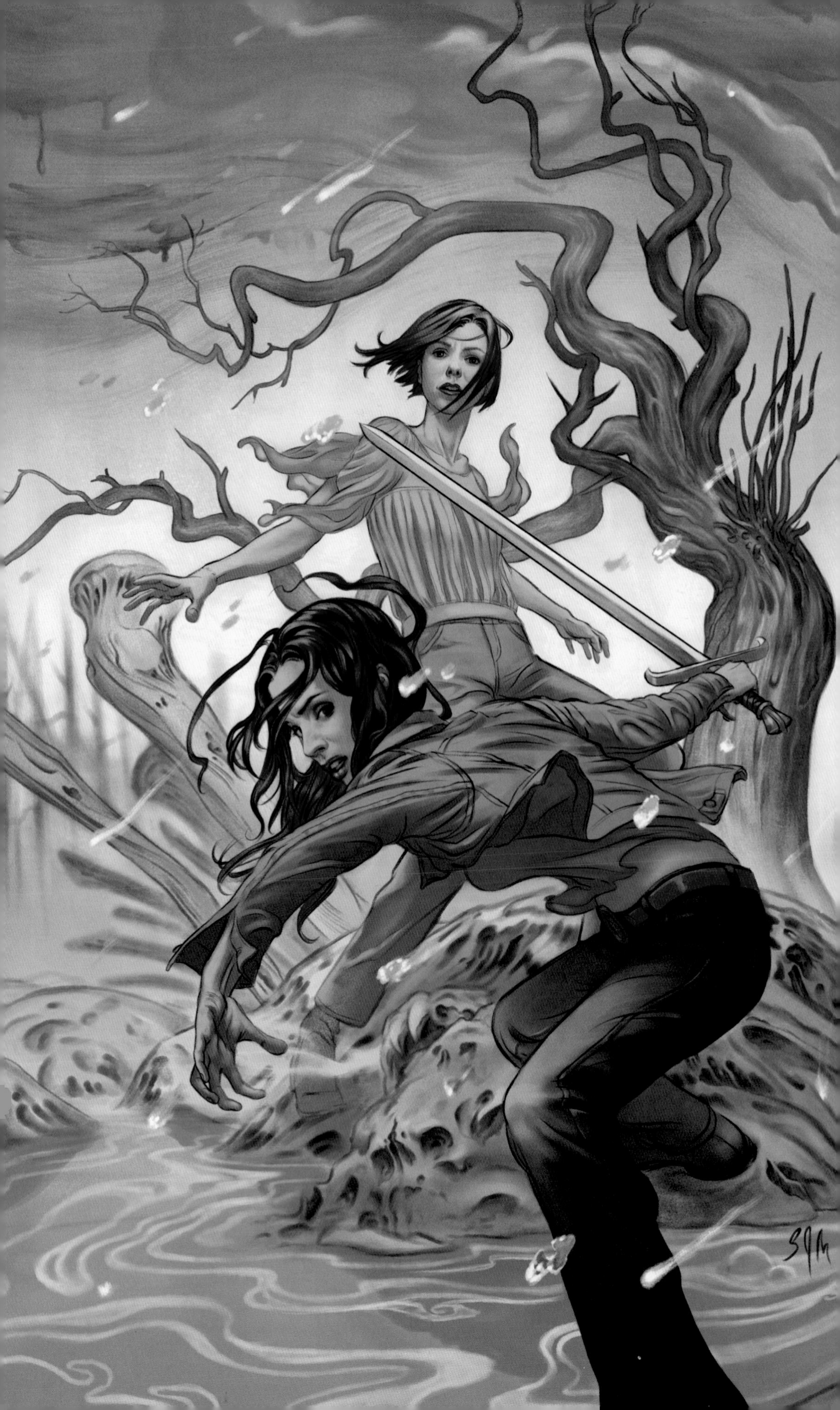

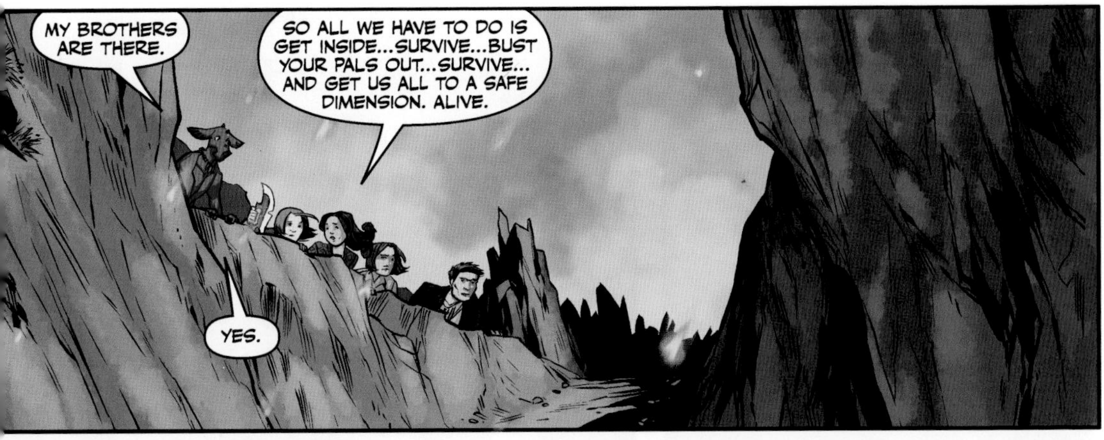
MY BROTHERS ARE THERE.
SO ALL WE HAVE TO DO IS GET INSIDE...SURVIVE...BUST YOUR PALS OUT...SURVIVE... AND GET US ALL TO A SAFE DIMENSION. ALIVE.
YES.

FAMILY REUNION

PART THREE

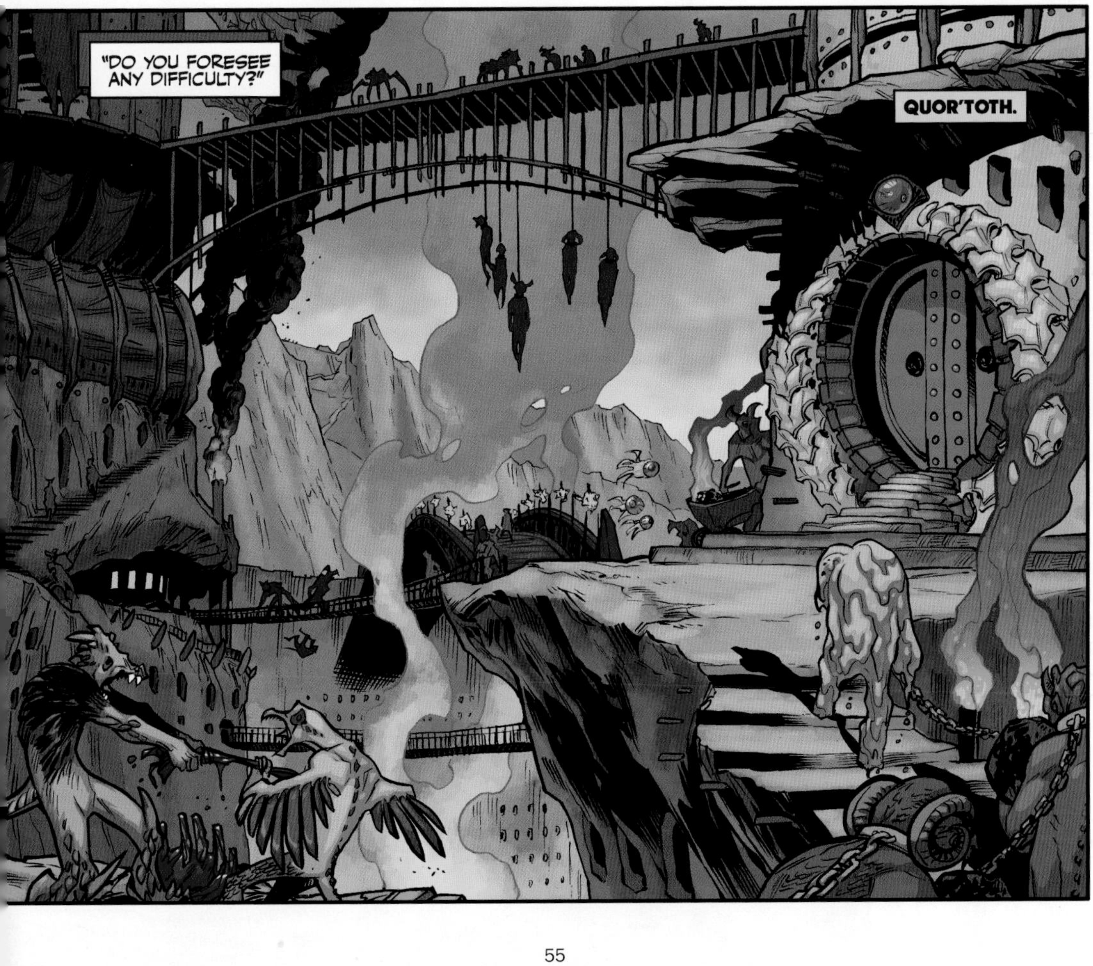
"DO YOU FORESEE ANY DIFFICULTY?"
QUOR'TOTH.

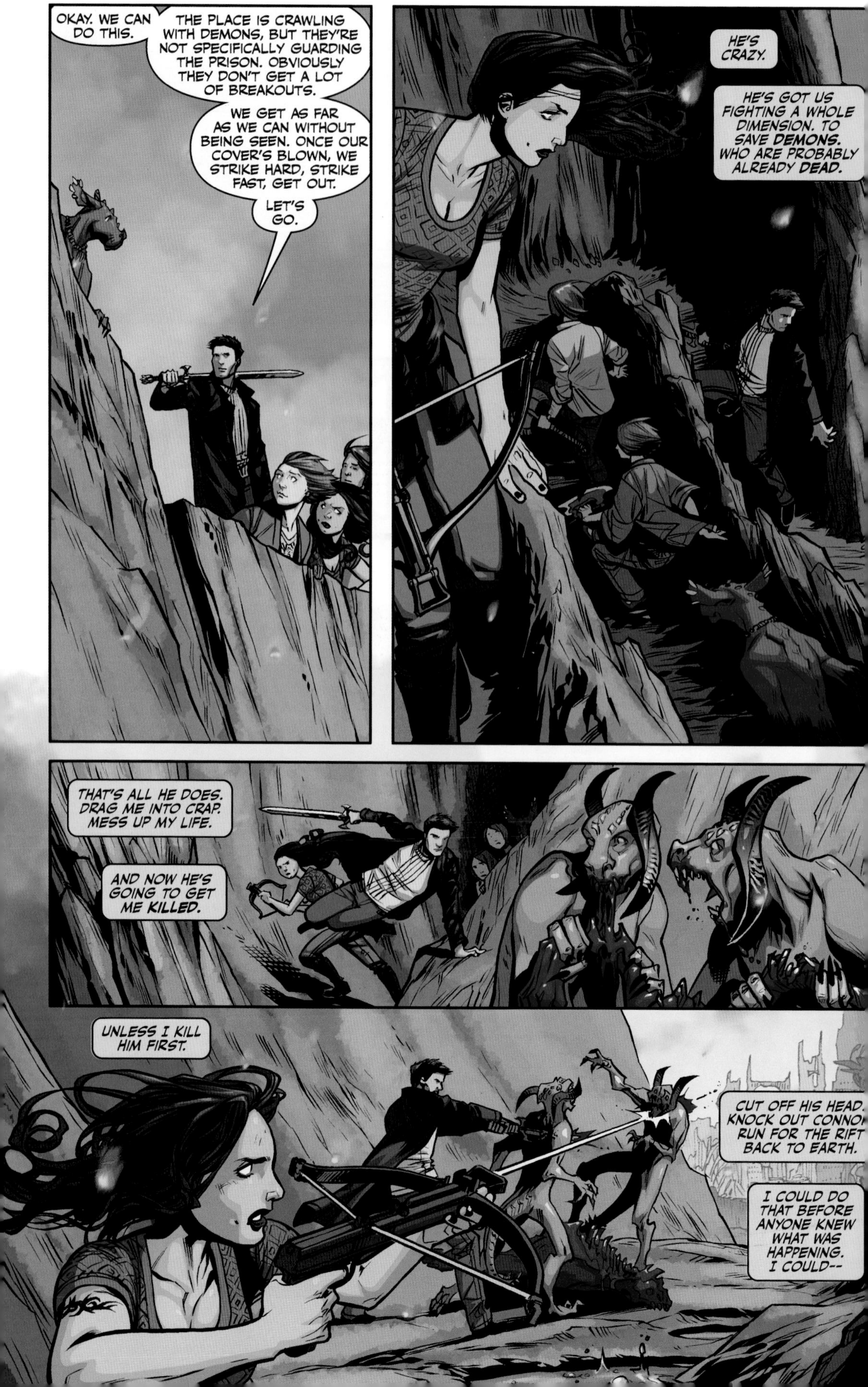
OKAY. WE CAN DO THIS.
THE PLACE IS CRAWLING WITH DEMONS, BUT THEY'RE NOT SPECIFICALLY GUARDING THE PRISON. OBVIOUSLY THEY DON'T GET A LOT OF BREAKOUTS.
WE GET AS FAR AS WE CAN WITHOUT BEING SEEN. ONCE OUR COVER'S BLOWN, WE STRIKE HARD, STRIKE FAST, GET OUT.
LET'S GO.
HE'S CRAZY.
HE'S GOT US FIGHTING A WHOLE DIMENSION. TO SAVE DEMONS. WHO ARE PROBABLY ALREADY DEAD.
THAT'S ALL HE DOES. DRAG ME INTO CRAP. MESS UP MY LIFE.
AND NOW HE'S GOING TO GET ME KILLED.
UNLESS I KILL HIM FIRST.
CUT OFF HIS HEAD. KNOCK OUT CONNO RUN FOR THE RIFT BACK TO EARTH.
I COULD DO THAT BEFORE ANYONE KNEW WHAT WAS HAPPENING. I COULD--

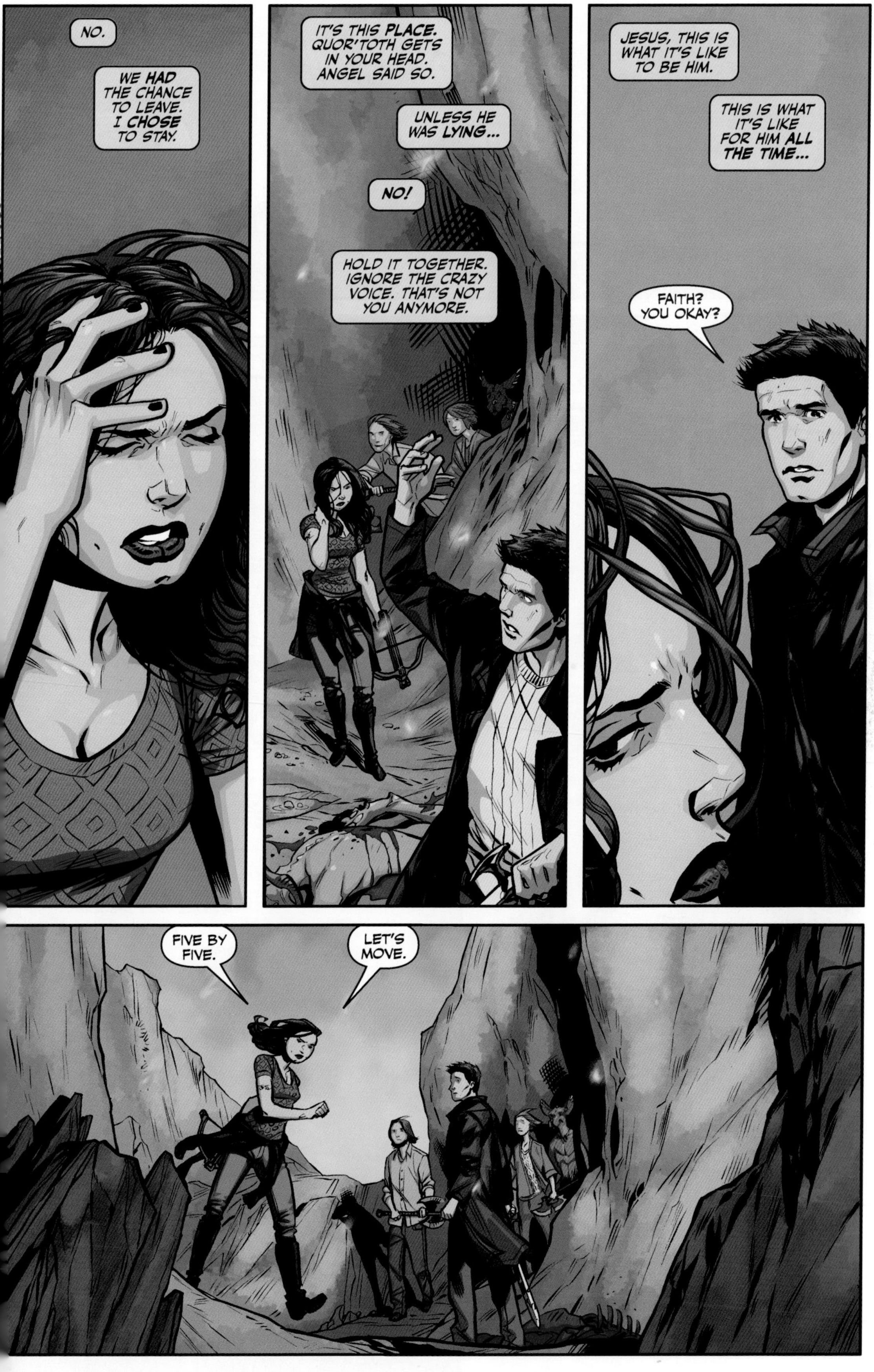
NO.
WE HAD THE CHANCE TO LEAVE. I CHOSE TO STAY.
IT'S THIS PLACE. QUOR'TOTH GETS IN YOUR HEAD. ANGEL SAID SO.
UNLESS HE WAS LYING...
NO!
HOLD IT TOGETHER. IGNORE THE CRAZY VOICE. THAT'S NOT YOU ANYMORE.
JESUS, THIS IS WHAT IT'S LIKE TO BE HIM.
THIS IS WHAT IT'S LIKE FOR HIM ALL THE TIME...
FAITH? YOU OKAY?
FIVE BY FIVE.
LET'S MOVE.

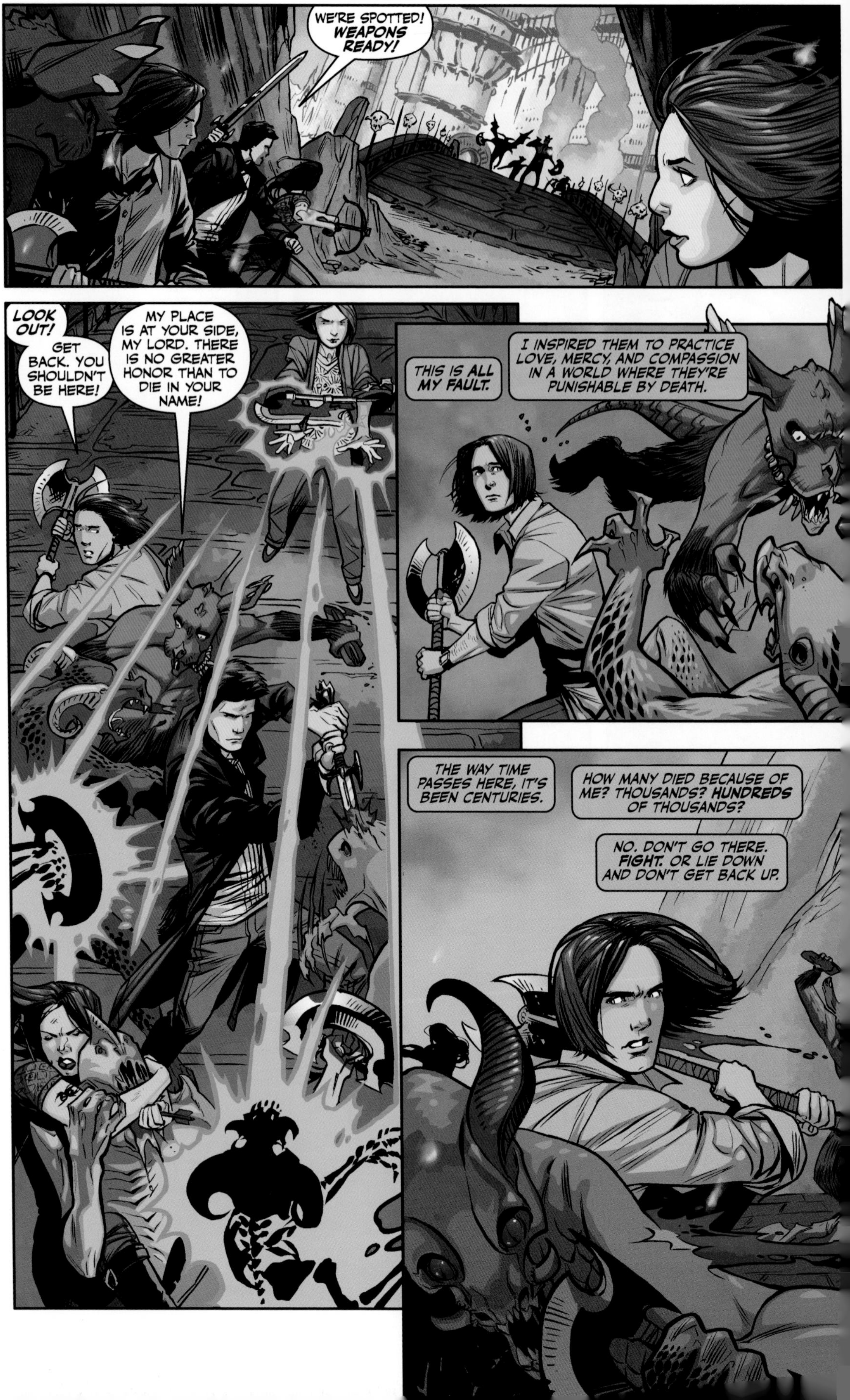
WE'RE SPOTTED! **WEAPONS READY!**
LOOK OUT!
GET BACK. YOU SHOULDN'T BE HERE!
MY PLACE IS AT YOUR SIDE, MY LORD. THERE IS NO GREATER HONOR THAN TO DIE IN YOUR NAME!
THIS IS **ALL MY FAULT.**
I INSPIRED THEM TO PRACTICE LOVE, MERCY, AND COMPASSION IN A WORLD WHERE THEY'RE PUNISHABLE BY DEATH.
THE WAY TIME PASSES HERE, IT'S BEEN CENTURIES.
HOW MANY DIED BECAUSE OF ME? THOUSANDS? **HUNDREDS** OF THOUSANDS?
NO. DON'T GO THERE. **FIGHT.** OR LIE DOWN AND DON'T GET BACK UP.

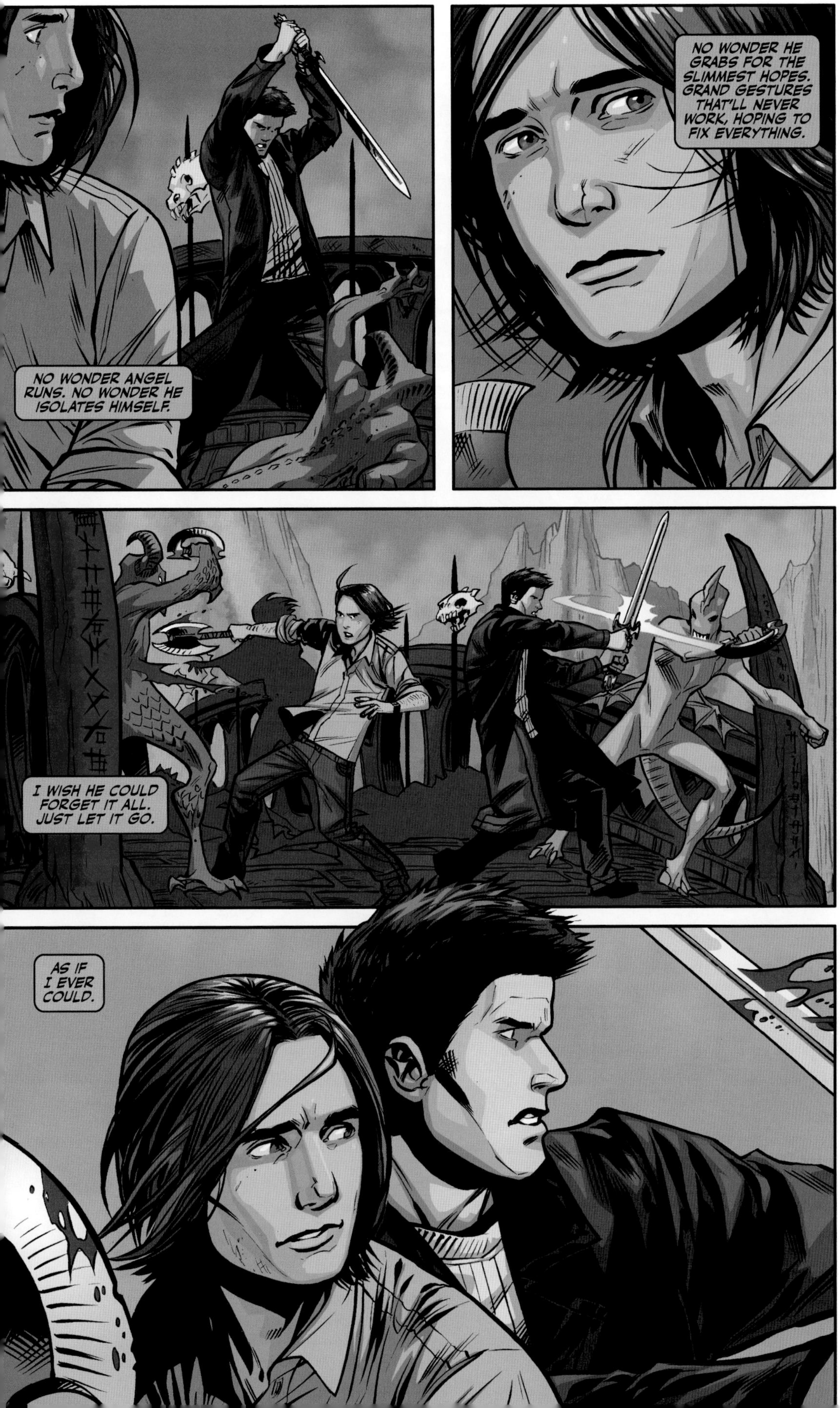
NO WONDER ANGEL RUNS. NO WONDER HE ISOLATES HIMSELF.
NO WONDER HE GRABS FOR THE SLIMMEST HOPES. GRAND GESTURES THAT'LL NEVER WORK, HOPING TO FIX EVERYTHING.
I WISH HE COULD FORGET IT ALL. JUST LET IT GO.
AS IF I EVER COULD.

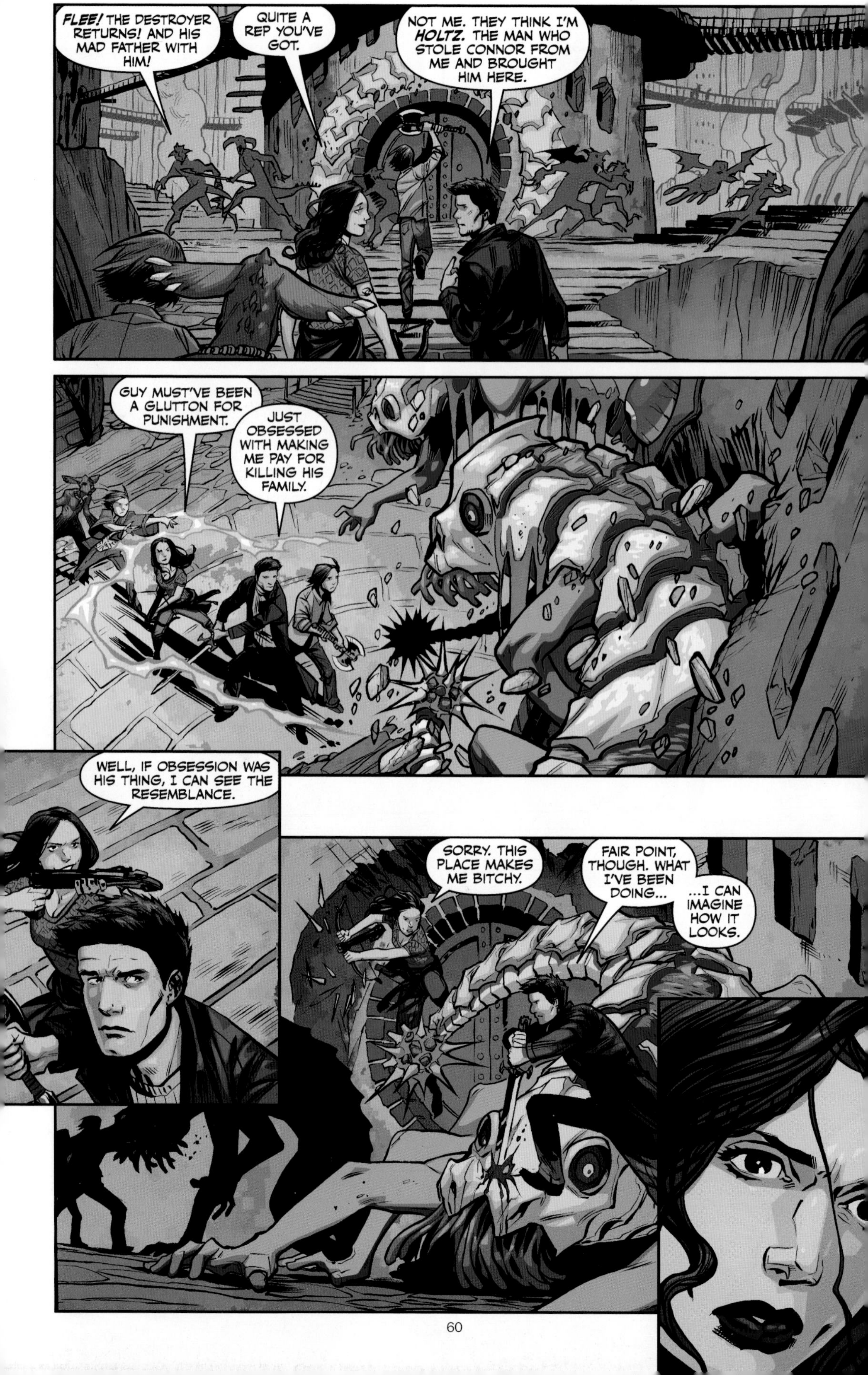

FLEE! THE DESTROYER RETURNS! AND HIS MAD FATHER WITH HIM!
QUITE A REP YOU'VE GOT.
NOT ME. THEY THINK I'M HOLTZ. THE MAN WHO STOLE CONNOR FROM ME AND BROUGHT HIM HERE.
GUY MUST'VE BEEN A GLUTTON FOR PUNISHMENT.
JUST OBSESSED WITH MAKING ME PAY FOR KILLING HIS FAMILY.
WELL, IF OBSESSION WAS HIS THING, I CAN SEE THE RESEMBLANCE.
SORRY. THIS PLACE MAKES ME BITCHY.
FAIR POINT, THOUGH. WHAT I'VE BEEN DOING...
...I CAN IMAGINE HOW IT LOOKS.

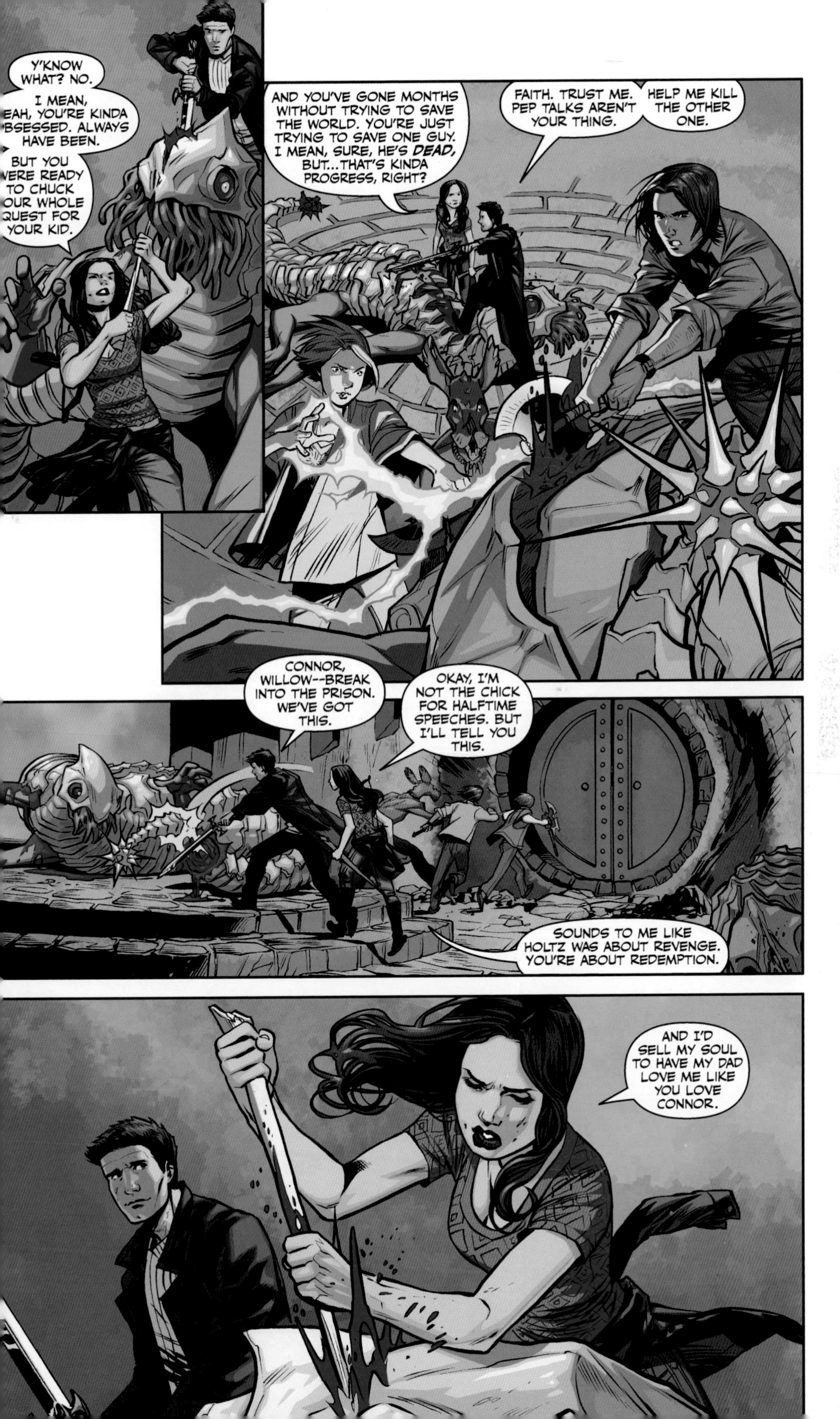

Y'KNOW WHAT? NO.
I MEAN, EAH, YOU'RE KINDA BSESSED. ALWAYS HAVE BEEN.
BUT YOU ERE READY TO CHUCK OUR WHOLE QUEST FOR YOUR KID.
AND YOU'VE GONE MONTHS WITHOUT TRYING TO SAVE THE WORLD. YOU'RE JUST TRYING TO SAVE ONE GUY. I MEAN, SURE, HE'S ***DEAD,*** BUT...THAT'S KINDA PROGRESS, RIGHT?
FAITH. TRUST ME. PEP TALKS AREN'T YOUR THING.
HELP ME KILL THE OTHER ONE.
CONNOR, WILLOW--BREAK INTO THE PRISON. WE'VE GOT THIS.
OKAY, I'M NOT THE CHICK FOR HALFTIME SPEECHES. BUT I'LL TELL YOU THIS.
SOUNDS TO ME LIKE HOLTZ WAS ABOUT REVENGE. YOU'RE ABOUT REDEMPTION.
AND I'D SELL MY SOUL TO HAVE MY DAD LOVE ME LIKE YOU LOVE CONNOR.

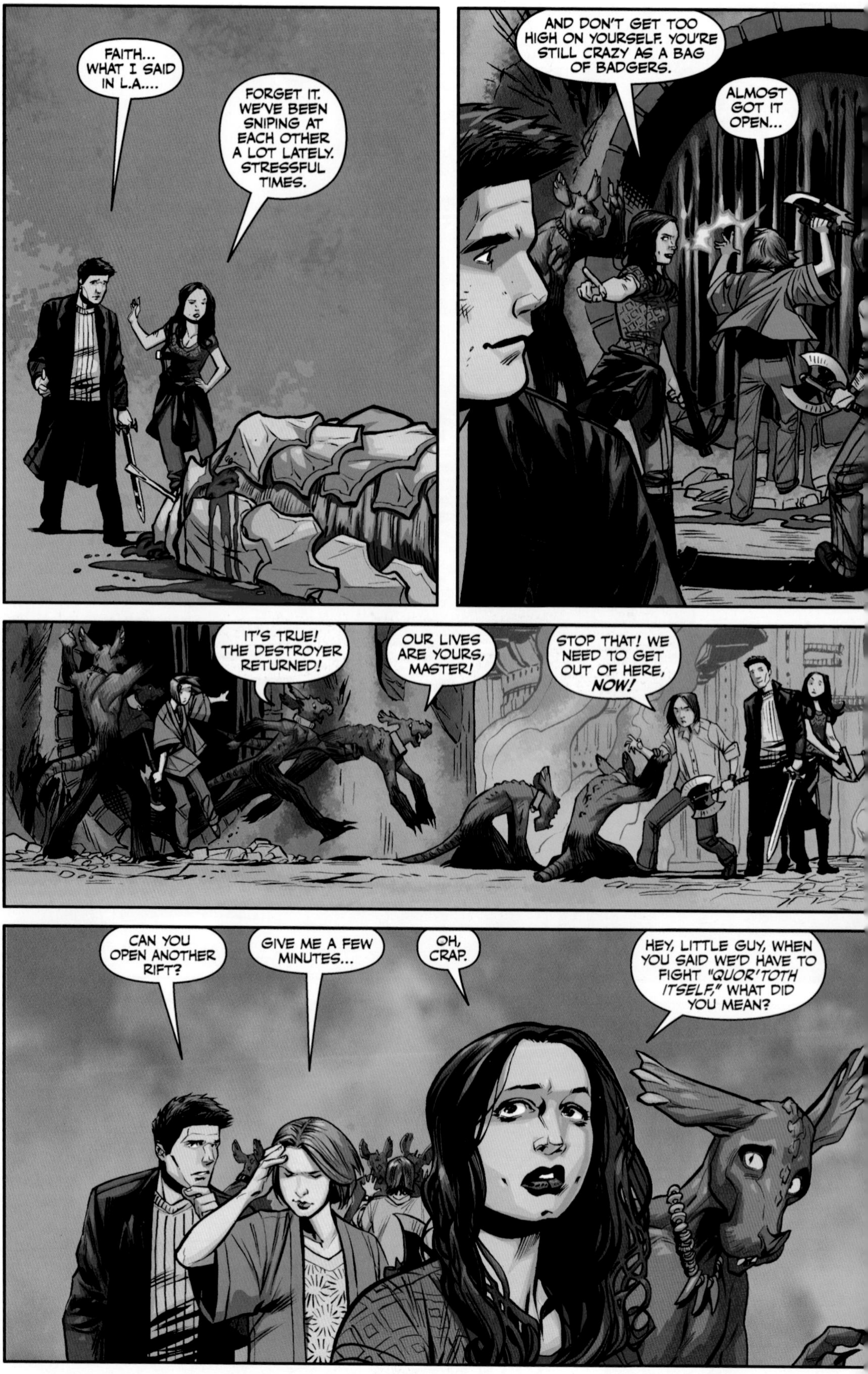
FAITH... WHAT I SAID IN L.A....
FORGET IT. WE'VE BEEN SNIPING AT EACH OTHER A LOT LATELY. STRESSFUL TIMES.
AND DON'T GET TOO HIGH ON YOURSELF. YOU'RE STILL CRAZY AS A BAG OF BADGERS.
ALMOST GOT IT OPEN...
IT'S TRUE! THE DESTROYER RETURNED!
OUR LIVES ARE YOURS, MASTER!
STOP THAT! WE NEED TO GET OUT OF HERE, NOW!
CAN YOU OPEN ANOTHER RIFT?
GIVE ME A FEW MINUTES...
OH, CRAP.
HEY, LITTLE GUY, WHEN YOU SAID WE'D HAVE TO FIGHT "QUOR'TOTH ITSELF," WHAT DID YOU MEAN?

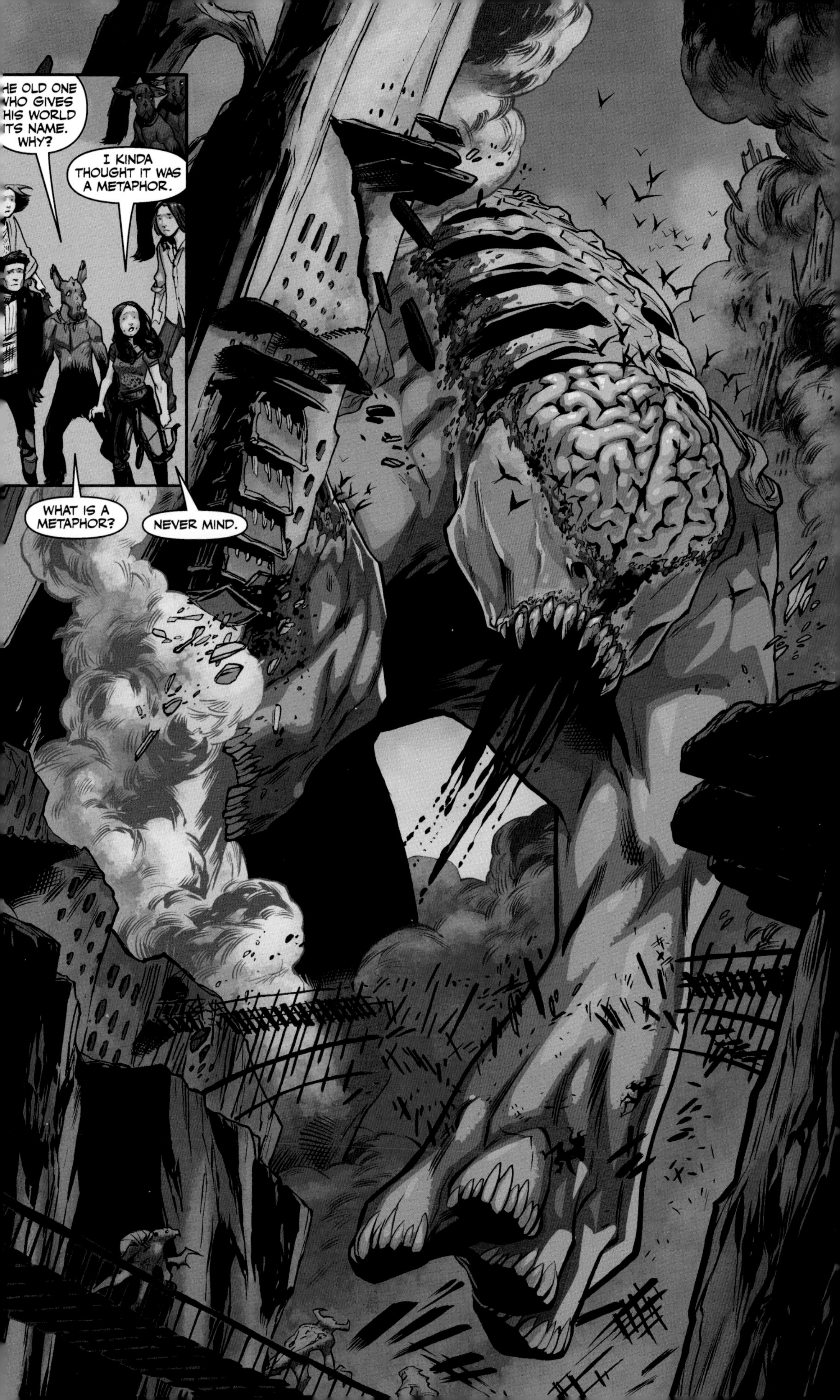
HE OLD ONE WHO GIVES HIS WORLD ITS NAME. WHY?
I KINDA THOUGHT IT WAS A METAPHOR.
WHAT IS A METAPHOR?
NEVER MIND.

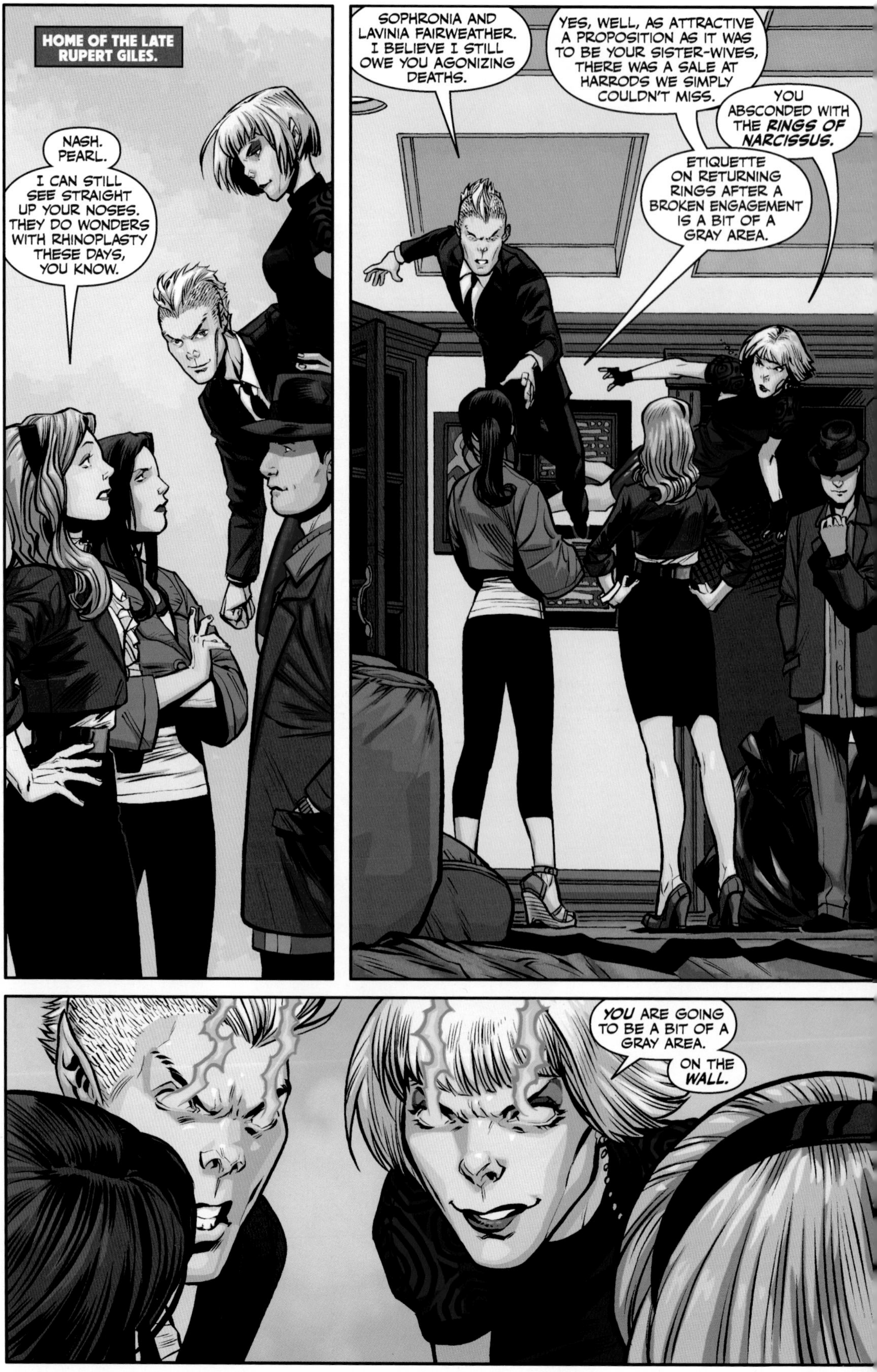
HOME OF THE LATE RUPERT GILES.
NASH. PEARL.
I CAN STILL SEE STRAIGHT UP YOUR NOSES. THEY DO WONDERS WITH RHINOPLASTY THESE DAYS, YOU KNOW.
SOPHRONIA AND LAVINIA FAIRWEATHER. I BELIEVE I STILL OWE YOU AGONIZING DEATHS.
YES, WELL, AS ATTRACTIVE A PROPOSITION AS IT WAS TO BE YOUR SISTER-WIVES, THERE WAS A SALE AT HARRODS WE SIMPLY COULDN'T MISS.
YOU ABSCONDED WITH THE RINGS OF NARCISSUS.
ETIQUETTE ON RETURNING RINGS AFTER A BROKEN ENGAGEMENT IS A BIT OF A GRAY AREA.
YOU ARE GOING TO BE A BIT OF A GRAY AREA.
ON THE WALL.

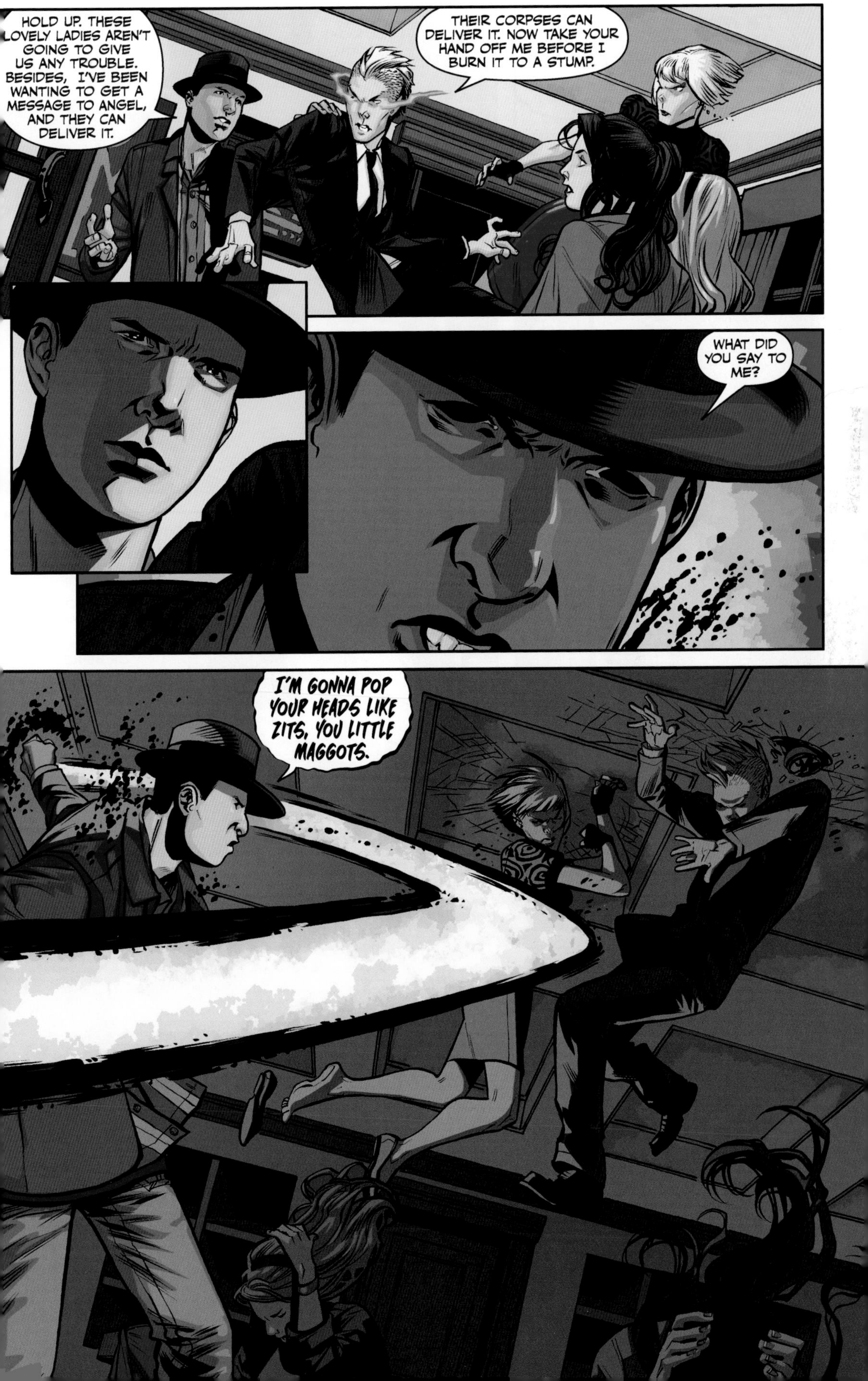
HOLD UP. THESE LOVELY LADIES AREN'T GOING TO GIVE US ANY TROUBLE. BESIDES, I'VE BEEN WANTING TO GET A MESSAGE TO ANGEL, AND THEY CAN DELIVER IT.
THEIR CORPSES CAN DELIVER IT. NOW TAKE YOUR HAND OFF ME BEFORE I BURN IT TO A STUMP.
WHAT DID YOU SAY TO ME?
I'M GONNA POP YOUR HEADS LIKE ZITS, YOU LITTLE MAGGOTS.

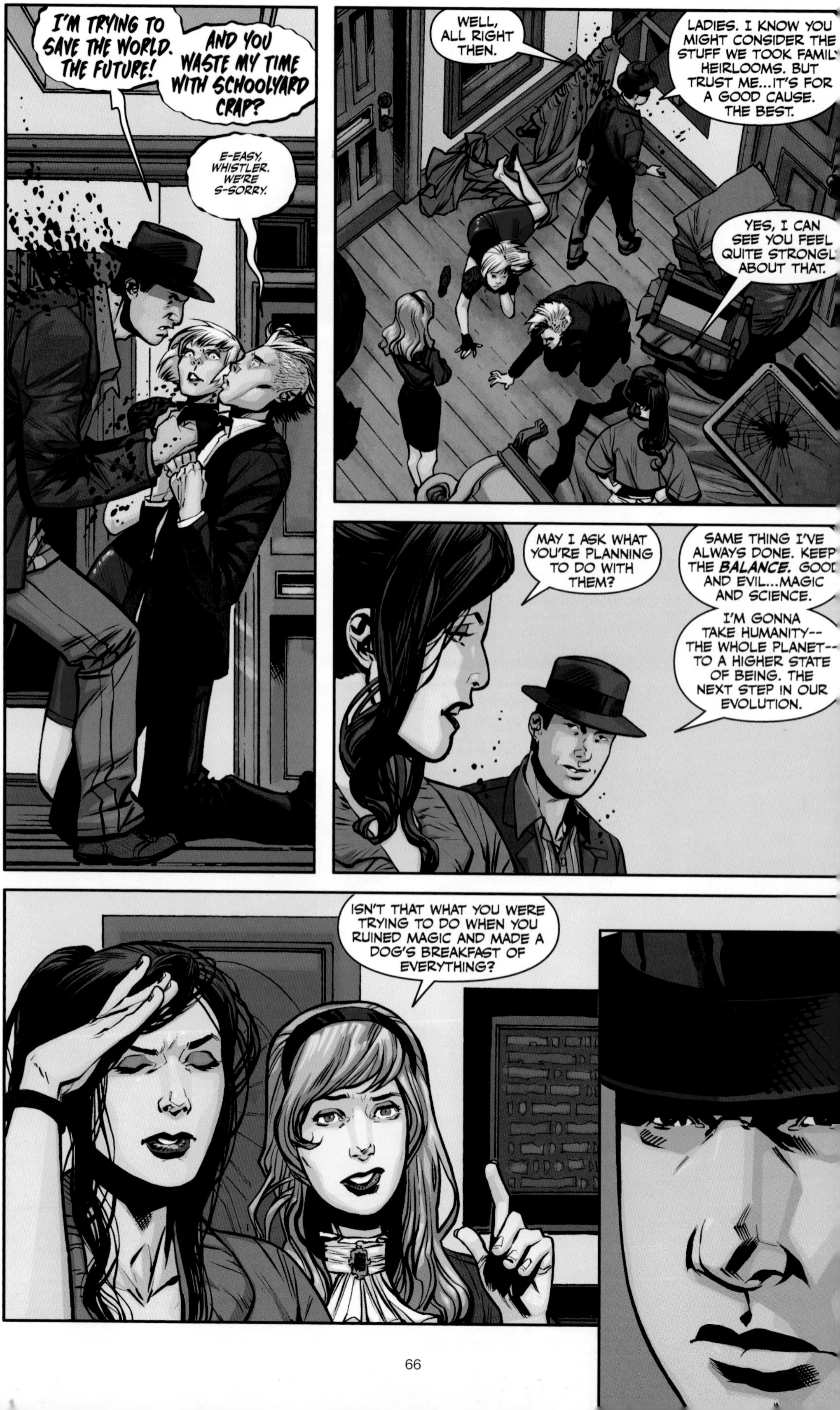
I'M TRYING TO SAVE THE WORLD. THE FUTURE!
AND YOU WASTE MY TIME WITH SCHOOLYARD CRAP?
E-EASY, WHISTLER. WE'RE S-SORRY.
WELL, ALL RIGHT THEN.
LADIES. I KNOW YOU MIGHT CONSIDER THE STUFF WE TOOK FAMIL HEIRLOOMS. BUT TRUST ME...IT'S FOR A GOOD CAUSE. THE BEST.
YES, I CAN SEE YOU FEEL QUITE STRONGL ABOUT THAT.
MAY I ASK WHAT YOU'RE PLANNING TO DO WITH THEM?
SAME THING I'VE ALWAYS DONE. KEEP THE *BALANCE.* GOOD AND EVIL...MAGIC AND SCIENCE.
I'M GONNA TAKE HUMANITY-- THE WHOLE PLANET-- TO A HIGHER STATE OF BEING. THE NEXT STEP IN OUR EVOLUTION.
ISN'T THAT WHAT YOU WERE TRYING TO DO WHEN YOU RUINED MAGIC AND MADE A DOG'S BREAKFAST OF EVERYTHING?

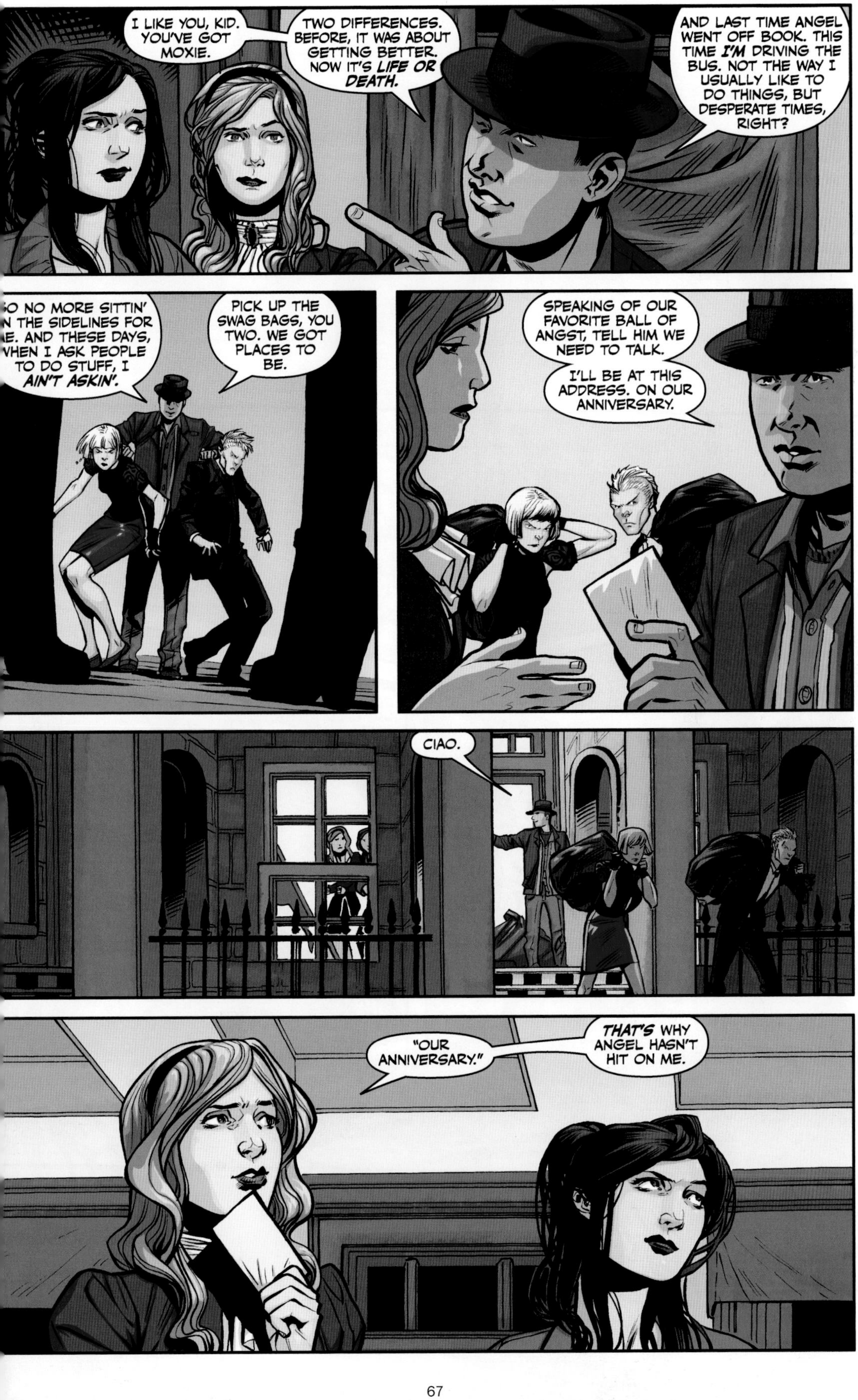

I LIKE YOU, KID. YOU'VE GOT MOXIE.
TWO DIFFERENCES. BEFORE, IT WAS ABOUT GETTING BETTER. NOW IT'S *LIFE OR DEATH.*
AND LAST TIME ANGEL WENT OFF BOOK. THIS TIME *I'M* DRIVING THE BUS. NOT THE WAY I USUALLY LIKE TO DO THINGS, BUT DESPERATE TIMES, RIGHT?
O NO MORE SITTIN' N THE SIDELINES FOR E. AND THESE DAYS, VHEN I ASK PEOPLE TO DO STUFF, I *AIN'T ASKIN'.*
PICK UP THE SWAG BAGS, YOU TWO. WE GOT PLACES TO BE.
SPEAKING OF OUR FAVORITE BALL OF ANGST, TELL HIM WE NEED TO TALK.
I'LL BE AT THIS ADDRESS. ON OUR ANNIVERSARY.
CIAO.
"OUR ANNIVERSARY."
THAT'S WHY ANGEL HASN'T HIT ON ME.

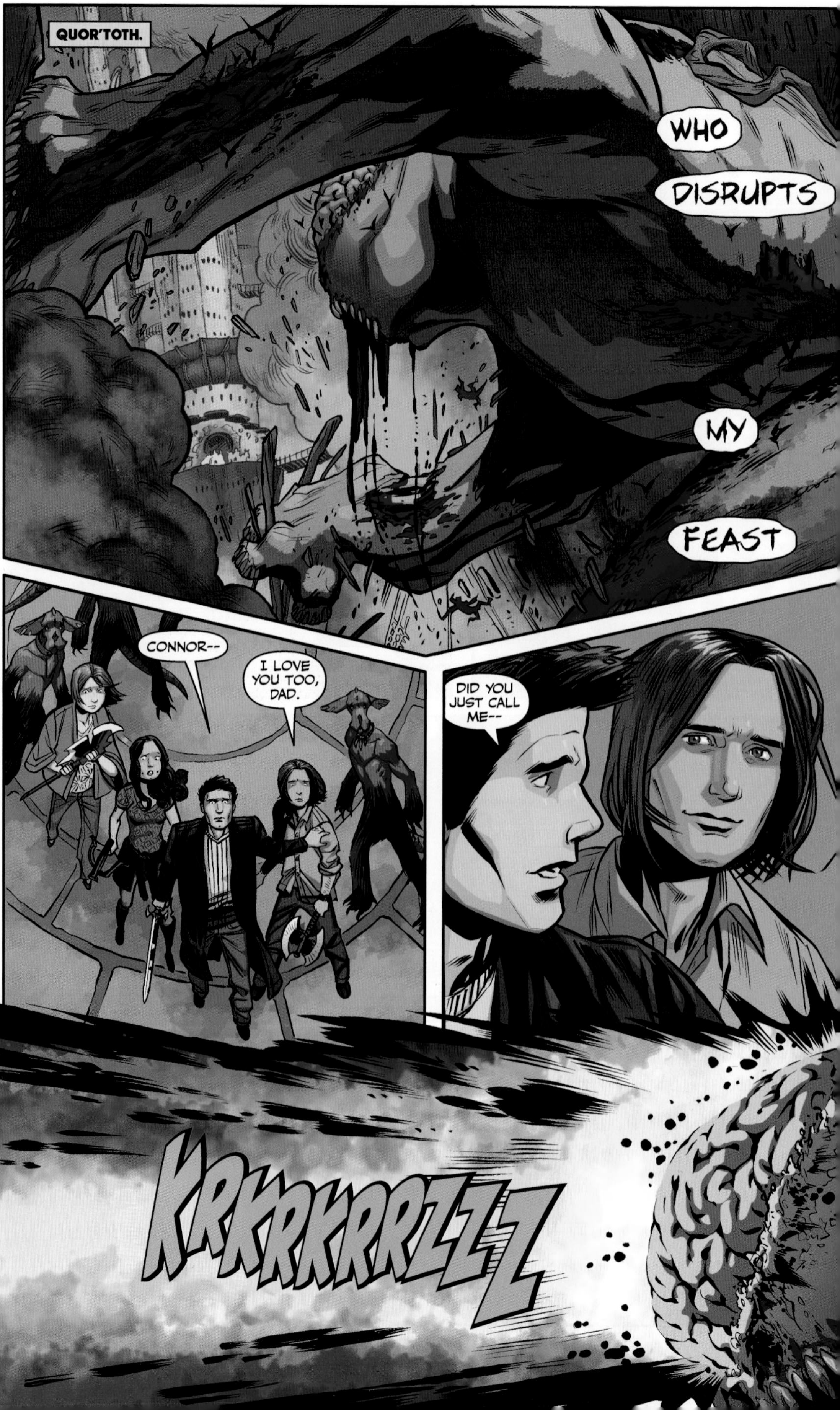
QUOR'TOTH.
WHO
DISRUPTS
MY
FEAST
CONNOR--
I LOVE YOU TOO, DAD.
DID YOU JUST CALL ME--
KRKRKRRZZZ

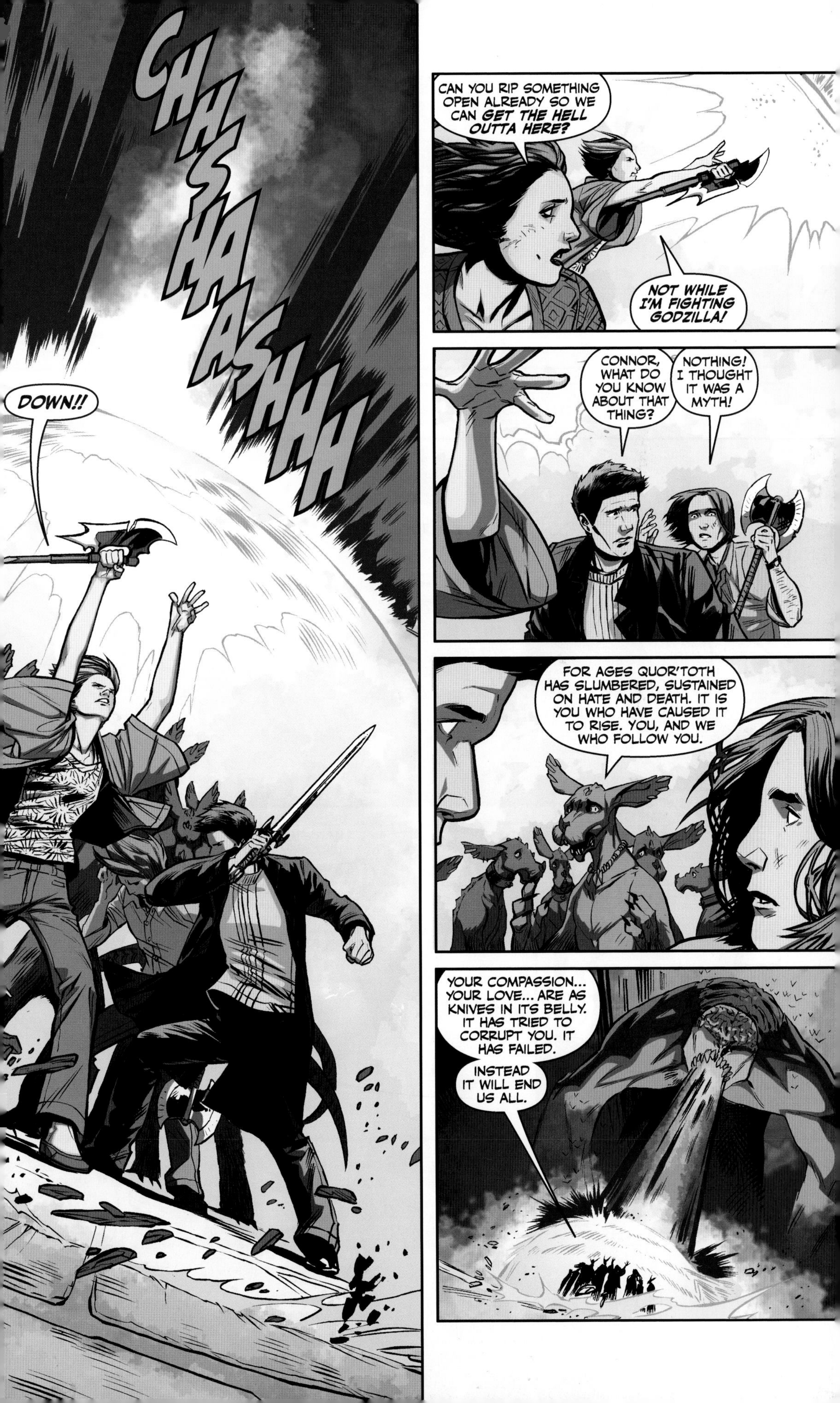
CHHSHAHASHHH
DOWN!!
CAN YOU RIP SOMETHING OPEN ALREADY SO WE CAN GET THE HELL OUTTA HERE?
NOT WHILE I'M FIGHTING GODZILLA!
CONNOR, WHAT DO YOU KNOW ABOUT THAT THING?
NOTHING! I THOUGHT IT WAS A MYTH!
FOR AGES QUOR'TOTH HAS SLUMBERED, SUSTAINED ON HATE AND DEATH. IT IS YOU WHO HAVE CAUSED IT TO RISE. YOU, AND WE WHO FOLLOW YOU.
YOUR COMPASSION... YOUR LOVE... ARE AS KNIVES IN ITS BELLY. IT HAS TRIED TO CORRUPT YOU. IT HAS FAILED.
INSTEAD IT WILL END US ALL.

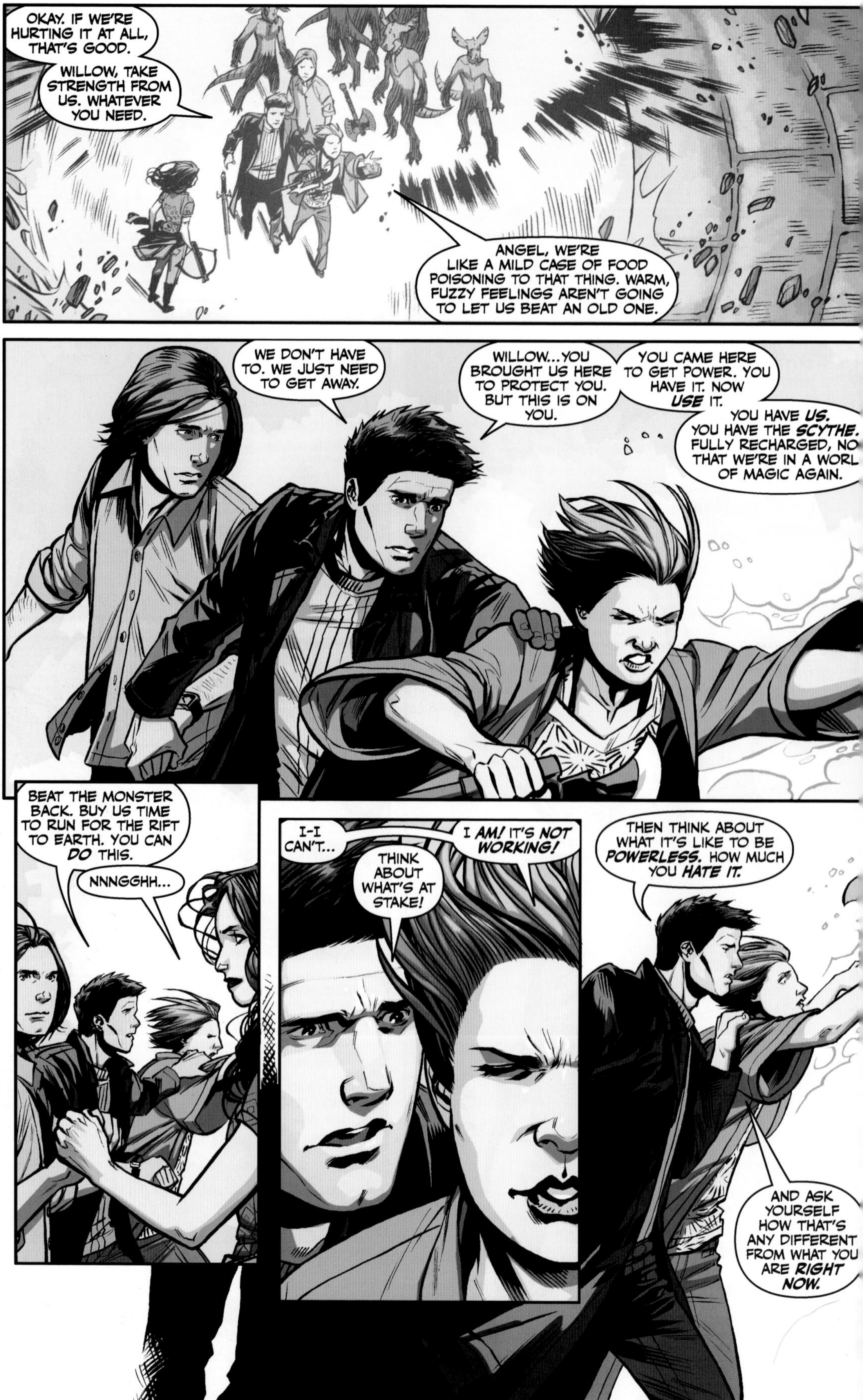
OKAY. IF WE'RE HURTING IT AT ALL, THAT'S GOOD.
WILLOW, TAKE STRENGTH FROM US. WHATEVER YOU NEED.
ANGEL, WE'RE LIKE A MILD CASE OF FOOD POISONING TO THAT THING. WARM, FUZZY FEELINGS AREN'T GOING TO LET US BEAT AN OLD ONE.
WE DON'T HAVE TO. WE JUST NEED TO GET AWAY.
WILLOW...YOU BROUGHT US HERE TO PROTECT YOU. BUT THIS IS ON YOU.
YOU CAME HERE TO GET POWER. YOU HAVE IT. NOW USE IT.
YOU HAVE US. YOU HAVE THE SCYTHE. FULLY RECHARGED, NO THAT WE'RE IN A WORL OF MAGIC AGAIN.
BEAT THE MONSTER BACK. BUY US TIME TO RUN FOR THE RIFT TO EARTH. YOU CAN DO THIS.
NNNGGHH...
I-I CAN'T...
THINK ABOUT WHAT'S AT STAKE!
I AM! IT'S NOT WORKING!
THEN THINK ABOUT WHAT IT'S LIKE TO BE POWERLESS. HOW MUCH YOU HATE IT.
AND ASK YOURSELF HOW THAT'S ANY DIFFERENT FROM WHAT YOU ARE RIGHT NOW.

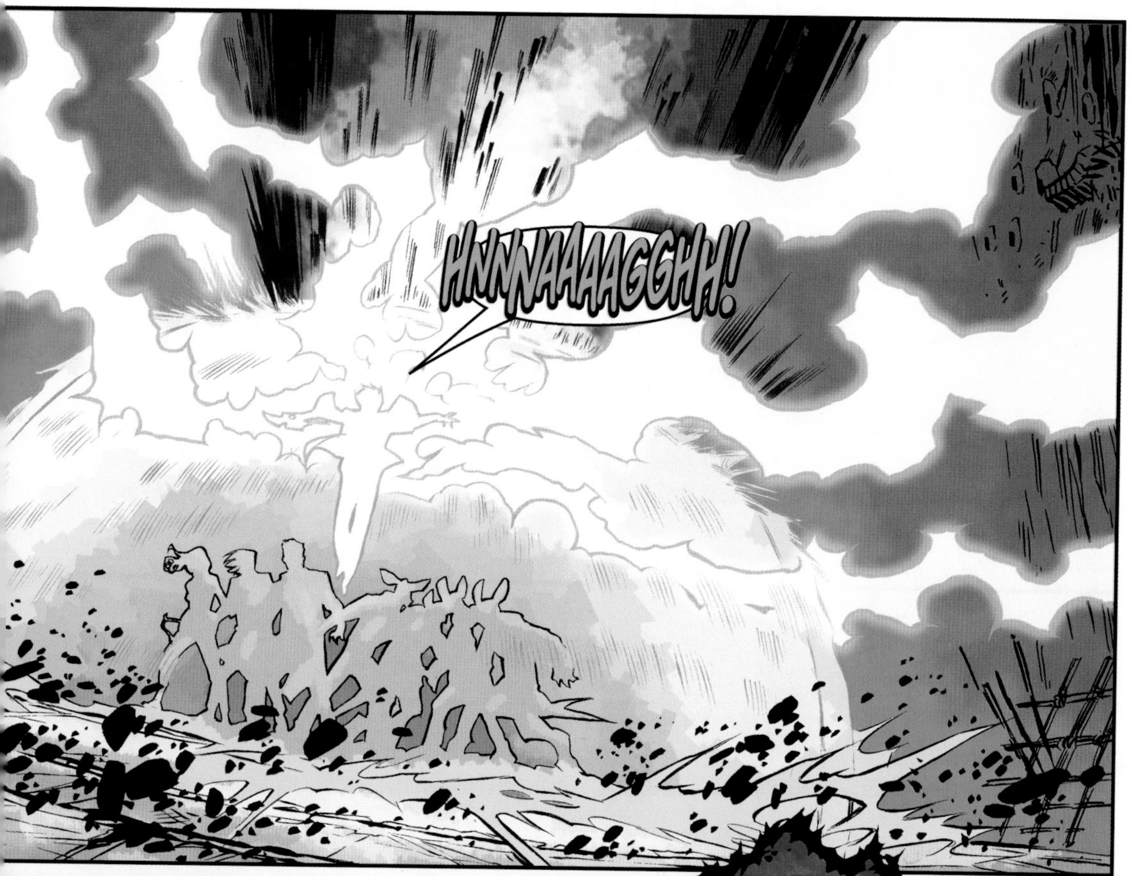
HNNNAAAAGGHH!

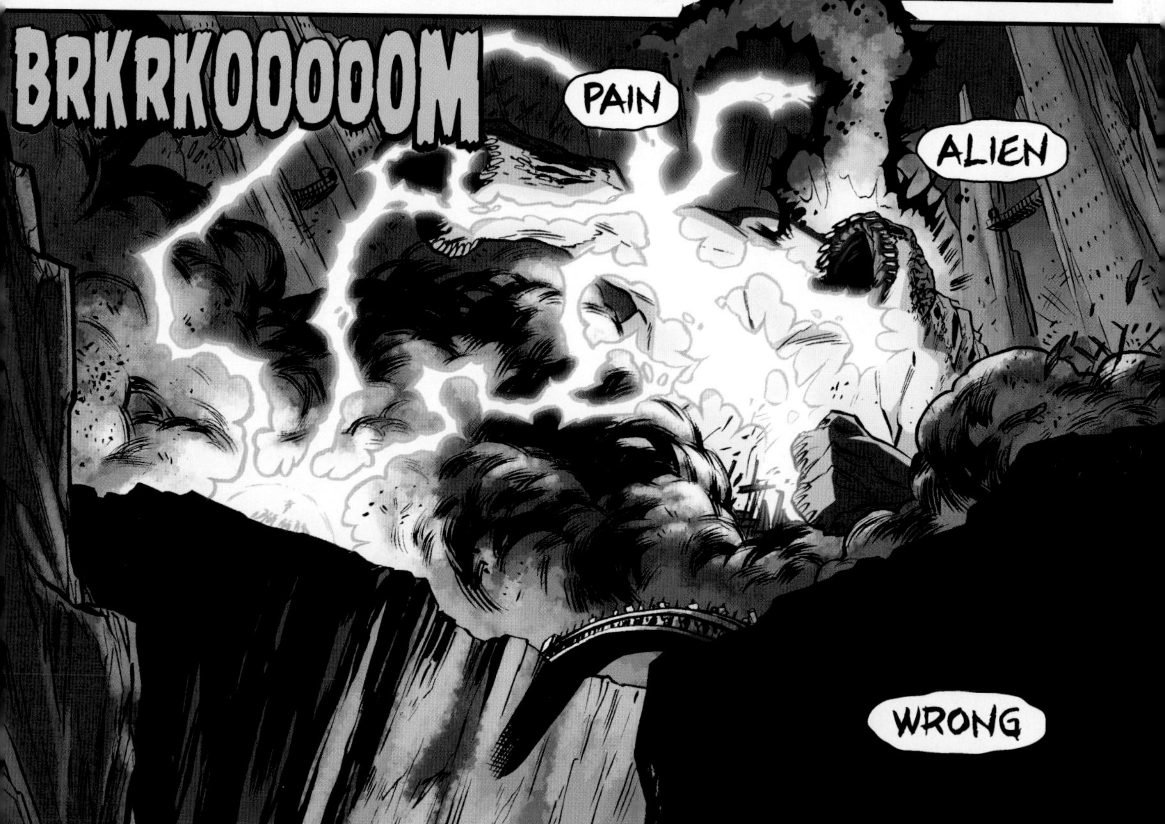
BRKRKOOOOOM
PAIN
ALIEN
WRONG

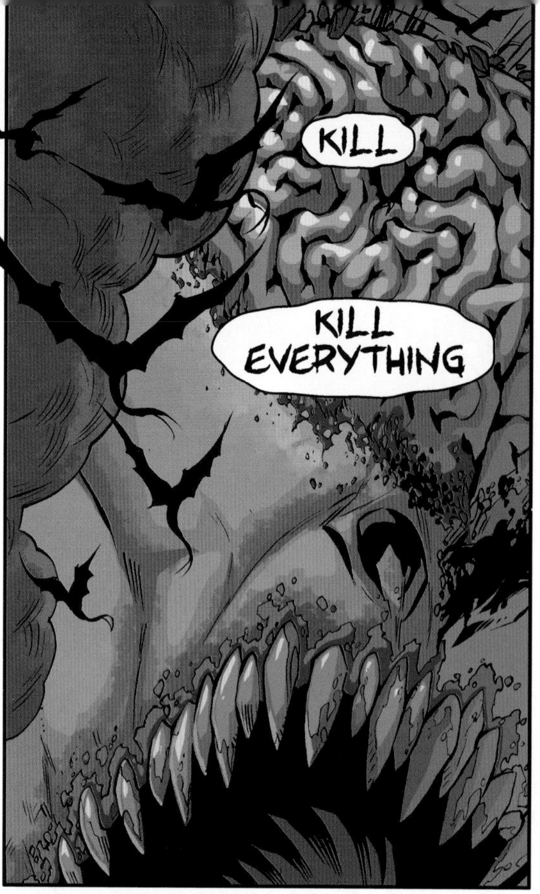
KILL
KILL EVERYTHING

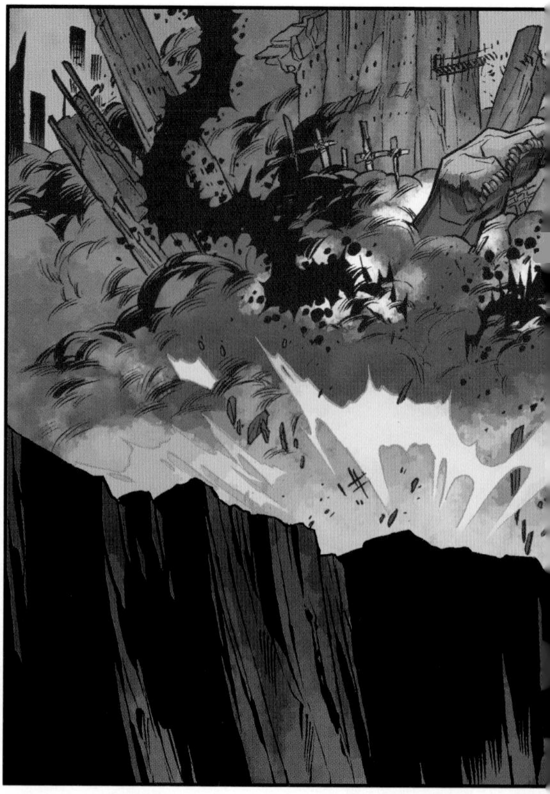

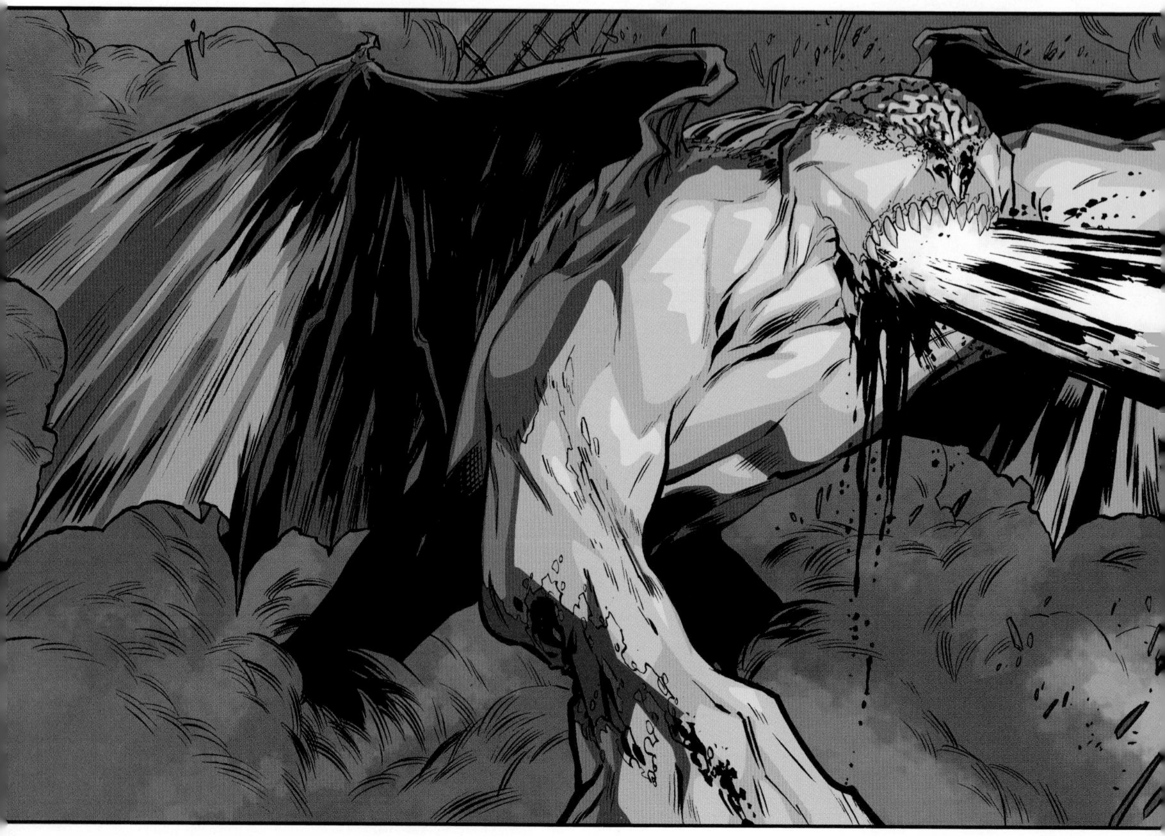

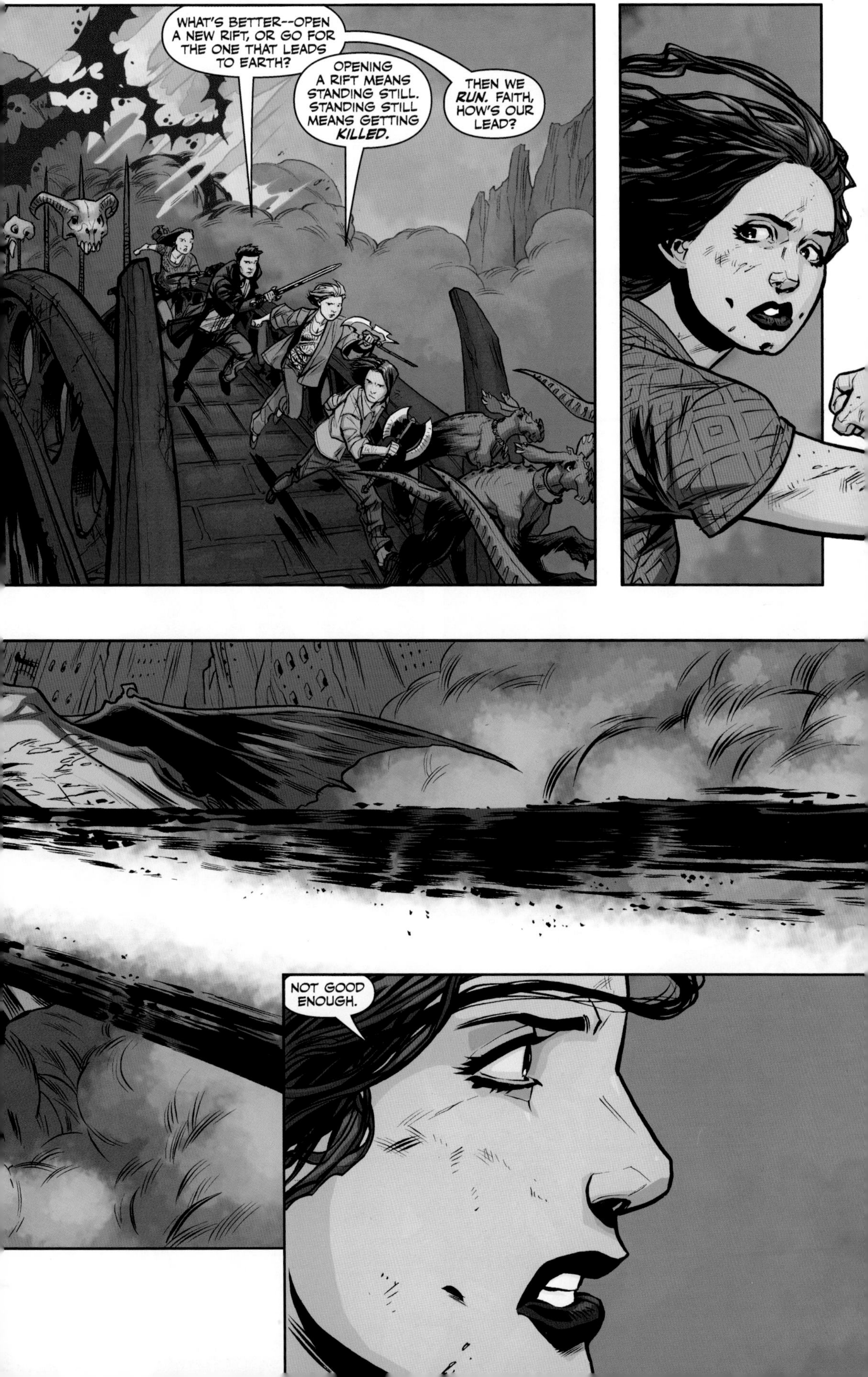

WHAT'S BETTER--OPEN A NEW RIFT, OR GO FOR THE ONE THAT LEADS TO EARTH?
OPENING A RIFT MEANS STANDING STILL. STANDING STILL MEANS GETTING KILLED.
THEN WE RUN. FAITH, HOW'S OUR LEAD?
NOT GOOD ENOUGH.

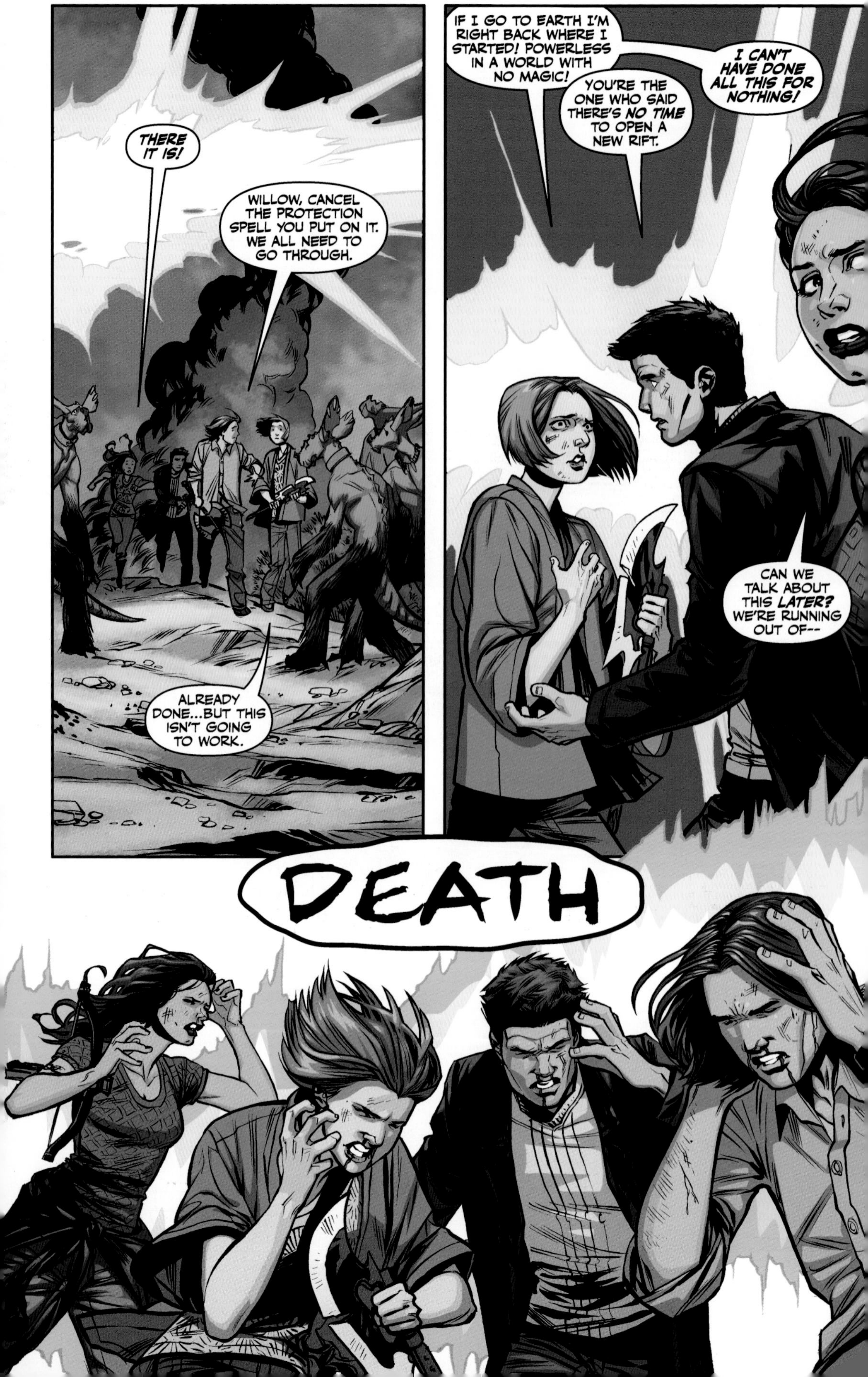
THERE IT IS!
WILLOW, CANCEL THE PROTECTION SPELL YOU PUT ON IT. WE ALL NEED TO GO THROUGH.
ALREADY DONE...BUT THIS ISN'T GOING TO WORK.
IF I GO TO EARTH I'M RIGHT BACK WHERE I STARTED! POWERLESS IN A WORLD WITH NO MAGIC!
YOU'RE THE ONE WHO SAID THERE'S NO TIME TO OPEN A NEW RIFT.
I CAN'T HAVE DONE ALL THIS FOR NOTHING!
CAN WE TALK ABOUT THIS LATER? WE'RE RUNNING OUT OF--
DEATH

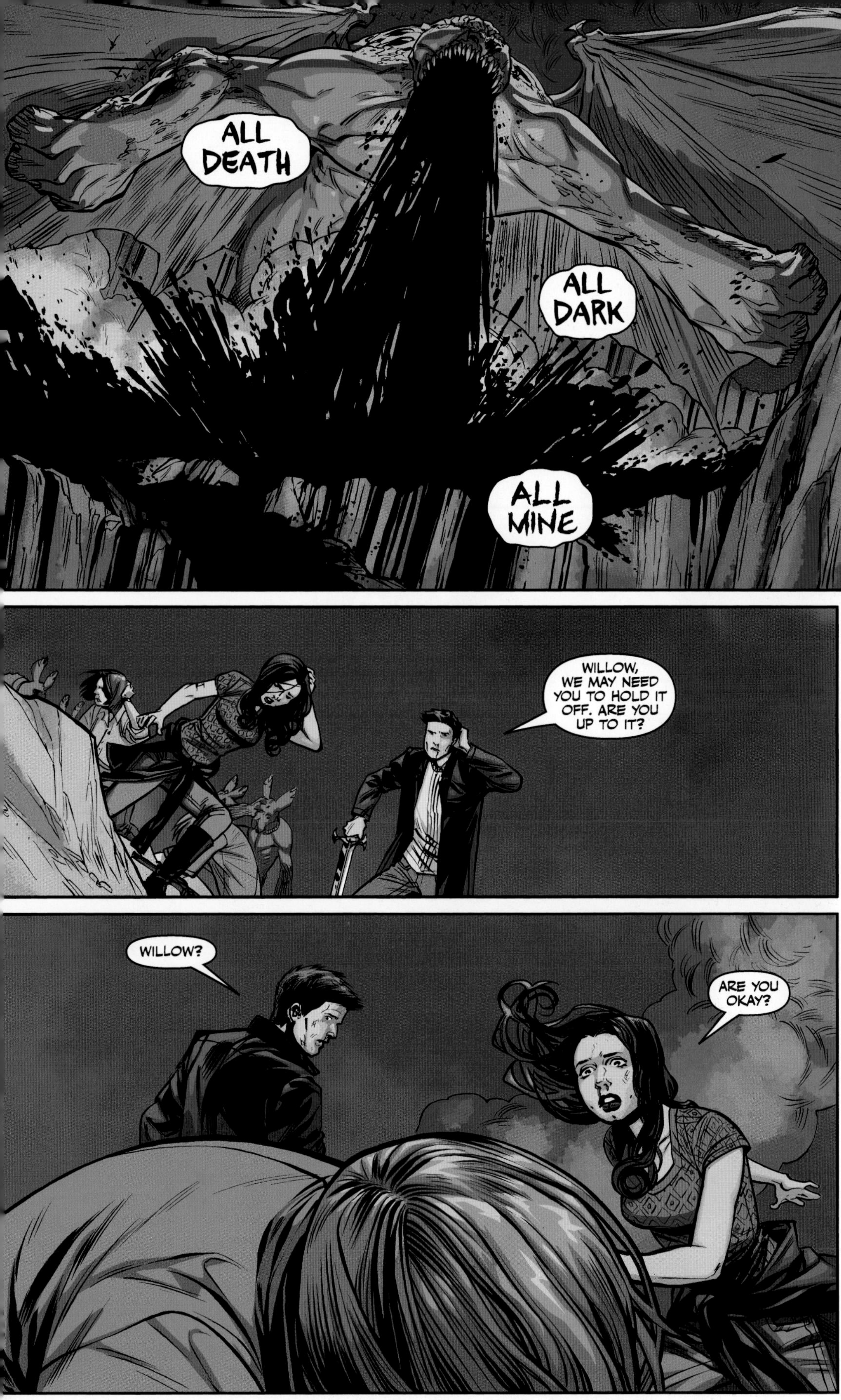
ALL DEATH
ALL DARK
ALL MINE
WILLOW, WE MAY NEED YOU TO HOLD IT OFF. ARE YOU UP TO IT?
WILLOW?
ARE YOU OKAY?

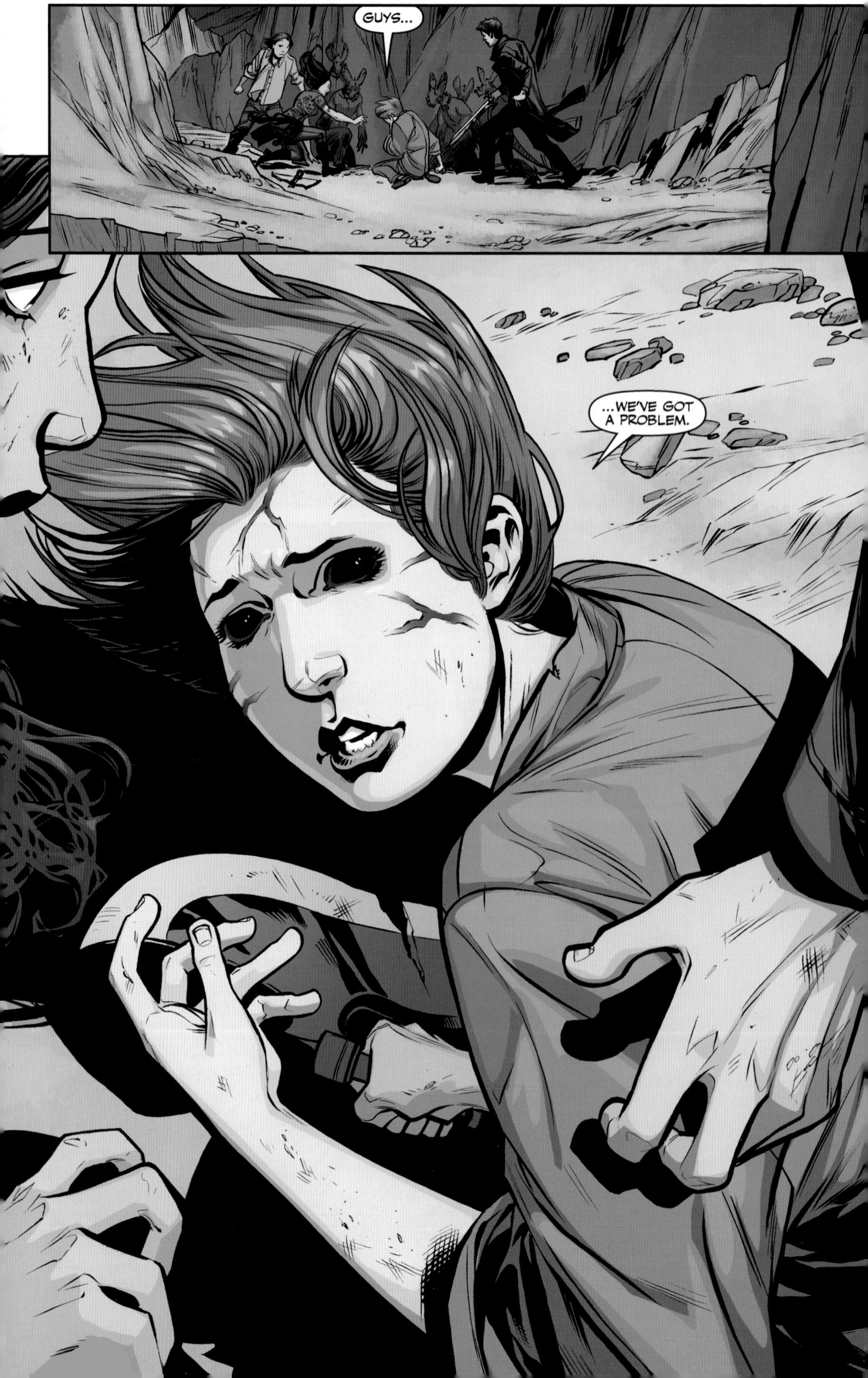
GUYS...
...WE'VE GOT A PROBLEM.

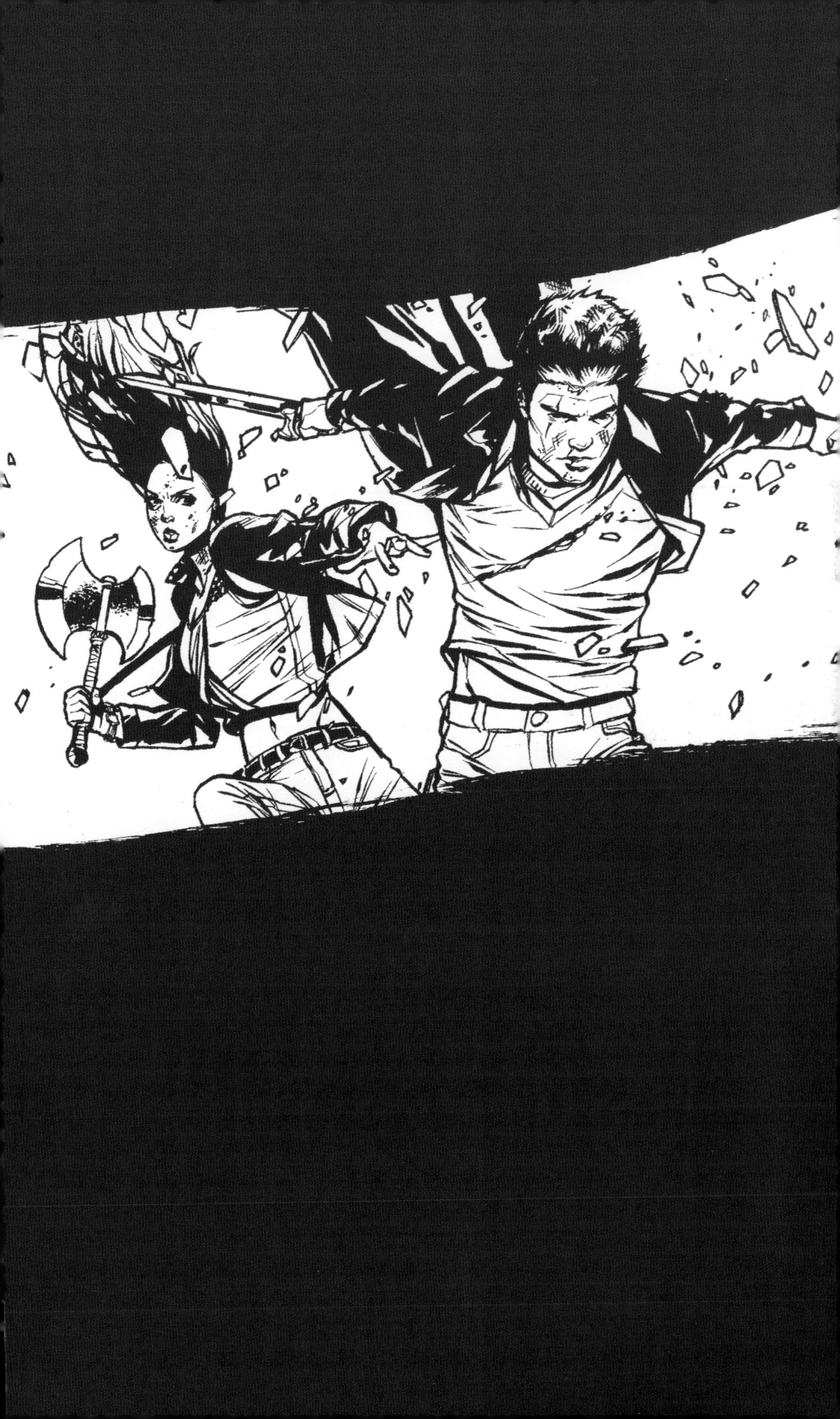

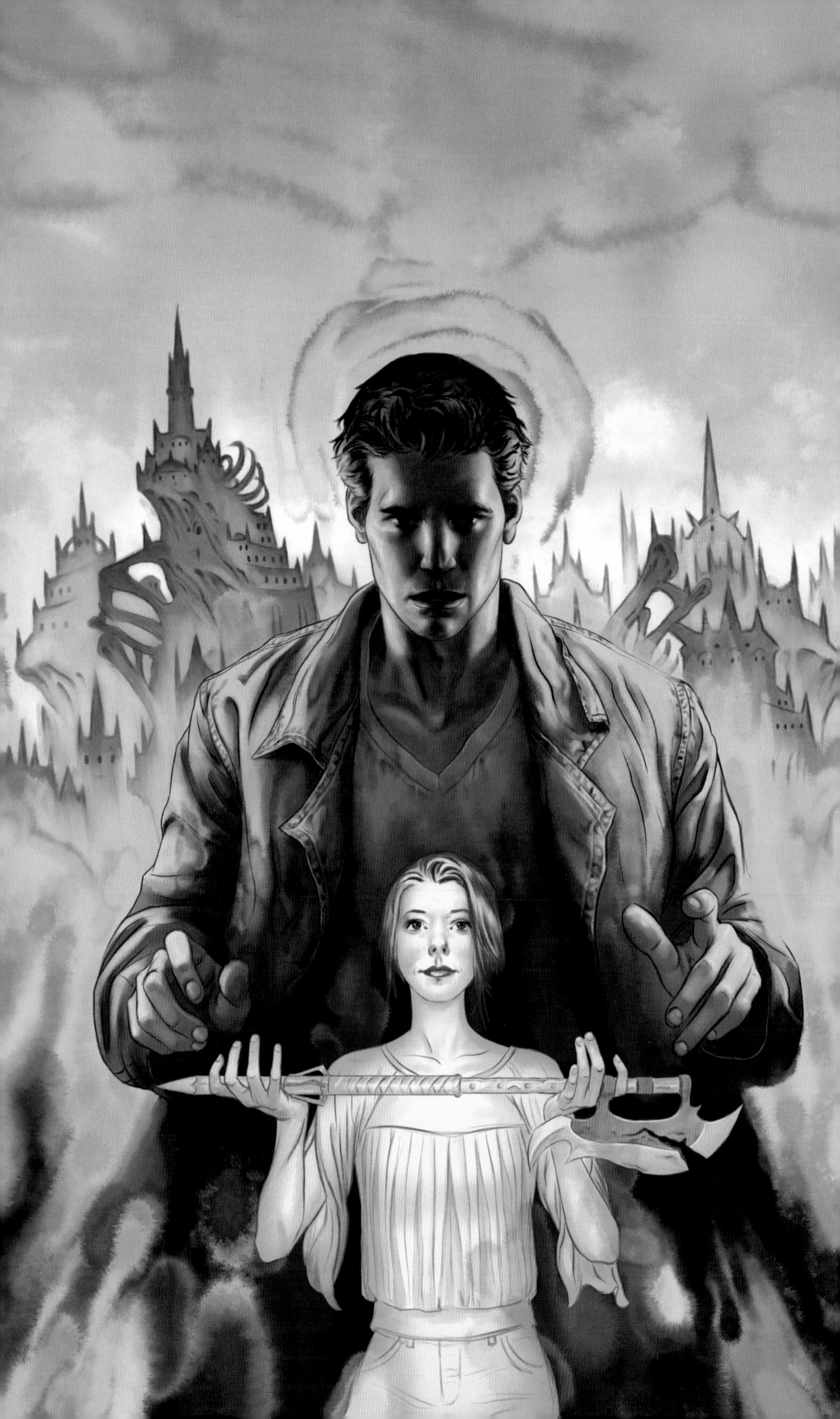

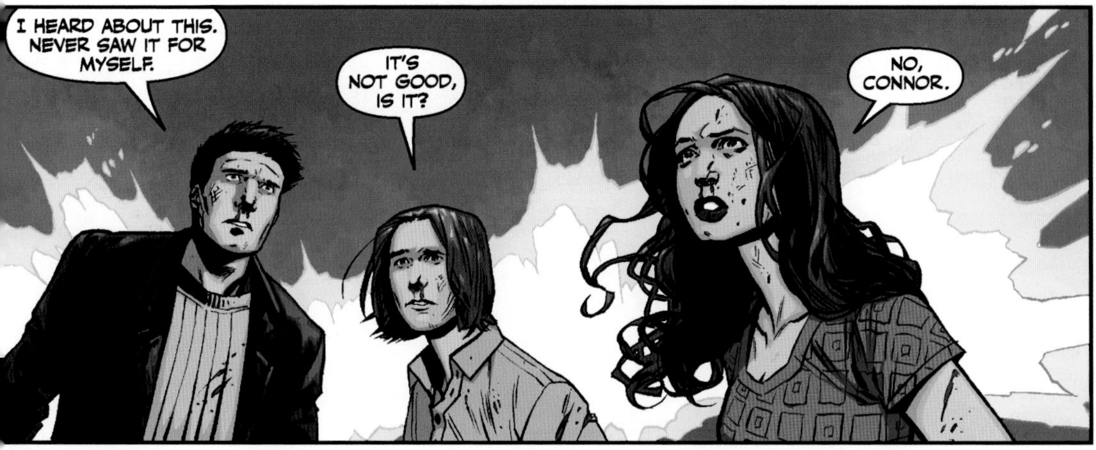
I HEARD ABOUT THIS. NEVER SAW IT FOR MYSELF.
IT'S NOT GOOD, IS IT?
NO, CONNOR.

FAMILY REUNION

PART FOUR

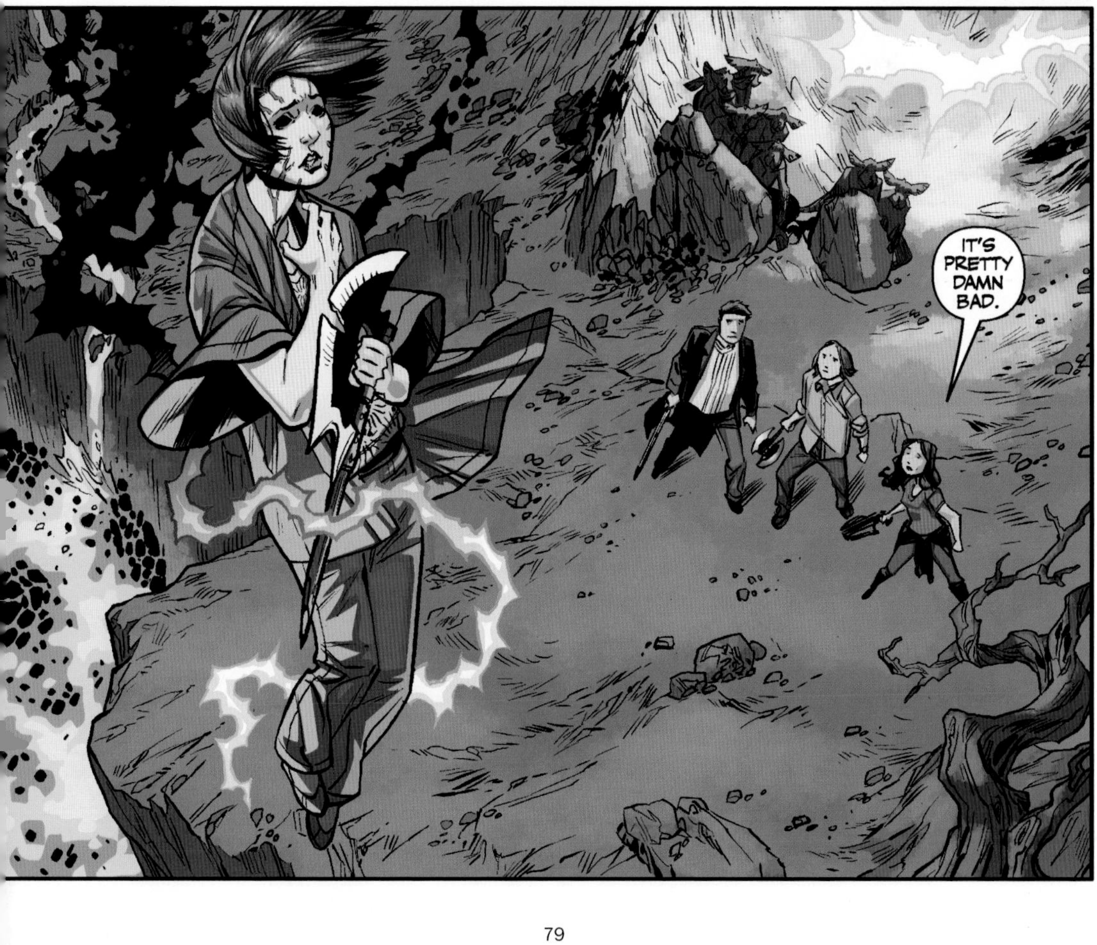
IT'S PRETTY DAMN BAD.

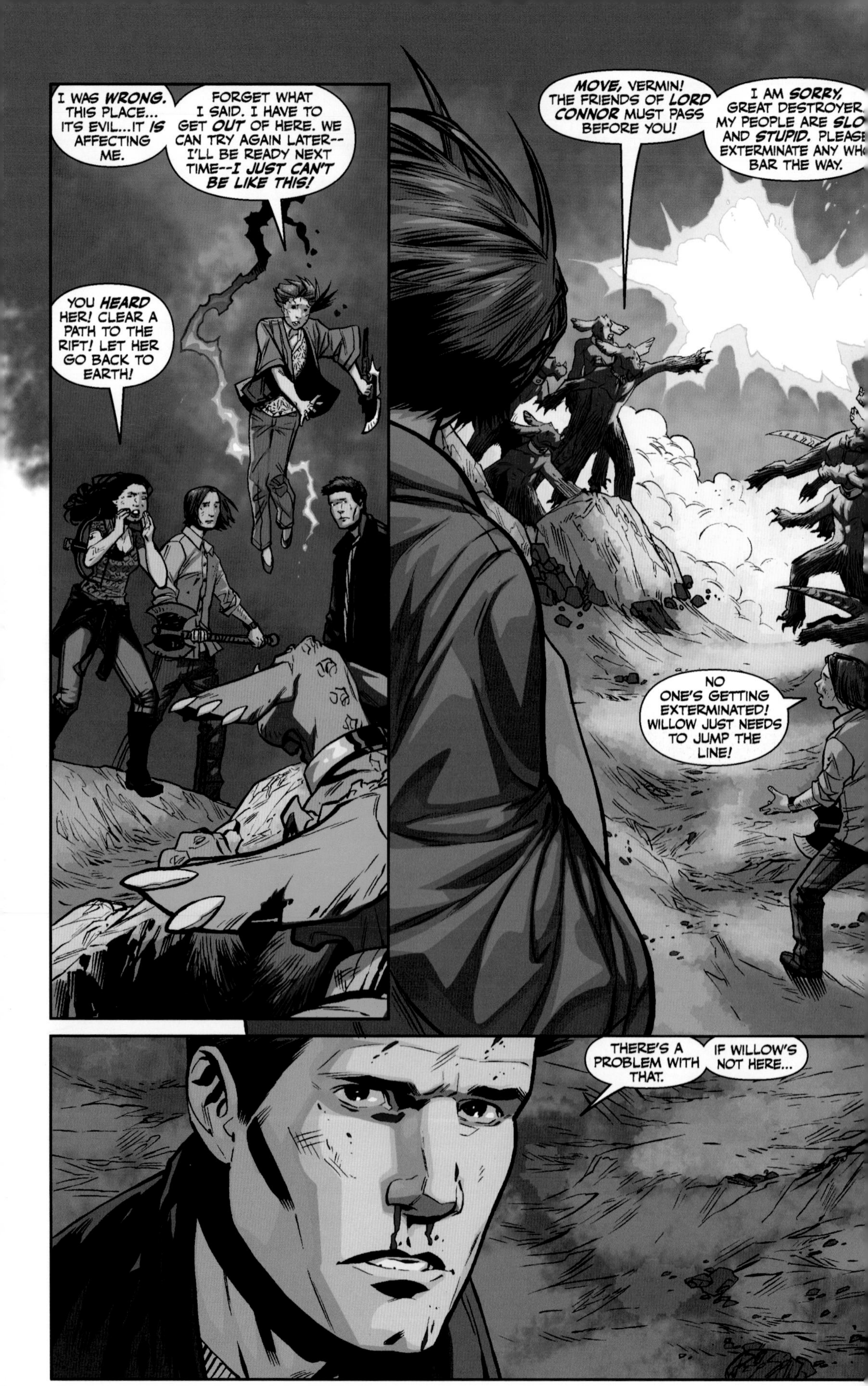
I WAS WRONG. THIS PLACE... IT'S EVIL...IT IS AFFECTING ME.
FORGET WHAT I SAID. I HAVE TO GET OUT OF HERE. WE CAN TRY AGAIN LATER-- I'LL BE READY NEXT TIME--I JUST CAN'T BE LIKE THIS!
YOU HEARD HER! CLEAR A PATH TO THE RIFT! LET HER GO BACK TO EARTH!
MOVE, VERMIN! THE FRIENDS OF LORD CONNOR MUST PASS BEFORE YOU!
I AM SORRY, GREAT DESTROYER. MY PEOPLE ARE SLO AND STUPID. PLEASE EXTERMINATE ANY WH BAR THE WAY.
NO ONE'S GETTING EXTERMINATED! WILLOW JUST NEEDS TO JUMP THE LINE!
THERE'S A PROBLEM WITH THAT.
IF WILLOW'S NOT HERE...

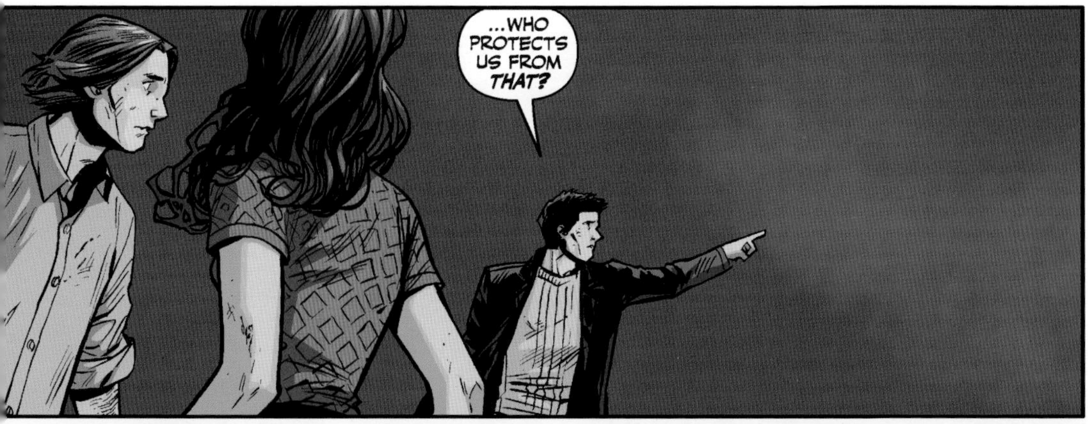
...WHO PROTECTS US FROM THAT?

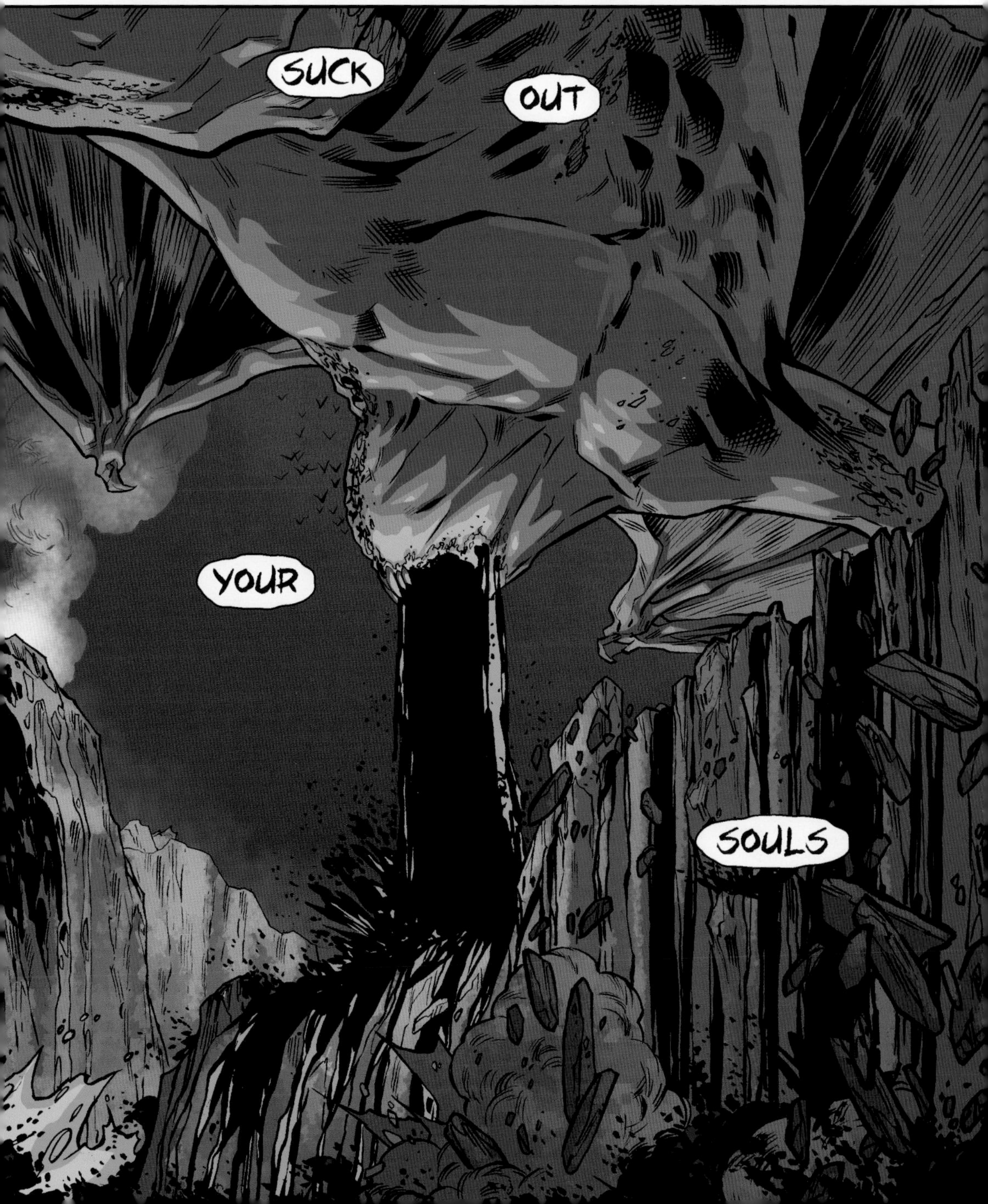
SUCK
OUT
YOUR
SOULS

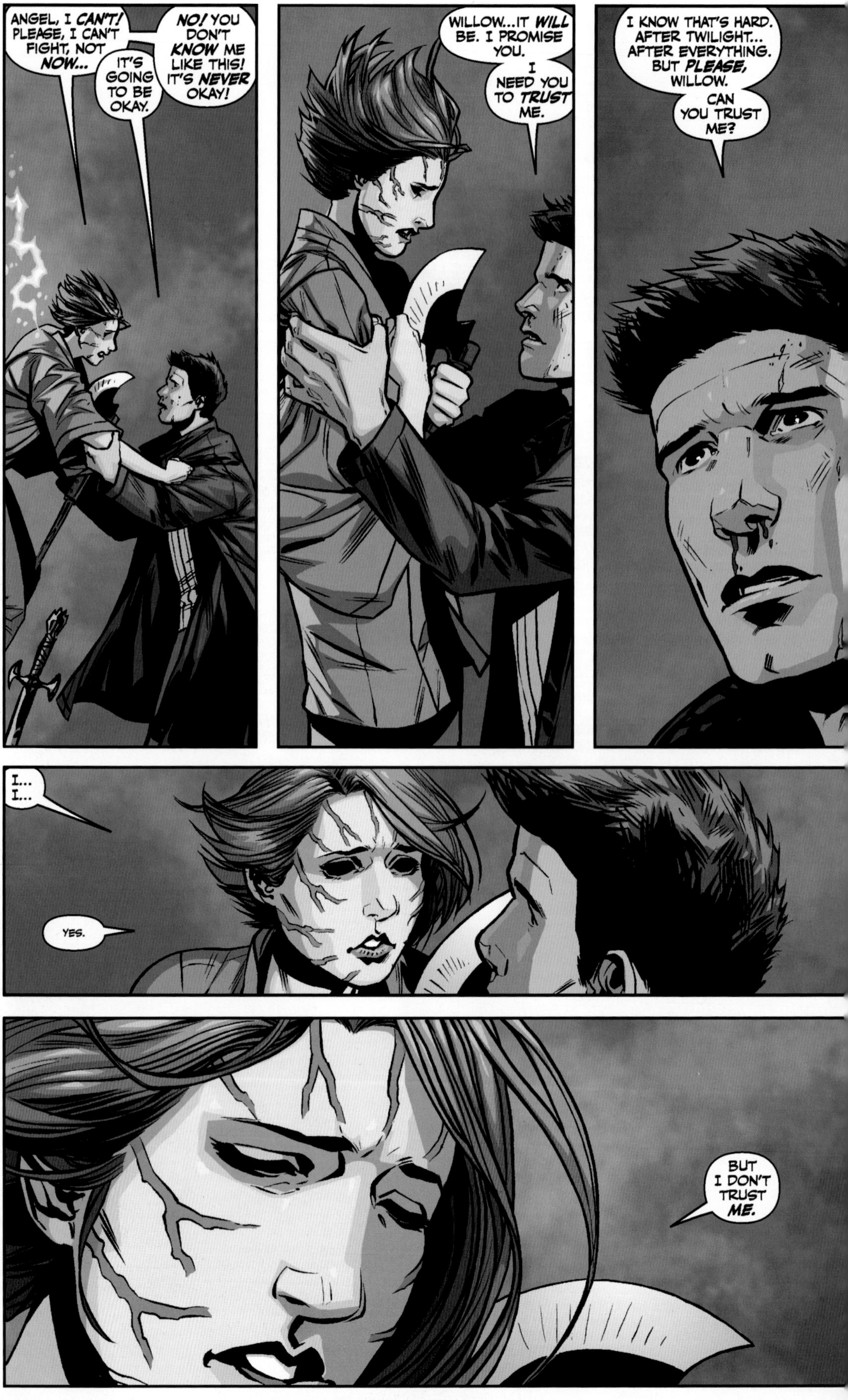

ANGEL, I *CAN'T!* PLEASE, I CAN'T FIGHT, NOT *NOW...*
IT'S GOING TO BE OKAY.
NO! YOU DON'T *KNOW* ME LIKE THIS! IT'S *NEVER* OKAY!
WILLOW...IT *WILL* BE. I PROMISE YOU.
I NEED YOU TO *TRUST* ME.
I KNOW THAT'S HARD. AFTER TWILIGHT... AFTER EVERYTHING. BUT *PLEASE,* WILLOW.
CAN YOU TRUST ME?
I... I...
YES.
BUT I DON'T TRUST *ME.*

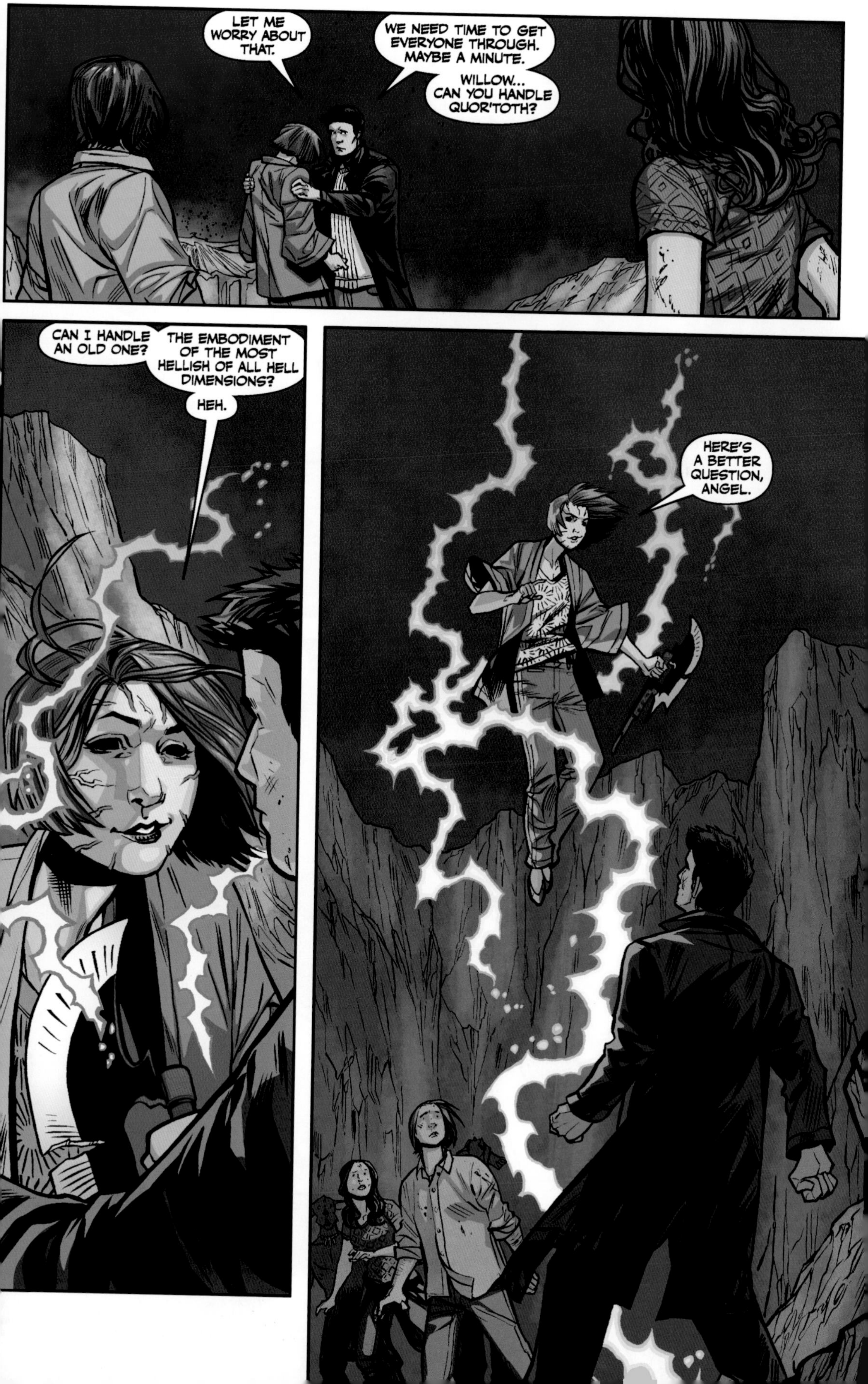
LET ME WORRY ABOUT THAT.
WE NEED TIME TO GET EVERYONE THROUGH. MAYBE A MINUTE.
WILLOW... CAN YOU HANDLE QUOR'TOTH?
CAN I HANDLE AN OLD ONE?
THE EMBODIMENT OF THE MOST HELLISH OF ALL HELL DIMENSIONS?
HEH.
HERE'S A BETTER QUESTION, ANGEL.

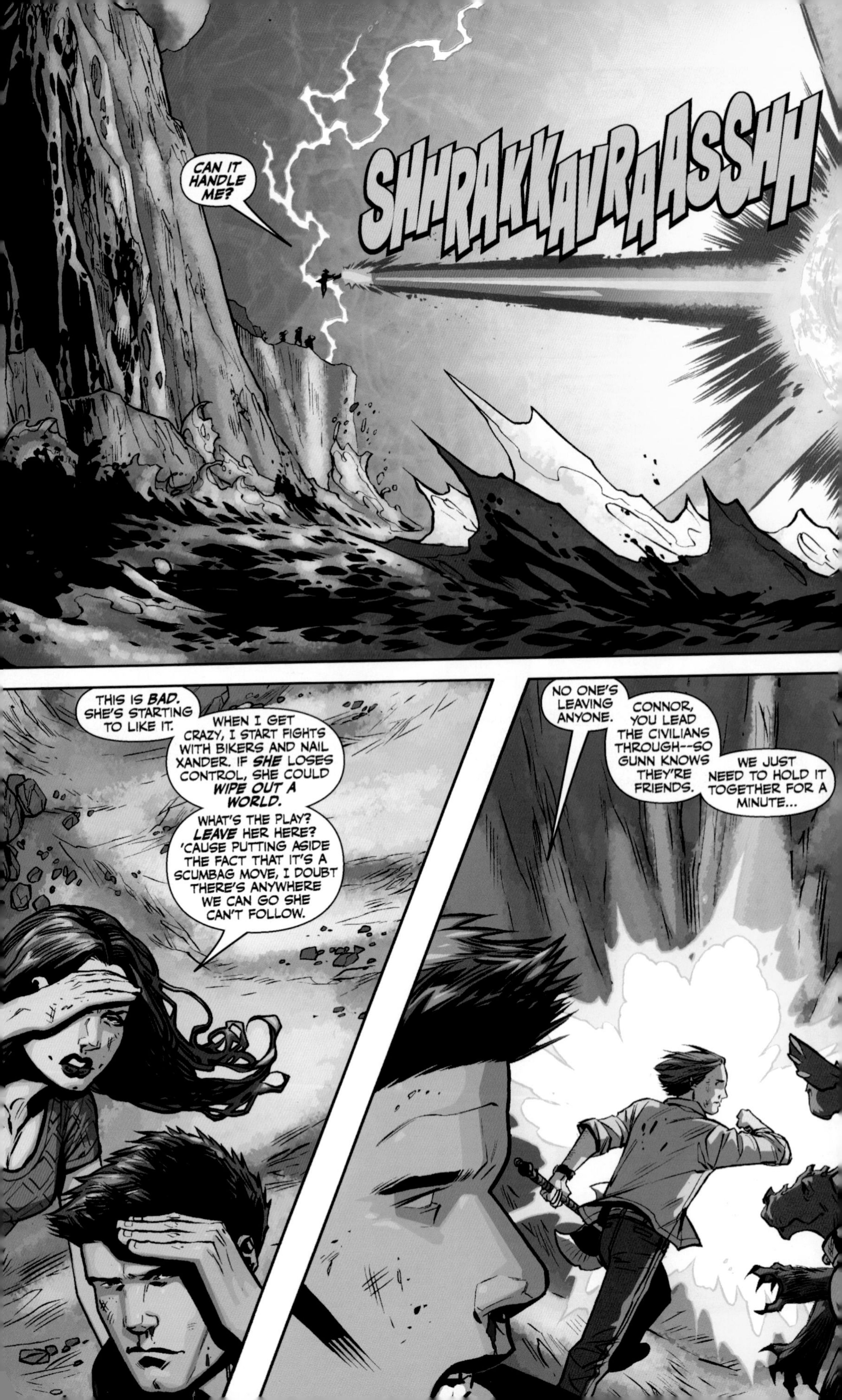
CAN IT HANDLE ME?
SHHRAKKAVRAASSHH
THIS IS BAD. SHE'S STARTING TO LIKE IT.
WHEN I GET CRAZY, I START FIGHTS WITH BIKERS AND NAIL XANDER. IF SHE LOSES CONTROL, SHE COULD WIPE OUT A WORLD.
WHAT'S THE PLAY? LEAVE HER HERE? 'CAUSE PUTTING ASIDE THE FACT THAT IT'S A SCUMBAG MOVE, I DOUBT THERE'S ANYWHERE WE CAN GO SHE CAN'T FOLLOW.
NO ONE'S LEAVING ANYONE.
CONNOR, YOU LEAD THE CIVILIANS THROUGH--SO GUNN KNOWS THEY'RE FRIENDS.
WE JUST NEED TO HOLD IT TOGETHER FOR A MINUTE...

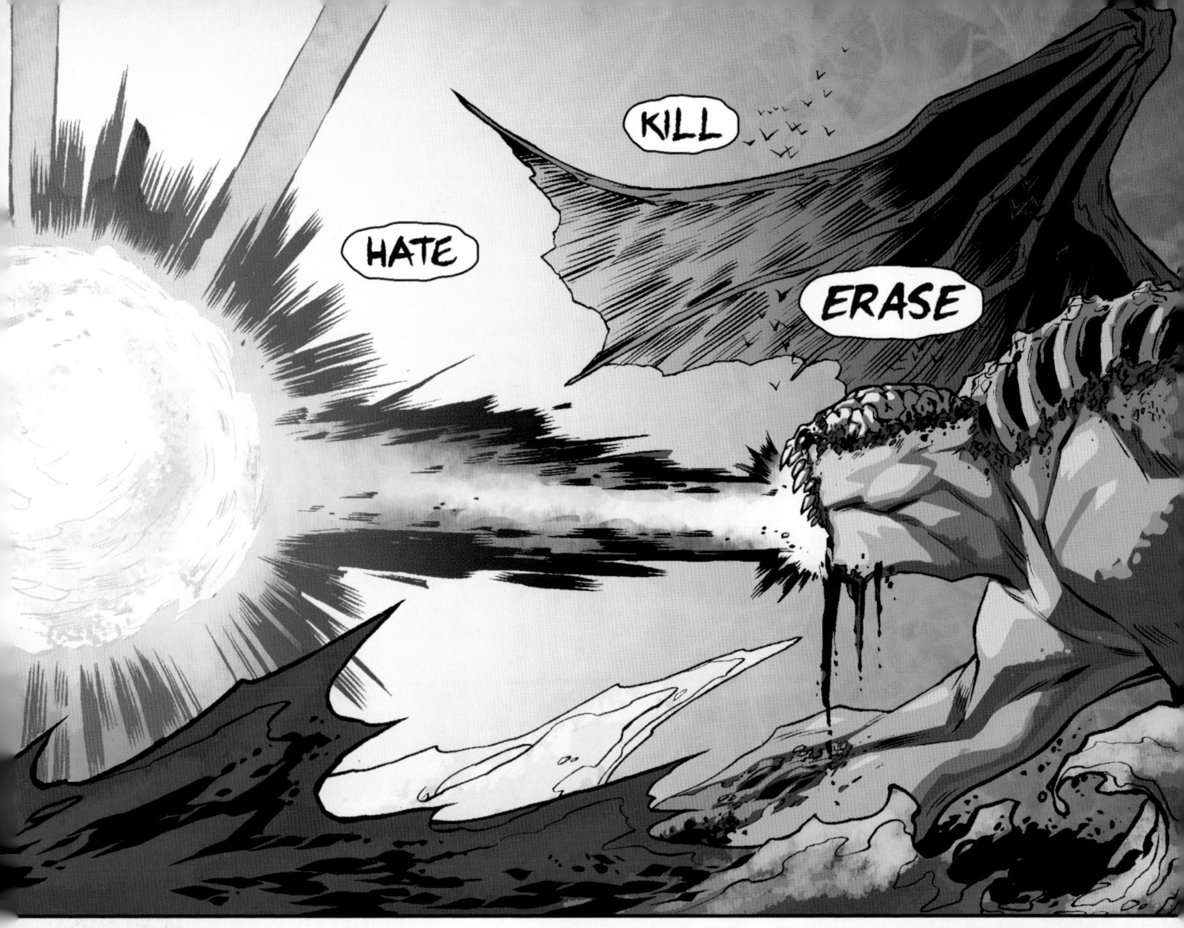
HATE
KILL
ERASE

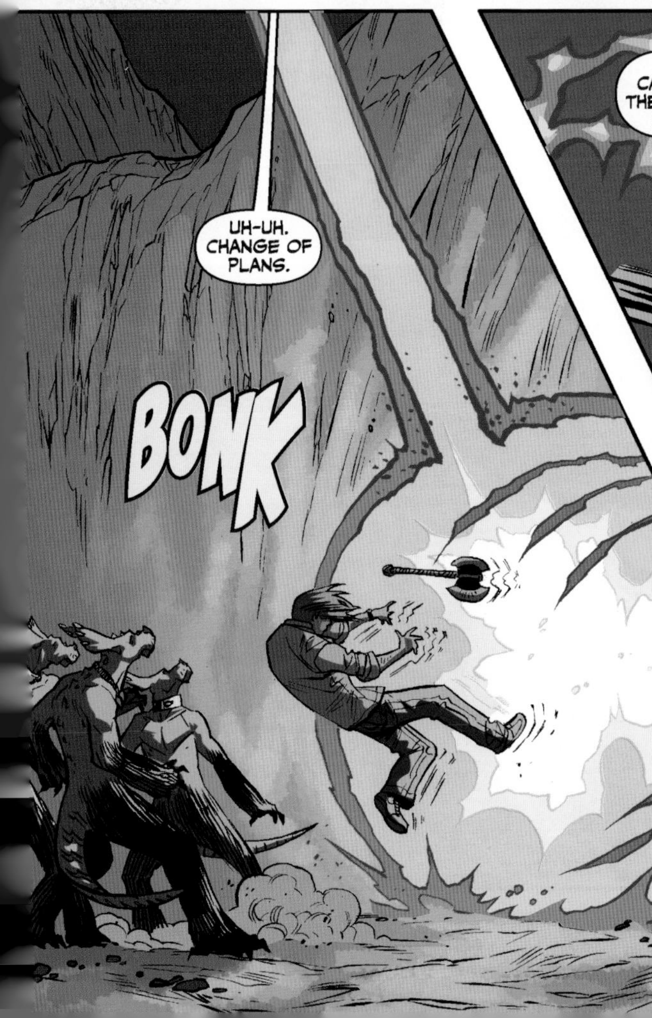
UH-UH. CHANGE OF PLANS.
BONK

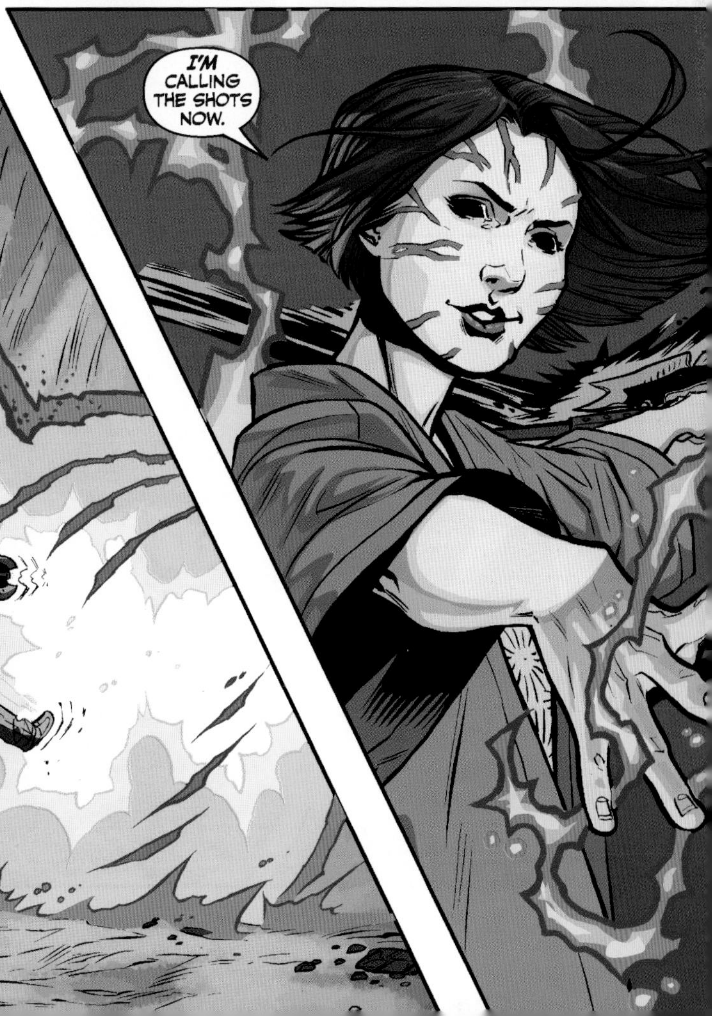
I'M CALLING THE SHOTS NOW.

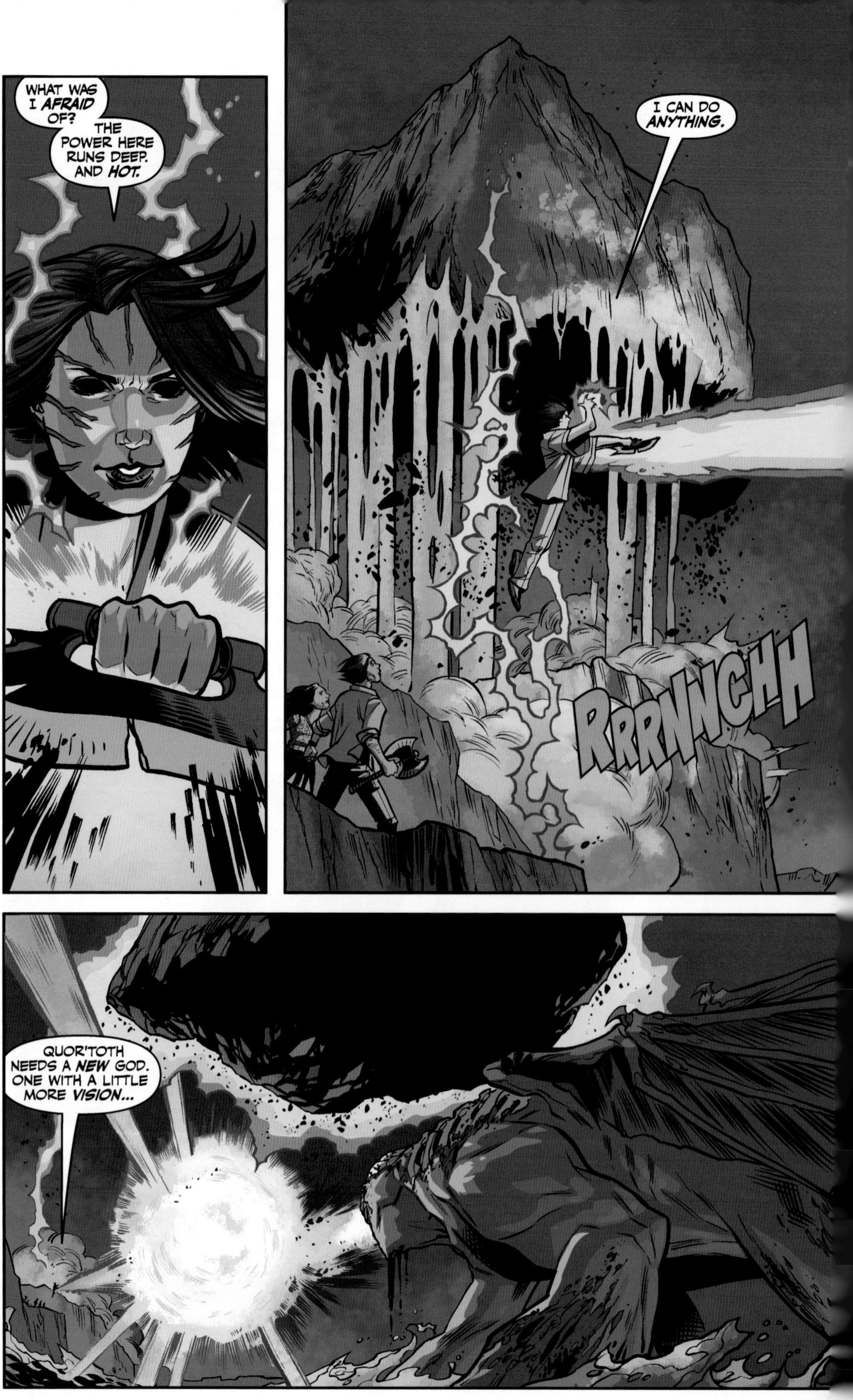
WHAT WAS I AFRAID OF?
THE POWER HERE RUNS DEEP. AND HOT.
I CAN DO ANYTHING.
RRRNNCHH
QUOR'TOTH NEEDS A NEW GOD. ONE WITH A LITTLE MORE VISION...

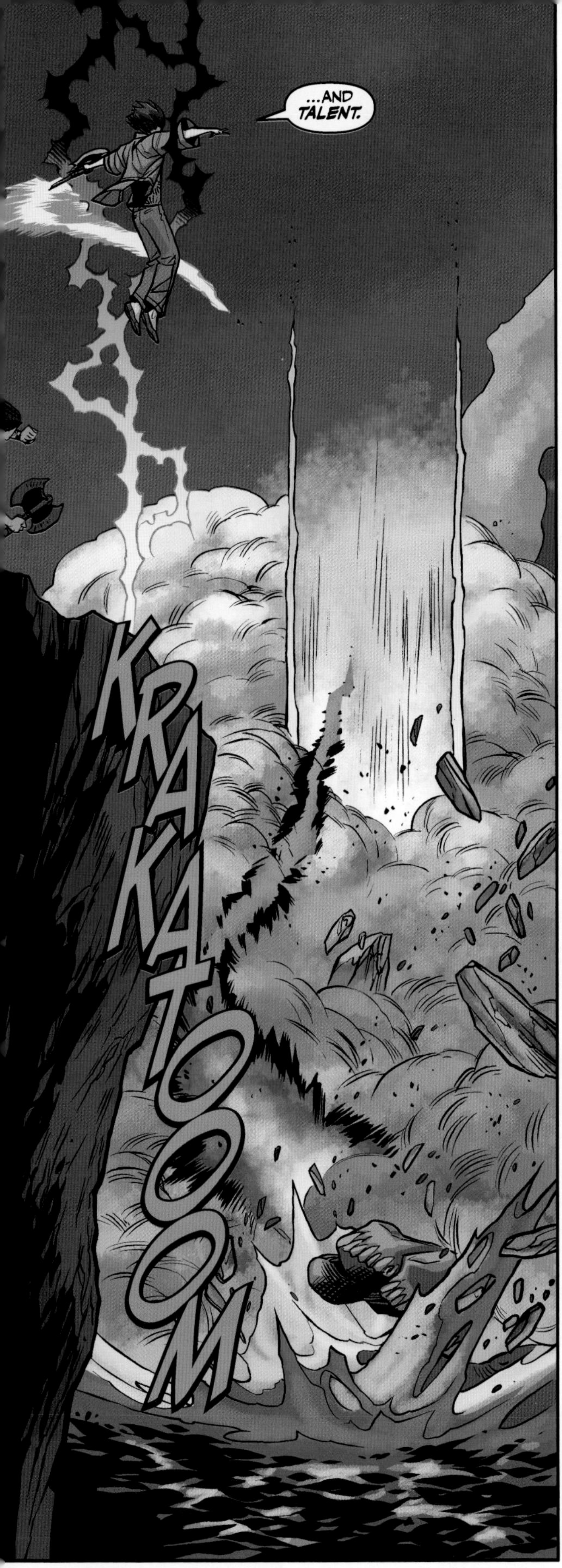
...AND TALENT.
KRAKATOOOOM

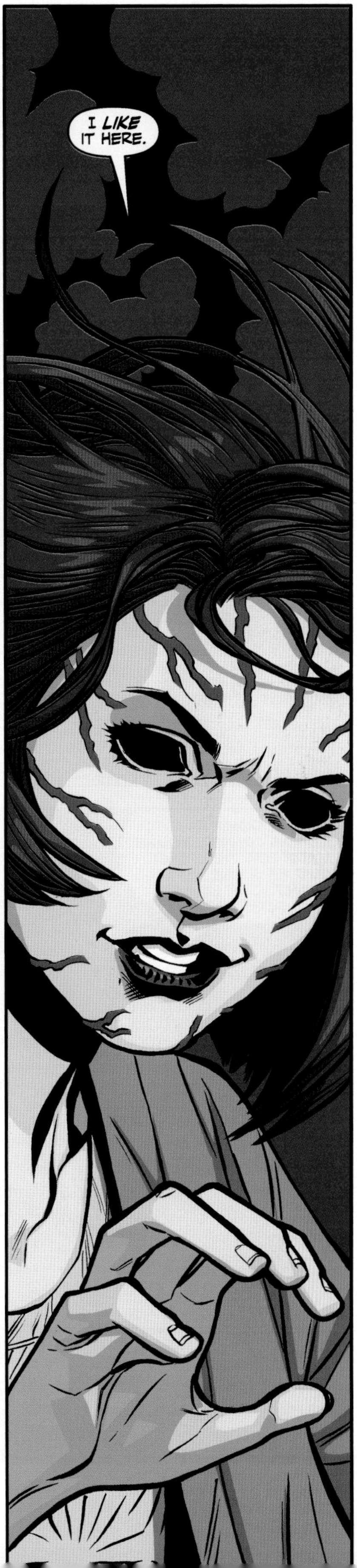
I LIKE IT HERE.

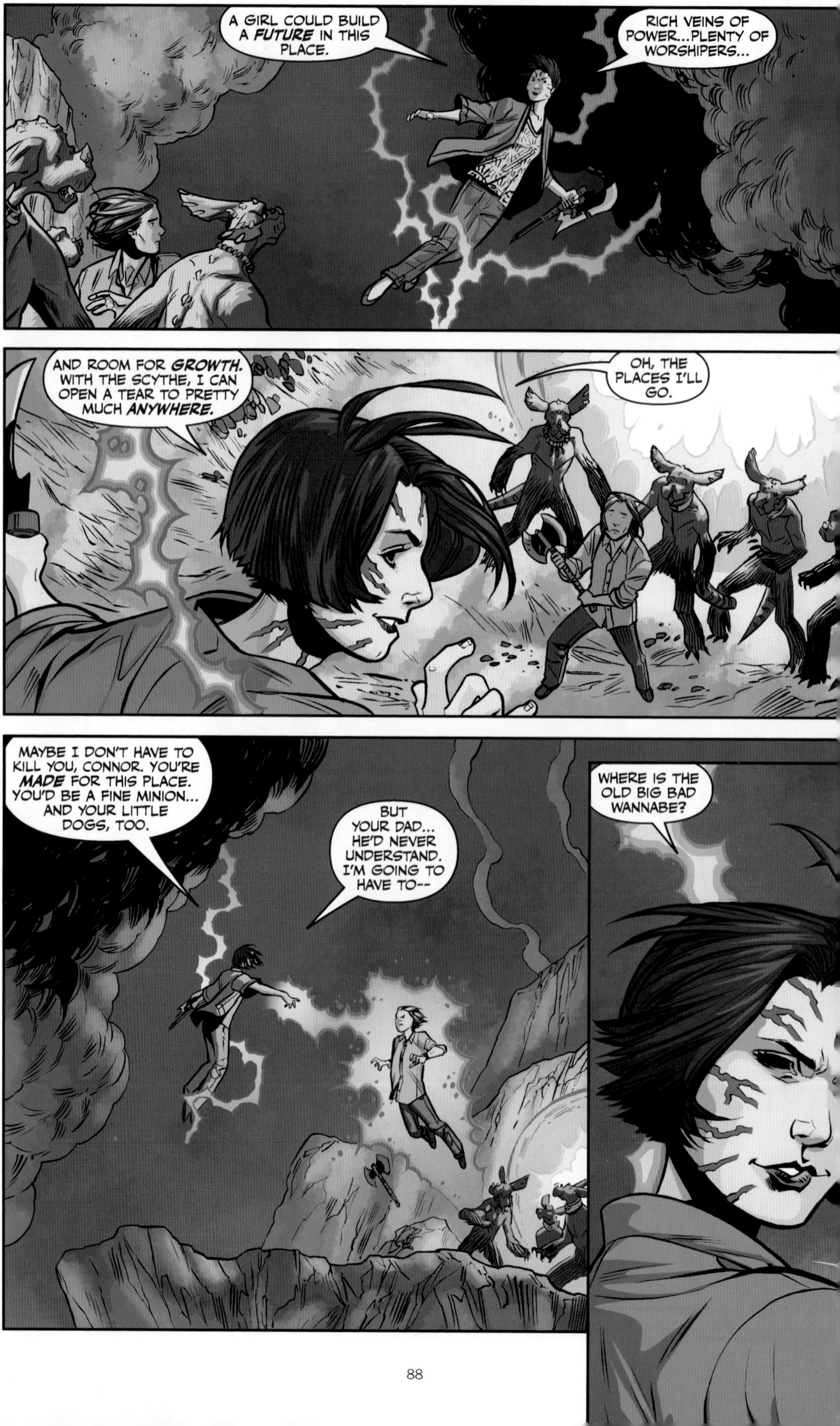
A GIRL COULD BUILD A *FUTURE* IN THIS PLACE.
RICH VEINS OF POWER...PLENTY OF WORSHIPERS...
AND ROOM FOR *GROWTH.* WITH THE SCYTHE, I CAN OPEN A TEAR TO PRETTY MUCH *ANYWHERE.*
OH, THE PLACES I'LL GO.
MAYBE I DON'T HAVE TO KILL YOU, CONNOR. YOU'RE *MADE* FOR THIS PLACE. YOU'D BE A FINE MINION... AND YOUR LITTLE DOGS, TOO.
BUT YOUR DAD... HE'D NEVER UNDERSTAND. I'M GOING TO HAVE TO--
WHERE IS THE OLD BIG BAD WANNABE?

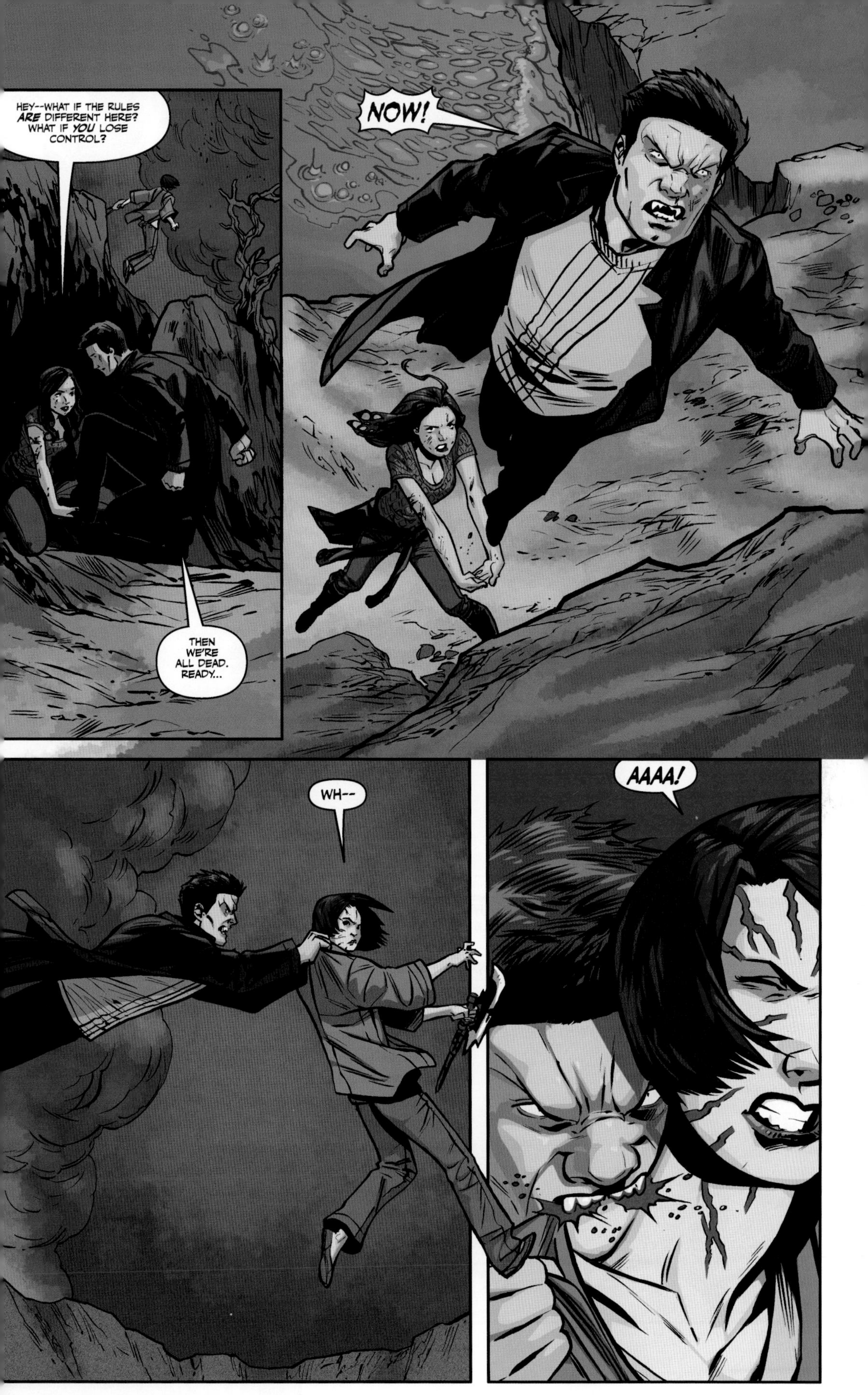
HEY--WHAT IF THE RULES *ARE* DIFFERENT HERE? WHAT IF *YOU* LOSE CONTROL?
THEN WE'RE ALL DEAD. READY...
NOW!
WH--
AAAA!

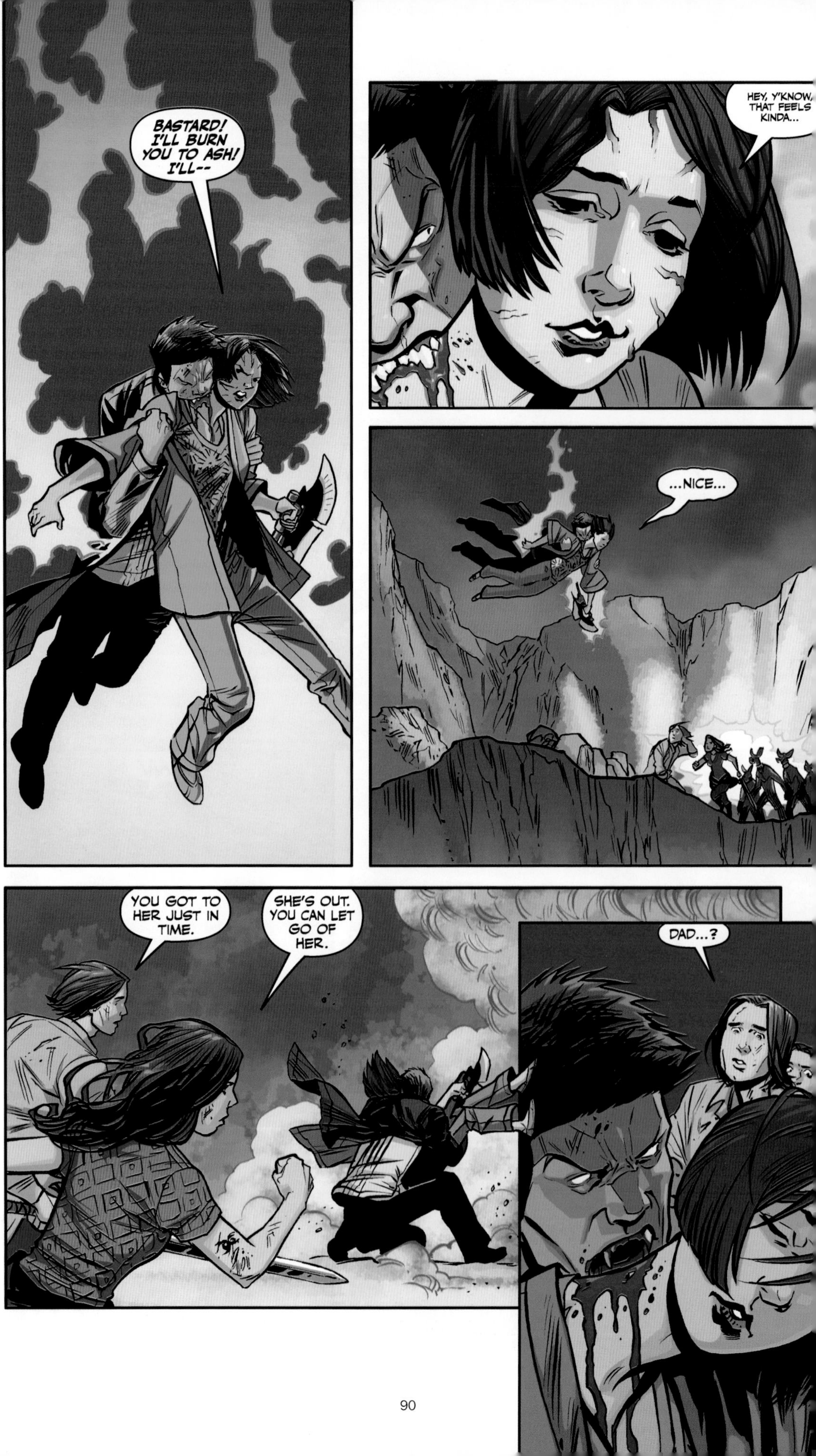
BASTARD! I'LL BURN YOU TO ASH! I'LL--
HEY, Y'KNOW, THAT FEELS KINDA...
...NICE...
YOU GOT TO HER JUST IN TIME.
SHE'S OUT. YOU CAN LET GO OF HER.
DAD...?

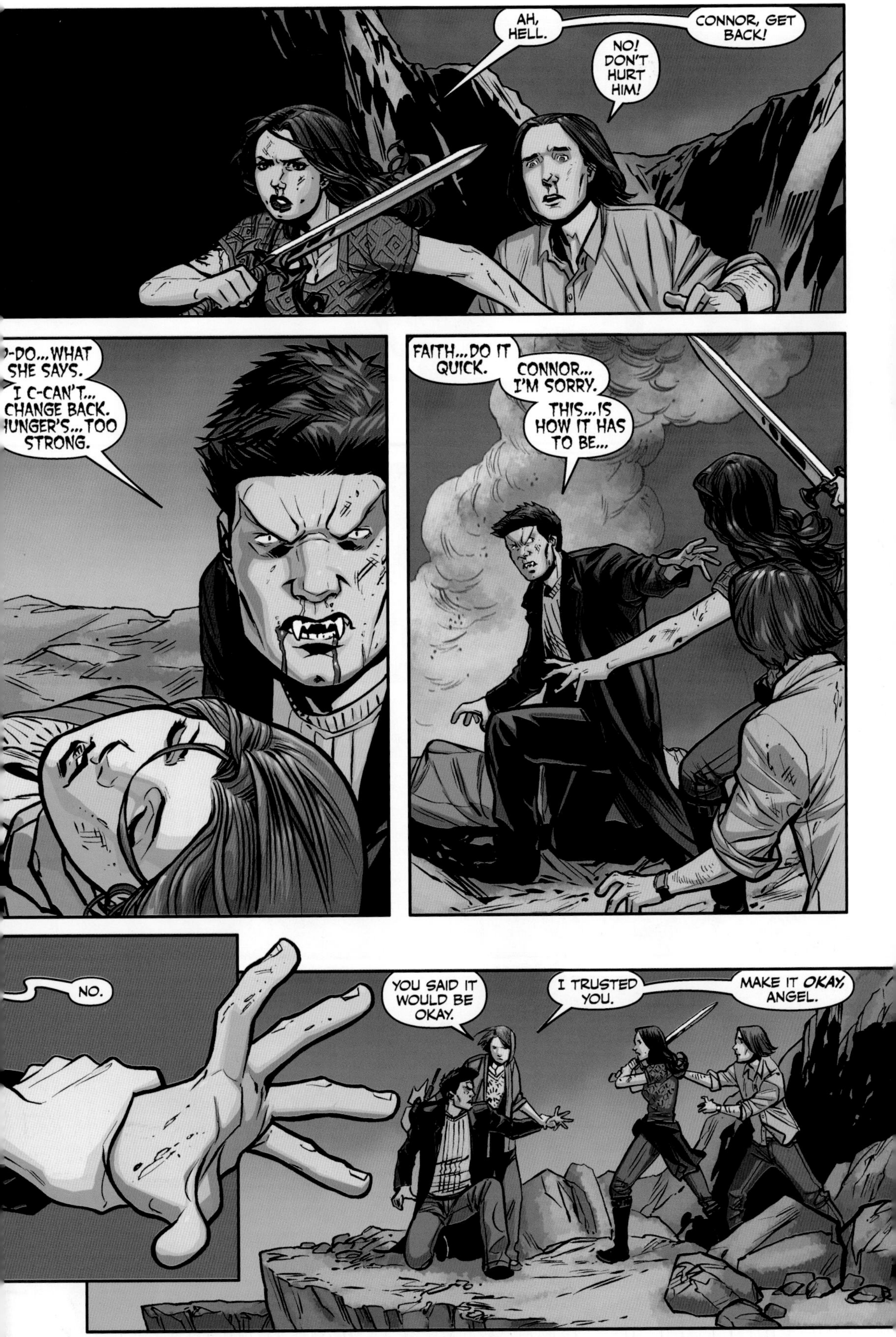
AH, HELL.
CONNOR, GET BACK!
NO! DON'T HURT HIM!
-DO...WHAT SHE SAYS.
I C-CAN'T... CHANGE BACK.
UNGER'S...TOO STRONG.
FAITH...DO IT QUICK.
CONNOR... I'M SORRY.
THIS...IS HOW IT HAS TO BE...
NO.
YOU SAID IT WOULD BE OKAY.
I TRUSTED YOU.
MAKE IT OKAY, ANGEL.

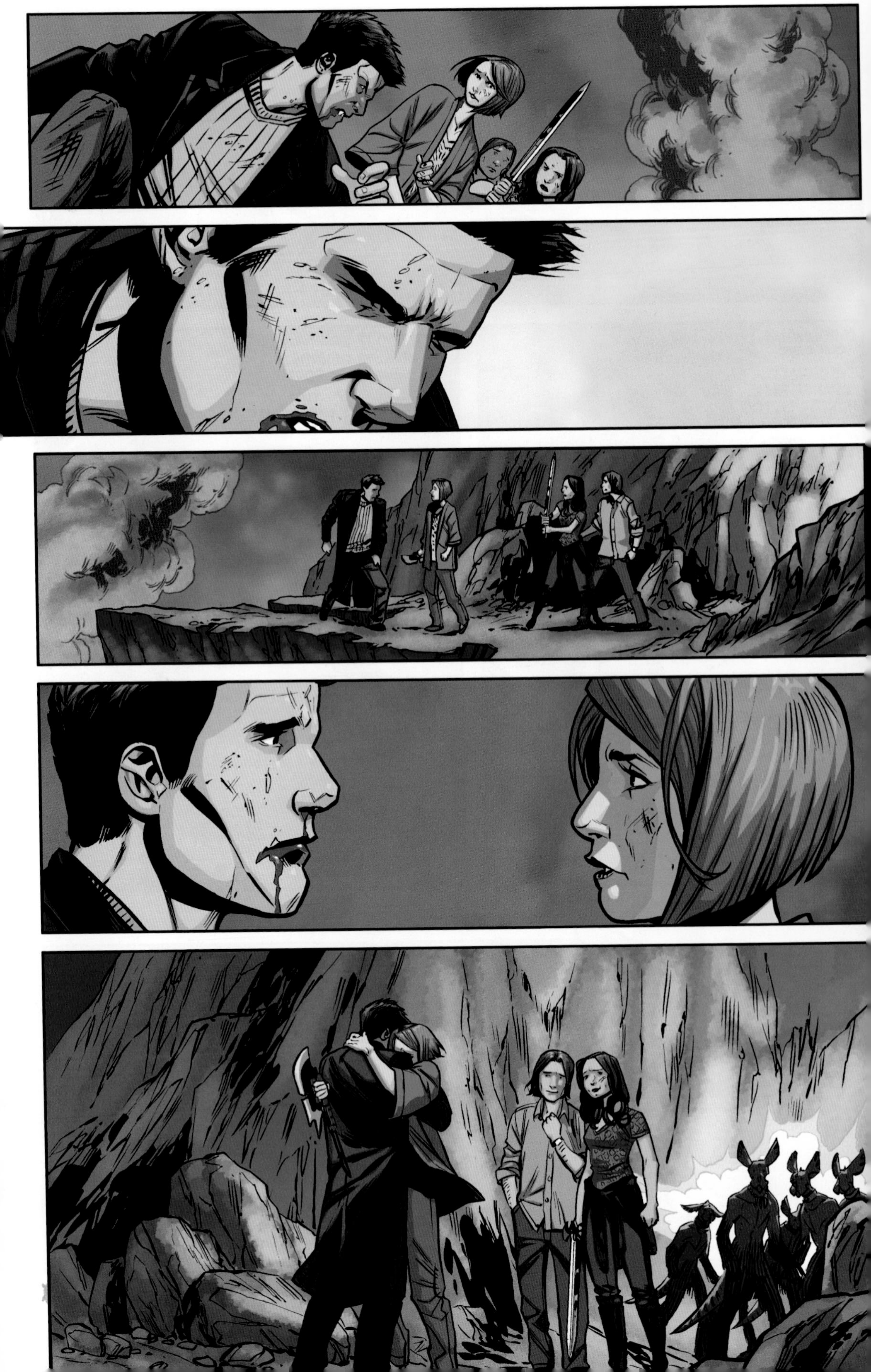

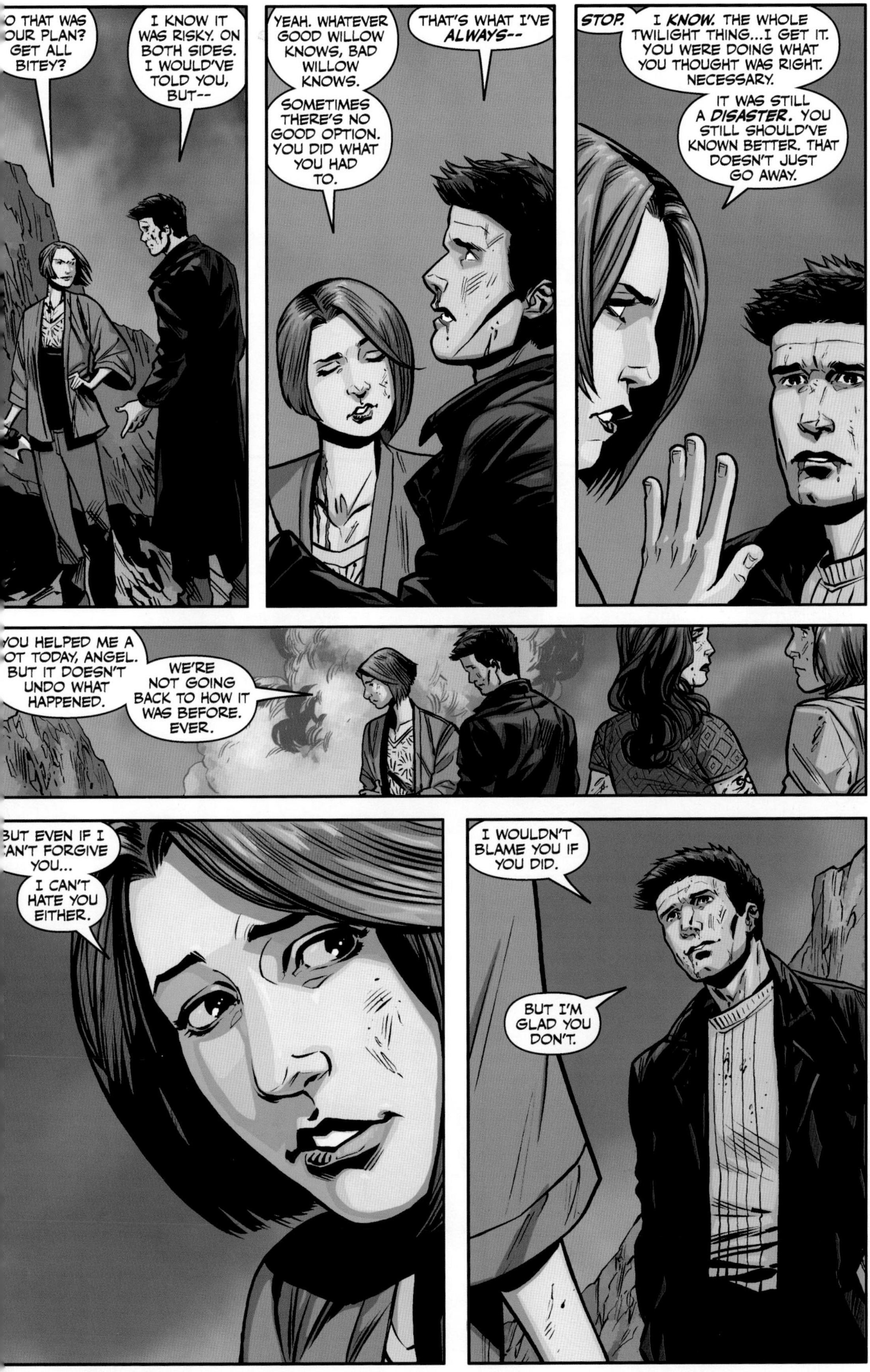
O THAT WAS OUR PLAN? GET ALL BITEY?
I KNOW IT WAS RISKY. ON BOTH SIDES. I WOULD'VE TOLD YOU, BUT--
YEAH. WHATEVER GOOD WILLOW KNOWS, BAD WILLOW KNOWS.
SOMETIMES THERE'S NO GOOD OPTION. YOU DID WHAT YOU HAD TO.
THAT'S WHAT I'VE ALWAYS--
STOP.
I KNOW. THE WHOLE TWILIGHT THING...I GET IT. YOU WERE DOING WHAT YOU THOUGHT WAS RIGHT. NECESSARY.
IT WAS STILL A DISASTER. YOU STILL SHOULD'VE KNOWN BETTER. THAT DOESN'T JUST GO AWAY.
YOU HELPED ME A OT TODAY, ANGEL. BUT IT DOESN'T UNDO WHAT HAPPENED.
WE'RE NOT GOING BACK TO HOW IT WAS BEFORE. EVER.
BUT EVEN IF I AN'T FORGIVE YOU...
I CAN'T HATE YOU EITHER.
I WOULDN'T BLAME YOU IF YOU DID.
BUT I'M GLAD YOU DON'T.

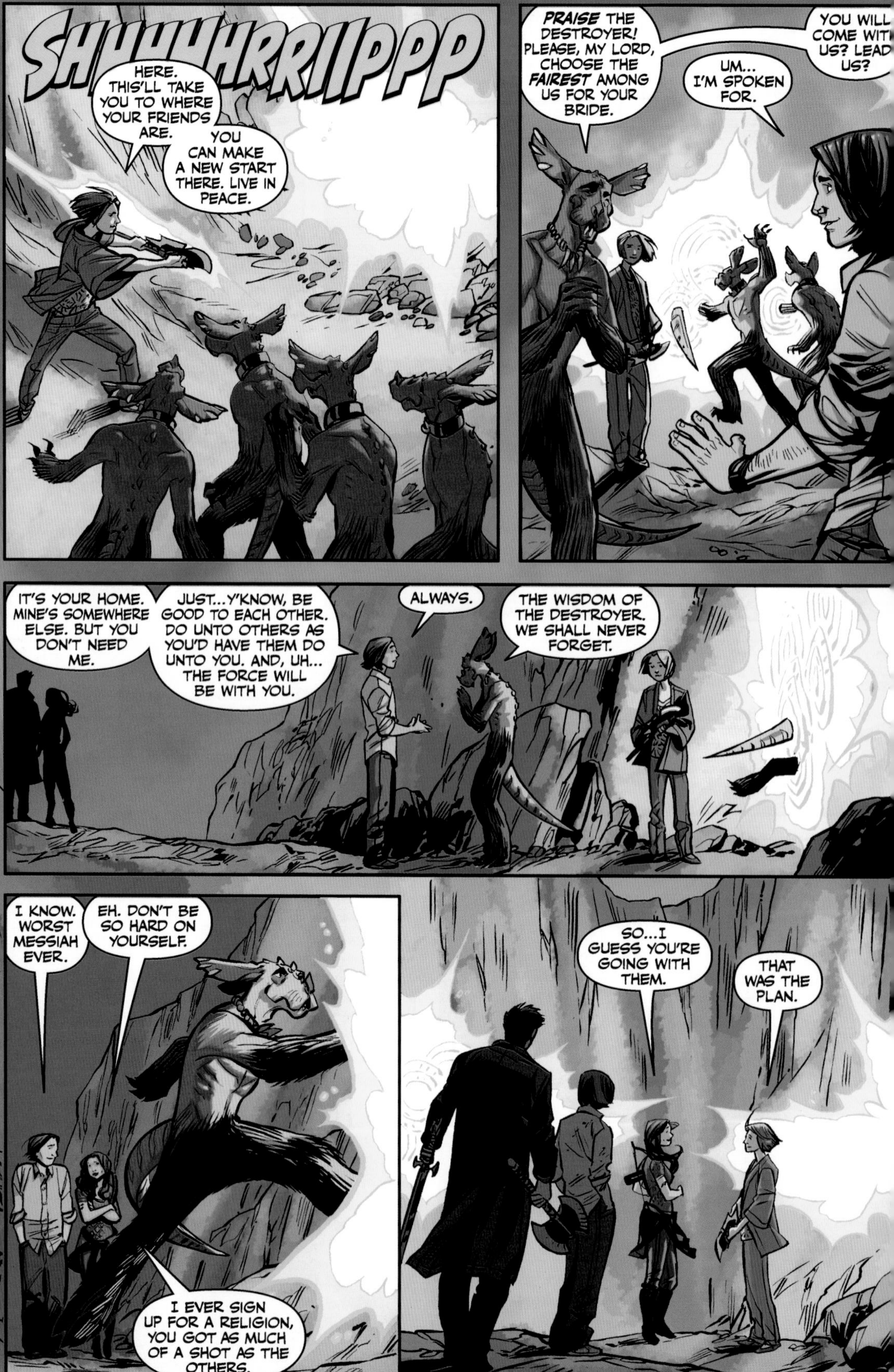
SHHHHHRRIIPPP
HERE. THIS'LL TAKE YOU TO WHERE YOUR FRIENDS ARE.
YOU CAN MAKE A NEW START THERE. LIVE IN PEACE.
PRAISE THE DESTROYER! PLEASE, MY LORD, CHOOSE THE FAIREST AMONG US FOR YOUR BRIDE.
YOU WILL COME WITH US? LEAD US?
UM... I'M SPOKEN FOR.
IT'S YOUR HOME. MINE'S SOMEWHERE ELSE. BUT YOU DON'T NEED ME.
JUST...Y'KNOW, BE GOOD TO EACH OTHER. DO UNTO OTHERS AS YOU'D HAVE THEM DO UNTO YOU. AND, UH... THE FORCE WILL BE WITH YOU.
ALWAYS.
THE WISDOM OF THE DESTROYER. WE SHALL NEVER FORGET.
I KNOW. WORST MESSIAH EVER.
EH. DON'T BE SO HARD ON YOURSELF.
I EVER SIGN UP FOR A RELIGION, YOU GOT AS MUCH OF A SHOT AS THE OTHERS.
SO...I GUESS YOU'RE GOING WITH THEM.
THAT WAS THE PLAN.

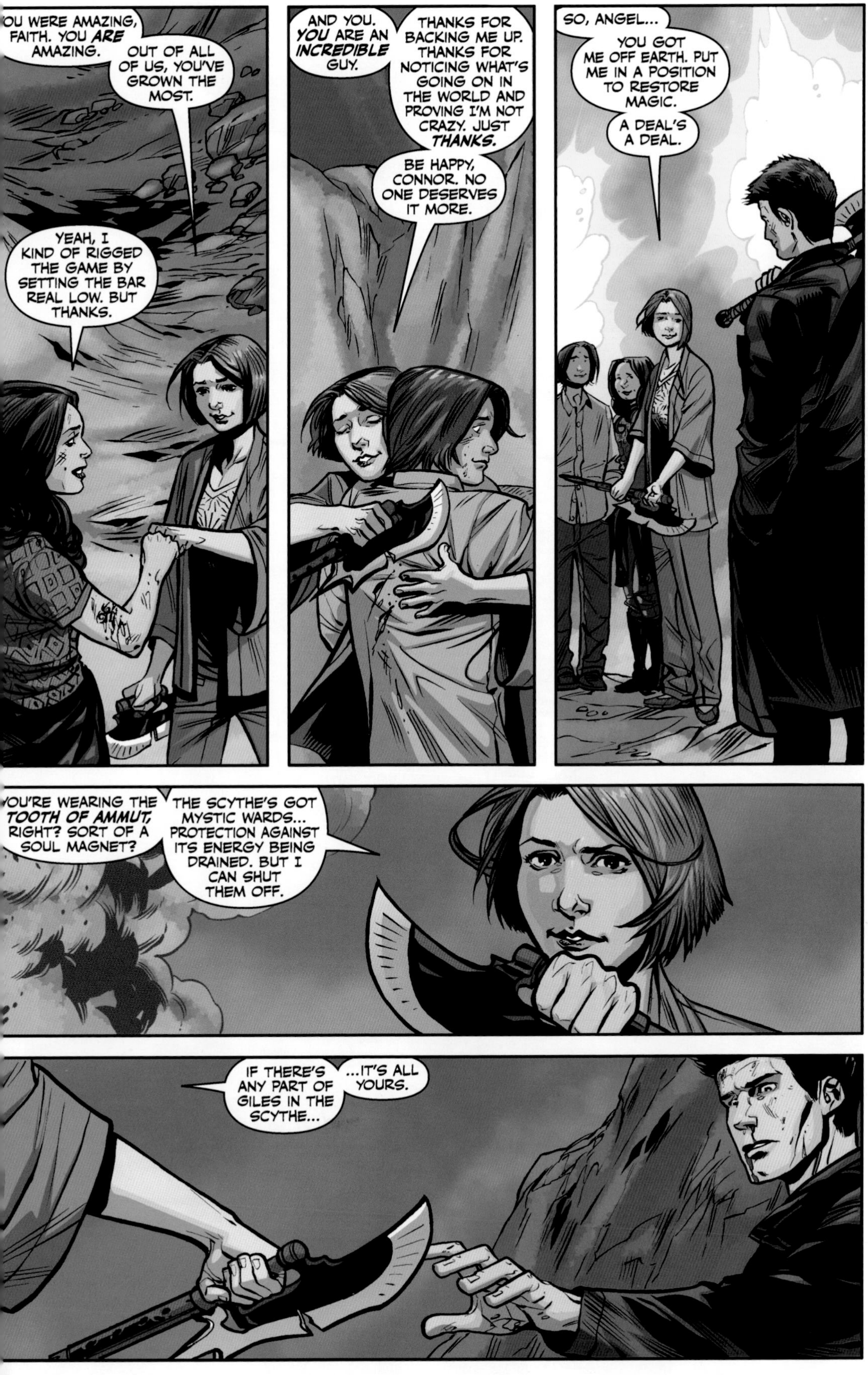
YOU WERE AMAZING, FAITH. YOU ARE AMAZING.
OUT OF ALL OF US, YOU'VE GROWN THE MOST.
YEAH, I KIND OF RIGGED THE GAME BY SETTING THE BAR REAL LOW. BUT THANKS.
AND YOU. YOU ARE AN INCREDIBLE GUY.
THANKS FOR BACKING ME UP. THANKS FOR NOTICING WHAT'S GOING ON IN THE WORLD AND PROVING I'M NOT CRAZY. JUST THANKS.
BE HAPPY, CONNOR. NO ONE DESERVES IT MORE.
SO, ANGEL...
YOU GOT ME OFF EARTH. PUT ME IN A POSITION TO RESTORE MAGIC.
A DEAL'S A DEAL.
YOU'RE WEARING THE TOOTH OF AMMUT, RIGHT? SORT OF A SOUL MAGNET?
THE SCYTHE'S GOT MYSTIC WARDS... PROTECTION AGAINST ITS ENERGY BEING DRAINED. BUT I CAN SHUT THEM OFF.
IF THERE'S ANY PART OF GILES IN THE SCYTHE...
...IT'S ALL YOURS.

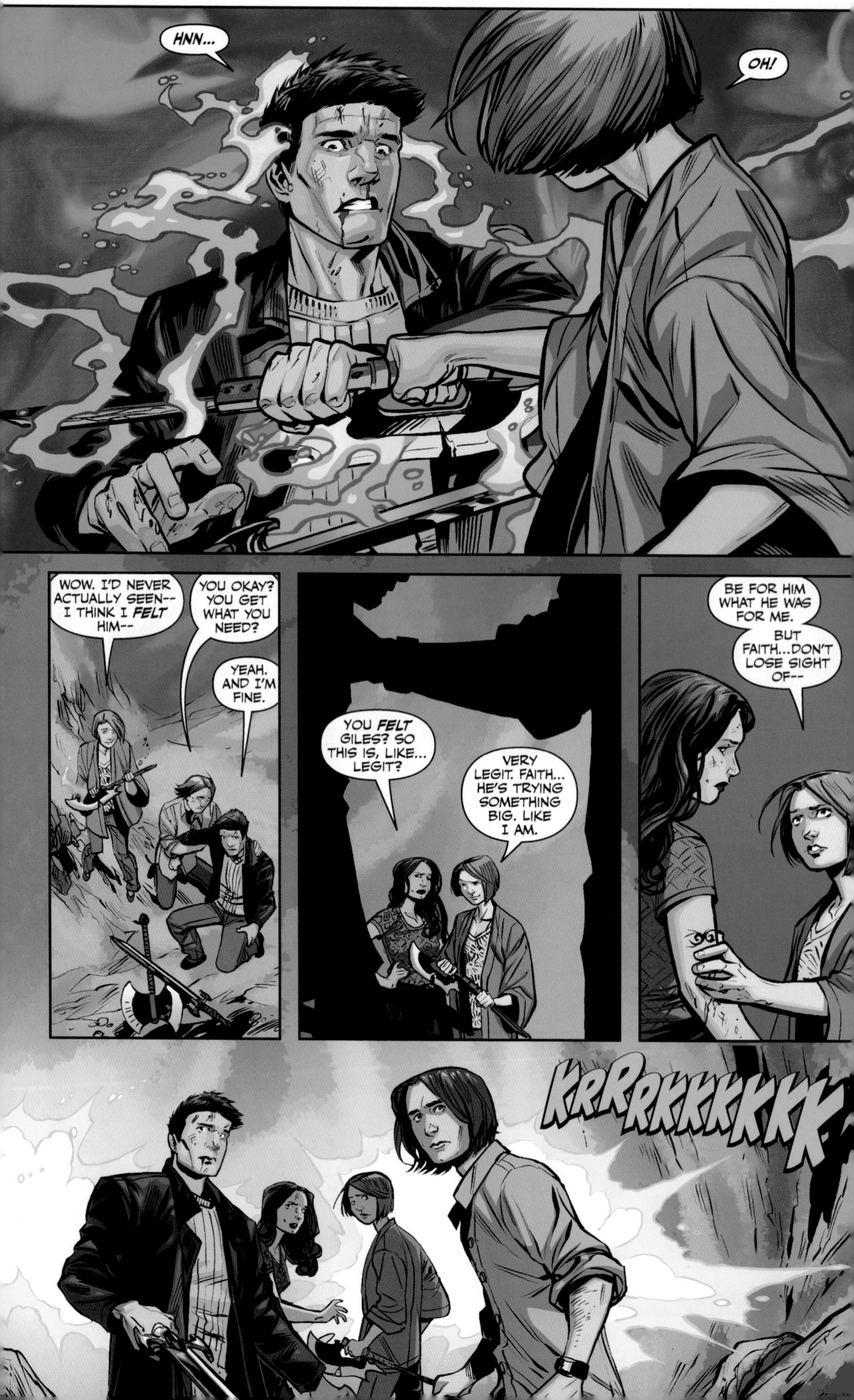
HNN...
OH!
WOW. I'D NEVER ACTUALLY SEEN-- I THINK I FELT HIM--
YOU OKAY? YOU GET WHAT YOU NEED?
YEAH. AND I'M FINE.
YOU FELT GILES? SO THIS IS, LIKE... LEGIT?
VERY LEGIT. FAITH... HE'S TRYING SOMETHING BIG. LIKE I AM.
BE FOR HIM WHAT HE WAS FOR ME.
BUT FAITH...DON'T LOSE SIGHT OF--
KRRRKKKKKKK

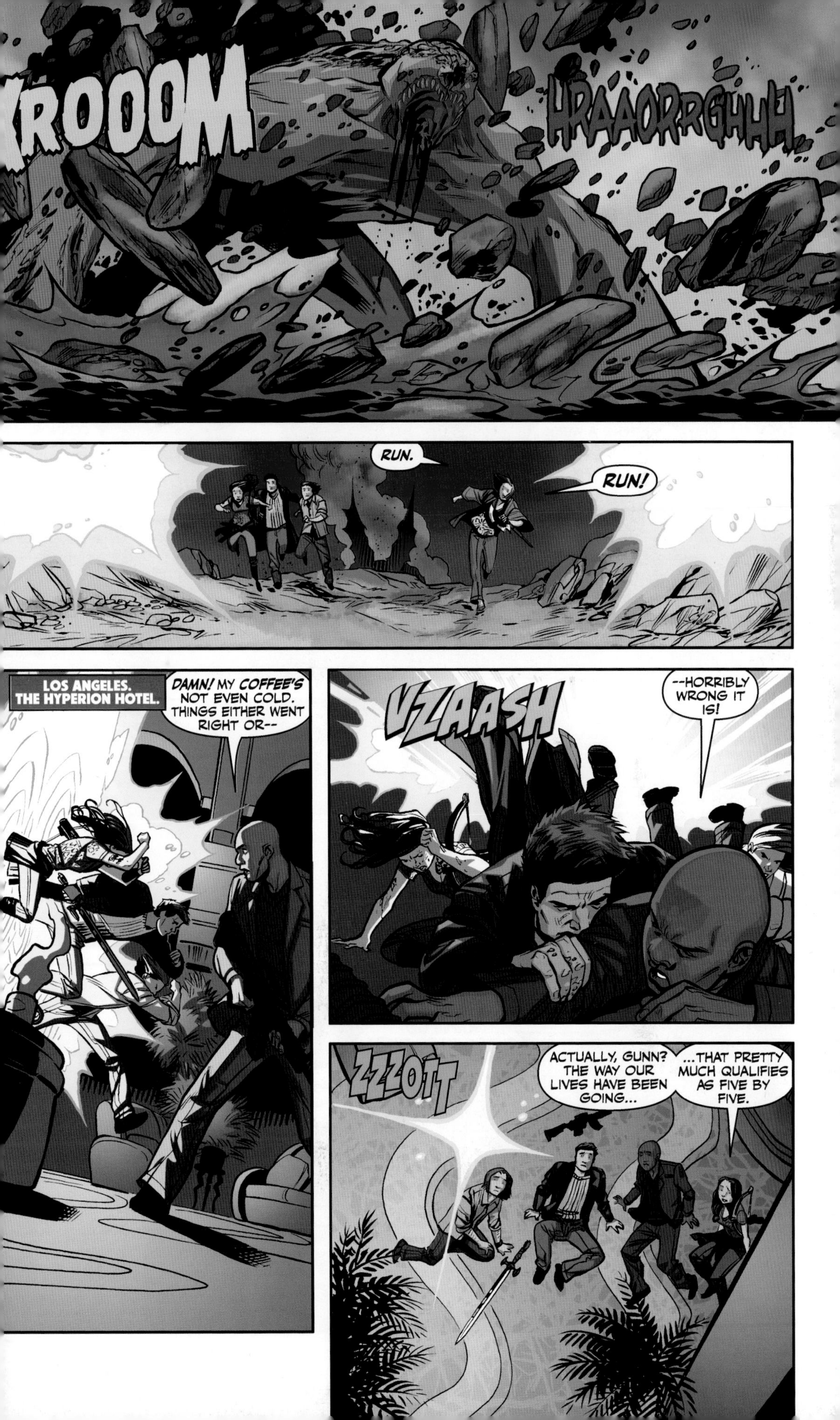
KROOOM
HRAAORRGHHH
RUN.
RUN!
LOS ANGELES. THE HYPERION HOTEL.
DAMN! MY COFFEE'S NOT EVEN COLD. THINGS EITHER WENT RIGHT OR--
VZAASH
--HORRIBLY WRONG IT IS!
ZZZOTT
ACTUALLY, GUNN? THE WAY OUR LIVES HAVE BEEN GOING...
...THAT PRETTY MUCH QUALIFIES AS FIVE BY FIVE.

SO THE RIFT CLOSING MEANS WILLOW TOOK CARE OF BUSINESS?

IT MEANS...

"...SHE'S ON HER WAY."

YOU ALL RIGHT?

NOTHING A WEEK OF SLEEP AND A LIFETIME OF THERAPY WON'T FIX.

CONNOR...I'M SORRY I PUT YOU THROUGH THAT.

IT WAS MY CHOICE. IF YOU USE THIS AS AN EXCUSE TO KEEP AVOIDING ME, *THEN* YOU CAN APOLOGIZE.

I WAS AFRAID I'D SCREW UP YOUR LIFE. BUT I SHOULD'VE KNOWN...YOU'RE WAY TOO STRONG FOR THAT.

ANY TIME YOU NEED ME, CONNOR--OR JUST WANT TO TALK-- I'M A PHONE CALL AWAY. OR A PLANE TRIP, IF YOU WANT TO COME VISIT. AND I HOPE YOU WILL.

RIGHT. I FIGURED...I MEAN, OF COURSE YOU GUYS WOULD BE HEADED STRAIGHT BACK TO LONDON.

YOU'VE GOT THINGS TO DO THERE. REALLY IMPORTANT STUFF.

YEAH. AND I'VE GOT TO GET BACK TO IT.

NEXT WEEK.

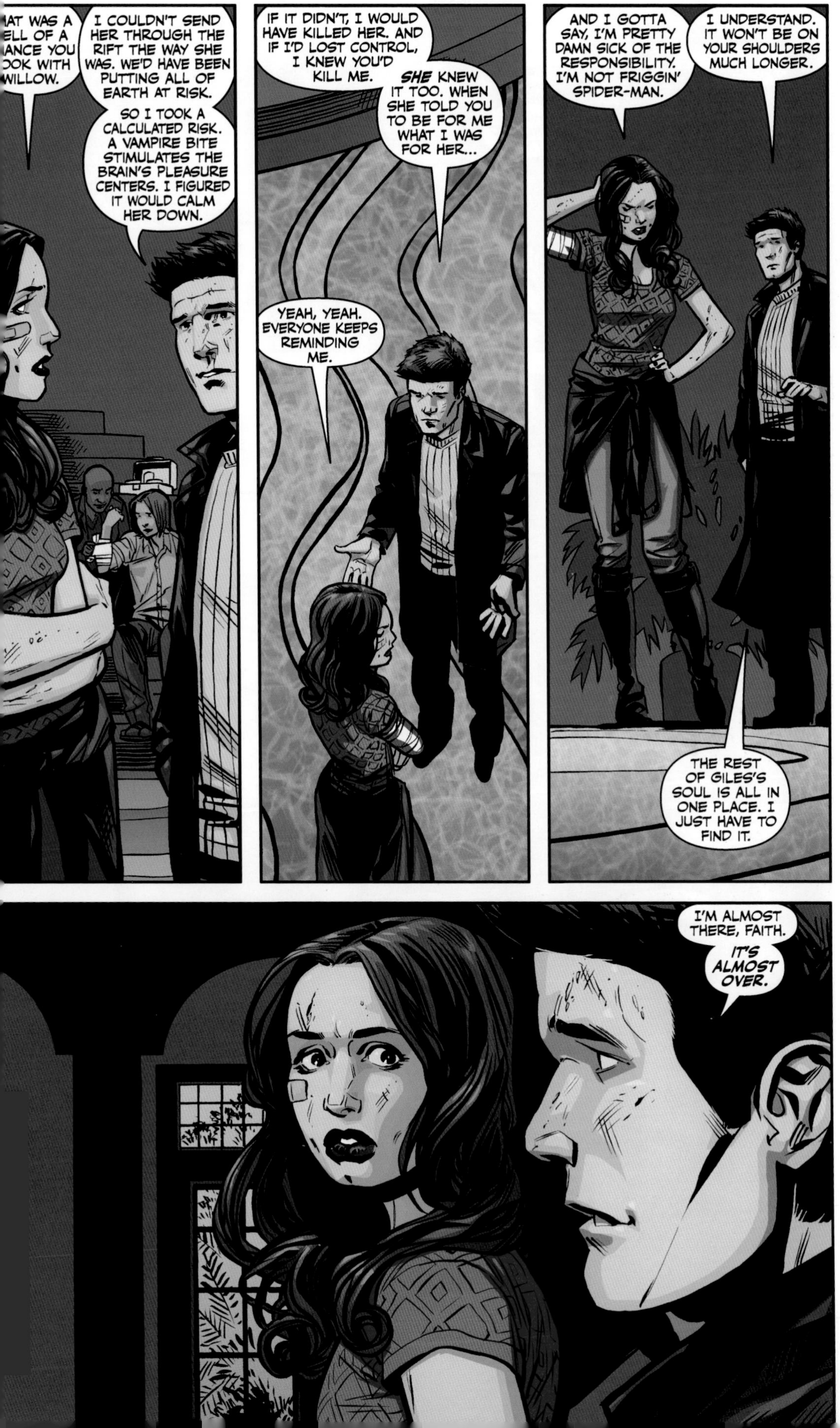

HAT WAS A
ELL OF A
ANCE YOU
OOK WITH
WILLOW.
I COULDN'T SEND HER THROUGH THE RIFT THE WAY SHE WAS. WE'D HAVE BEEN PUTTING ALL OF EARTH AT RISK.
SO I TOOK A CALCULATED RISK. A VAMPIRE BITE STIMULATES THE BRAIN'S PLEASURE CENTERS. I FIGURED IT WOULD CALM HER DOWN.
IF IT DIDN'T, I WOULD HAVE KILLED HER. AND IF I'D LOST CONTROL, I KNEW YOU'D KILL ME.
SHE KNEW IT TOO. WHEN SHE TOLD YOU TO BE FOR ME WHAT I WAS FOR HER...
YEAH, YEAH. EVERYONE KEEPS REMINDING ME.
AND I GOTTA SAY, I'M PRETTY DAMN SICK OF THE RESPONSIBILITY. I'M NOT FRIGGIN' SPIDER-MAN.
I UNDERSTAND. IT WON'T BE ON YOUR SHOULDERS MUCH LONGER.
THE REST OF GILES'S SOUL IS ALL IN ONE PLACE. I JUST HAVE TO FIND IT.
I'M ALMOST THERE, FAITH.
IT'S ALMOST OVER.

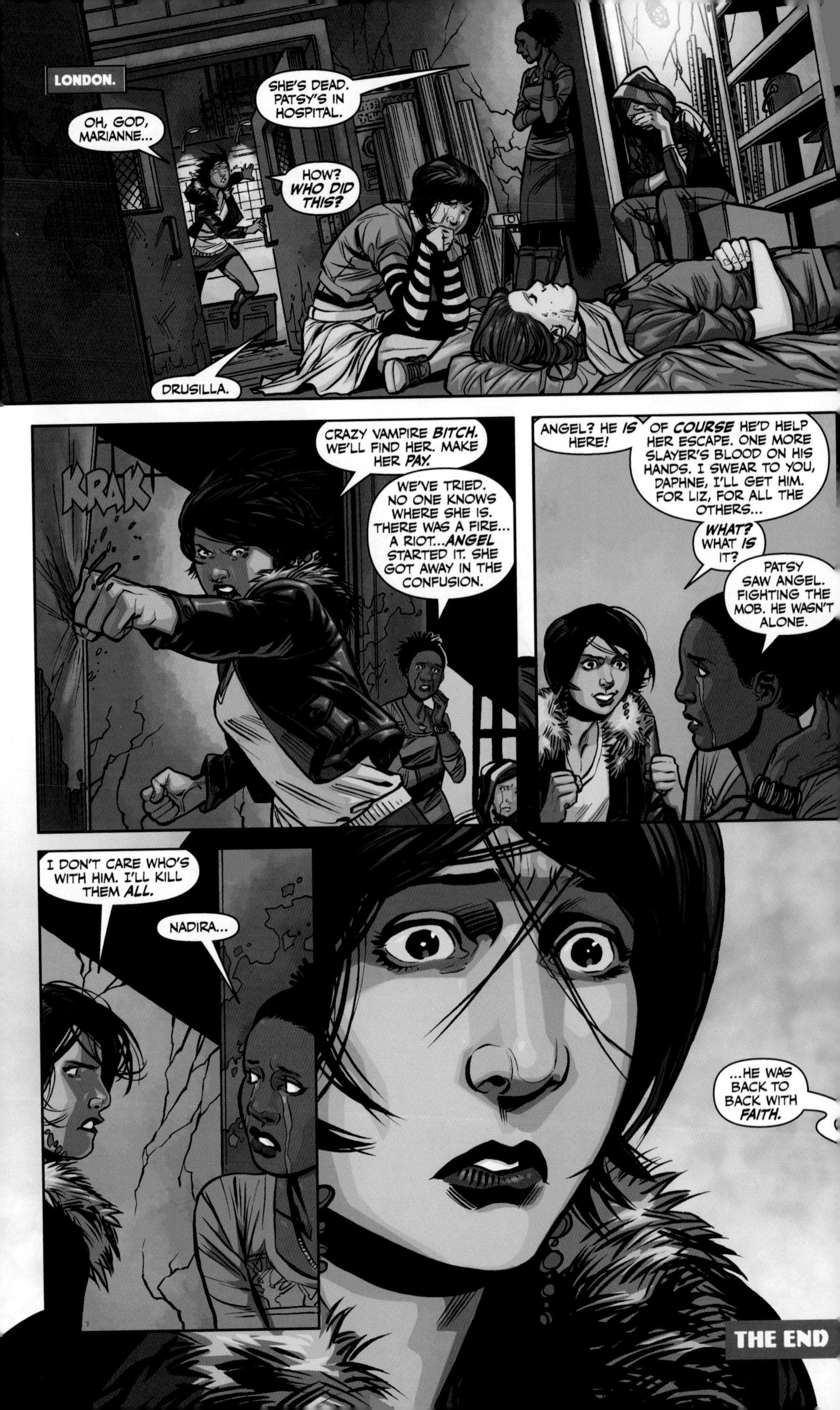
LONDON.
OH, GOD, MARIANNE...
SHE'S DEAD. PATSY'S IN HOSPITAL.
HOW? WHO DID THIS?
DRUSILLA.
KRAK
CRAZY VAMPIRE BITCH. WE'LL FIND HER. MAKE HER PAY.
WE'VE TRIED. NO ONE KNOWS WHERE SHE IS. THERE WAS A FIRE... A RIOT...ANGEL STARTED IT. SHE GOT AWAY IN THE CONFUSION.
ANGEL? HE IS HERE!
OF COURSE HE'D HELP HER ESCAPE. ONE MORE SLAYER'S BLOOD ON HIS HANDS. I SWEAR TO YOU, DAPHNE, I'LL GET HIM. FOR LIZ, FOR ALL THE OTHERS...
WHAT? WHAT IS IT?
PATSY SAW ANGEL. FIGHTING THE MOB. HE WASN'T ALONE.
I DON'T CARE WHO'S WITH HIM. I'LL KILL THEM ALL.
NADIRA...
...HE WAS BACK TO BACK WITH FAITH.
THE END

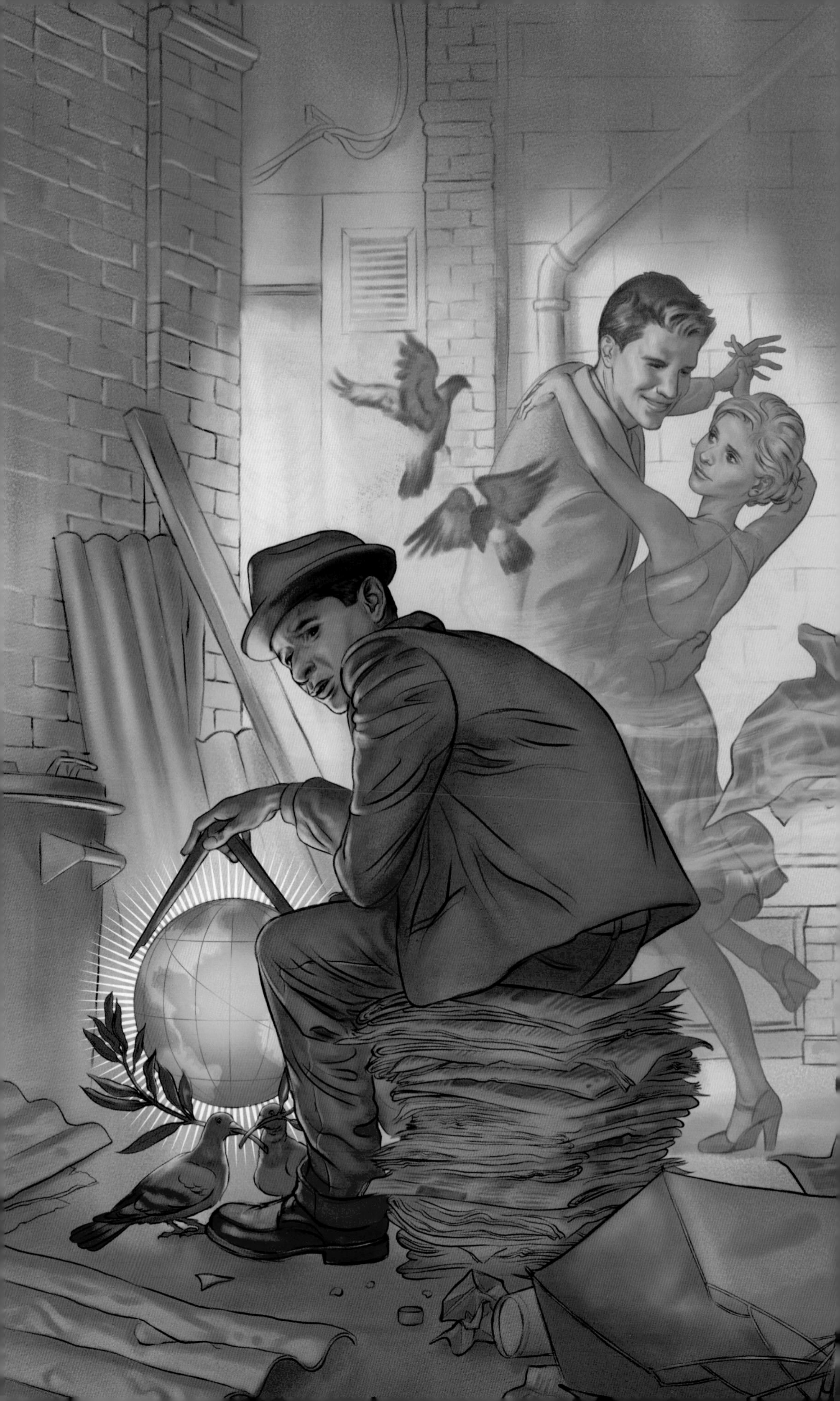

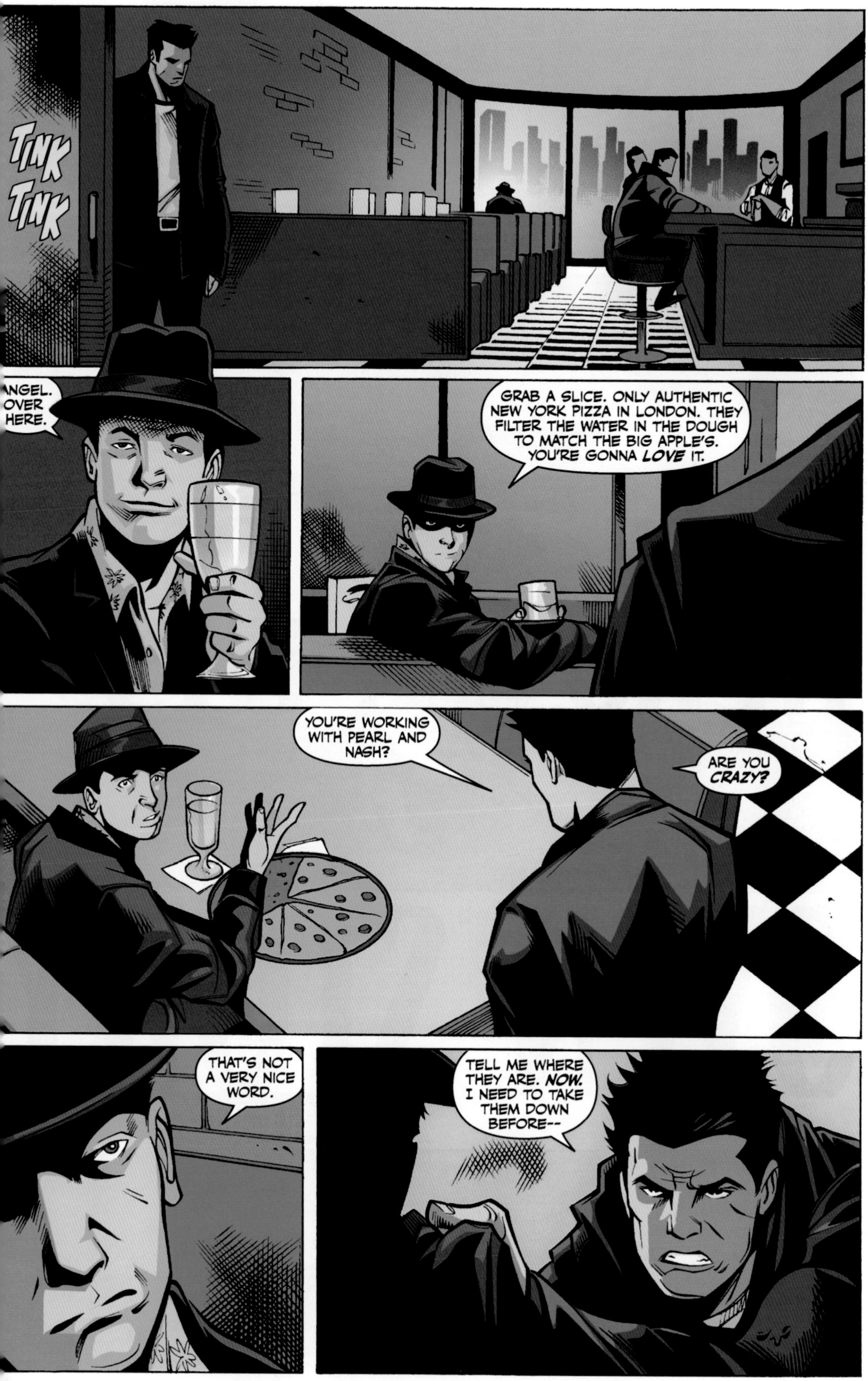
TINK
TINK
NGEL. OVER HERE.
GRAB A SLICE. ONLY AUTHENTIC NEW YORK PIZZA IN LONDON. THEY FILTER THE WATER IN THE DOUGH TO MATCH THE BIG APPLE'S. YOU'RE GONNA LOVE IT.
YOU'RE WORKING WITH PEARL AND NASH?
ARE YOU CRAZY?
THAT'S NOT A VERY NICE WORD.
TELL ME WHERE THEY ARE. NOW. I NEED TO TAKE THEM DOWN BEFORE--

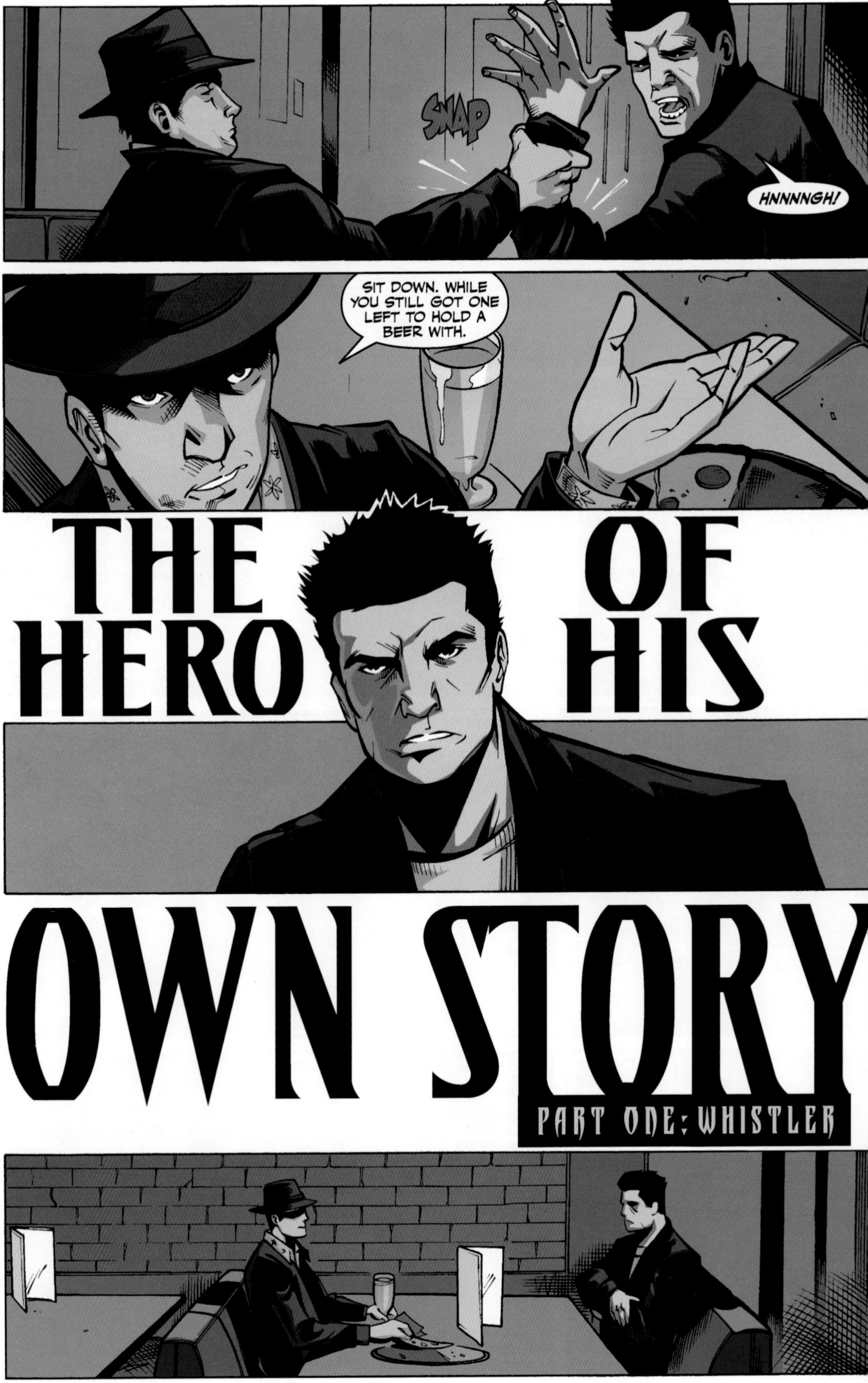
SNAP
HNNNNGH!
SIT DOWN. WHILE YOU STILL GOT ONE LEFT TO HOLD A BEER WITH.
THE HERO OF HIS OWN STORY
PART ONE: WHISTLER

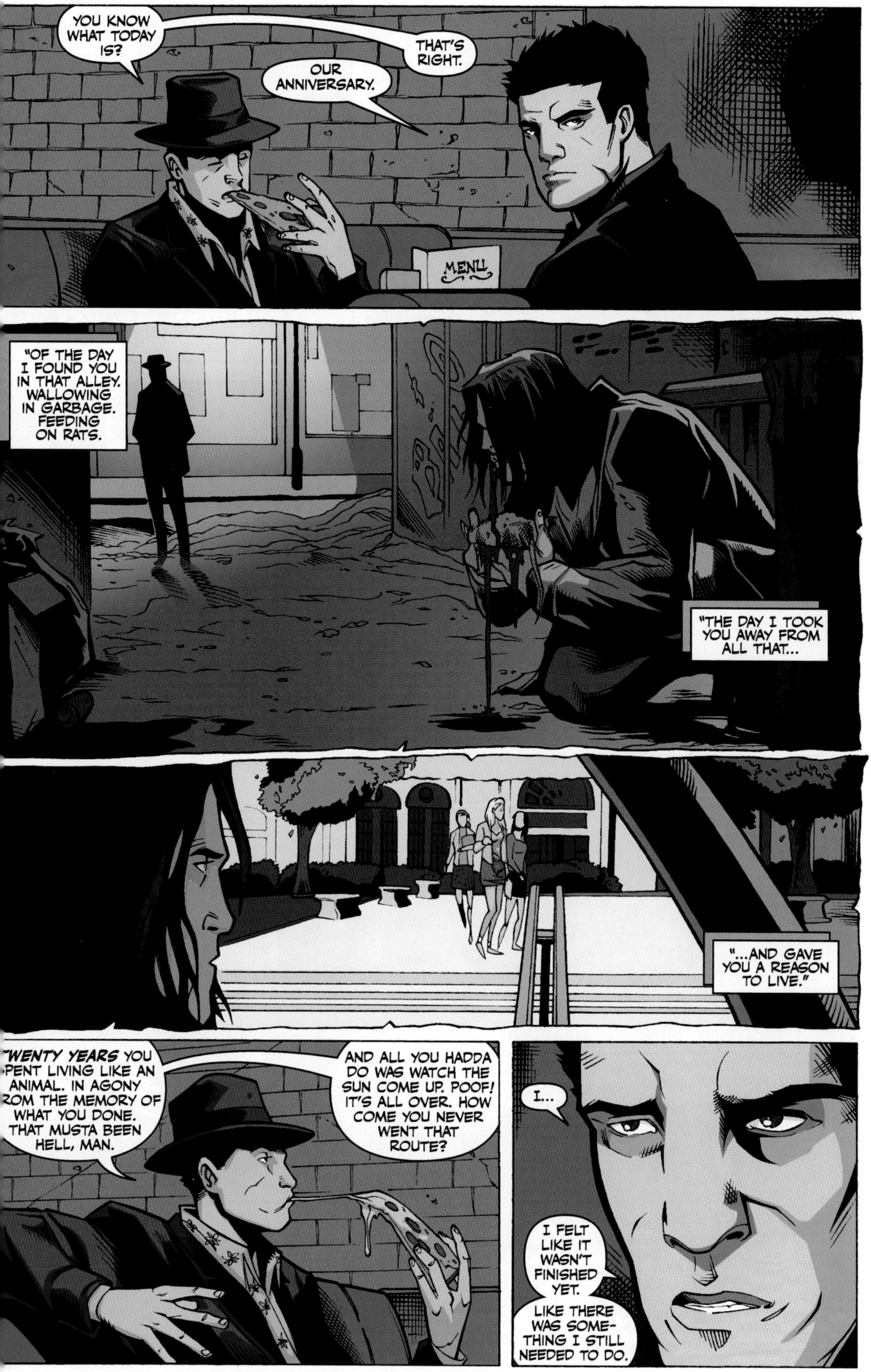
YOU KNOW WHAT TODAY IS?
OUR ANNIVERSARY.
THAT'S RIGHT.
"OF THE DAY I FOUND YOU IN THAT ALLEY. WALLOWING IN GARBAGE. FEEDING ON RATS.
"THE DAY I TOOK YOU AWAY FROM ALL THAT...
"...AND GAVE YOU A REASON TO LIVE."
WENTY YEARS YOU PENT LIVING LIKE AN ANIMAL. IN AGONY ROM THE MEMORY OF WHAT YOU DONE. THAT MUSTA BEEN HELL, MAN.
AND ALL YOU HADDA DO WAS WATCH THE SUN COME UP. POOF! IT'S ALL OVER. HOW COME YOU NEVER WENT THAT ROUTE?
I...
I FELT LIKE IT WASN'T FINISHED YET.
LIKE THERE WAS SOME-THING I STILL NEEDED TO DO.

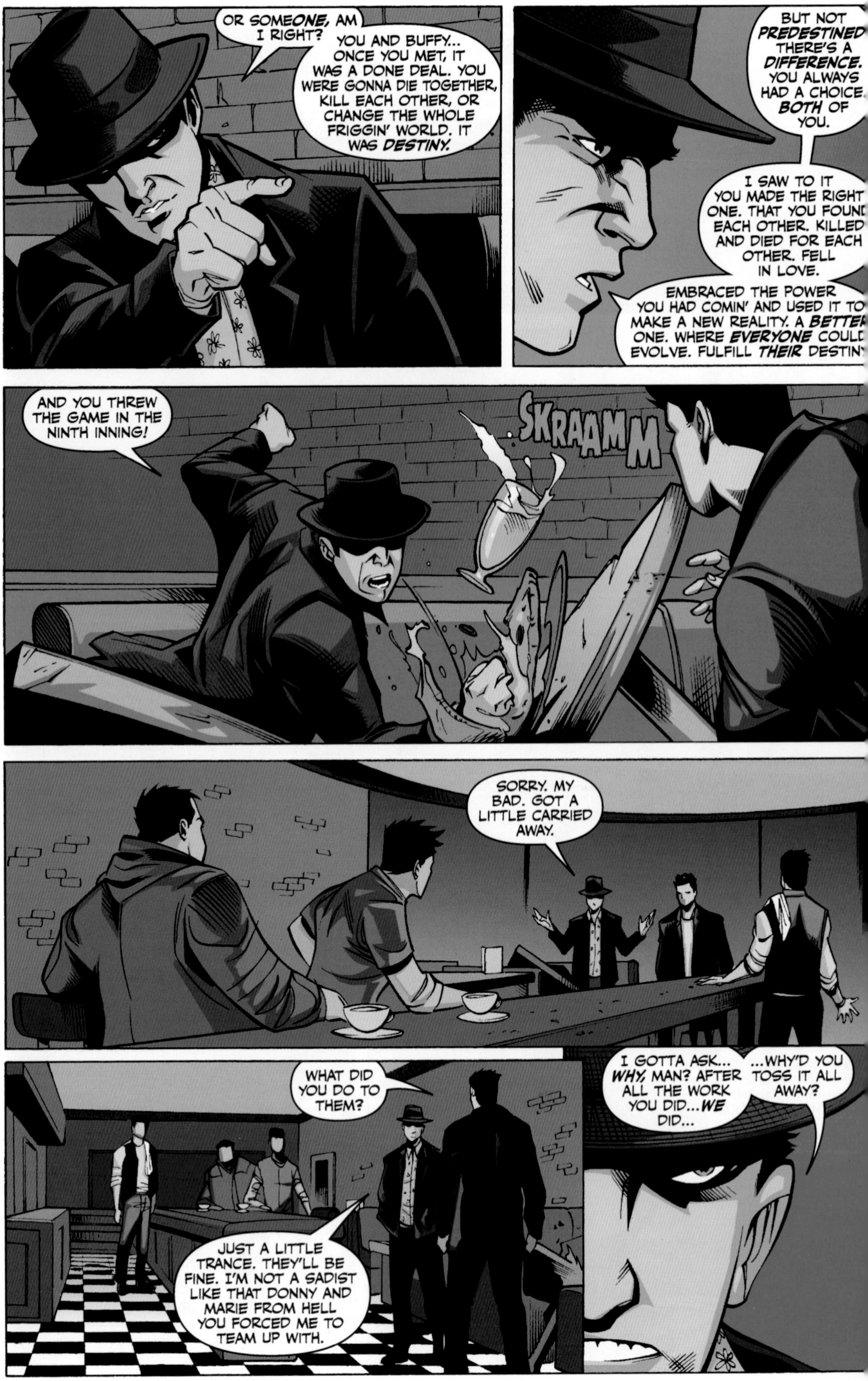
OR SOMEONE, AM I RIGHT?
YOU AND BUFFY... ONCE YOU MET, IT WAS A DONE DEAL. YOU WERE GONNA DIE TOGETHER, KILL EACH OTHER, OR CHANGE THE WHOLE FRIGGIN' WORLD. IT WAS DESTINY.
BUT NOT PREDESTINED. THERE'S A DIFFERENCE. YOU ALWAYS HAD A CHOICE. BOTH OF YOU.
I SAW TO IT YOU MADE THE RIGHT ONE. THAT YOU FOUND EACH OTHER. KILLED AND DIED FOR EACH OTHER. FELL IN LOVE.
EMBRACED THE POWER YOU HAD COMIN' AND USED IT TO MAKE A NEW REALITY. A BETTER ONE. WHERE EVERYONE COULD EVOLVE. FULFILL THEIR DESTINY.
AND YOU THREW THE GAME IN THE NINTH INNING!
SKRAAMM
SORRY. MY BAD. GOT A LITTLE CARRIED AWAY.
WHAT DID YOU DO TO THEM?
JUST A LITTLE TRANCE. THEY'LL BE FINE. I'M NOT A SADIST LIKE THAT DONNY AND MARIE FROM HELL YOU FORCED ME TO TEAM UP WITH.
I GOTTA ASK... WHY, MAN? AFTER ALL THE WORK YOU DID... WE DID...
...WHY'D YOU TOSS IT ALL AWAY?

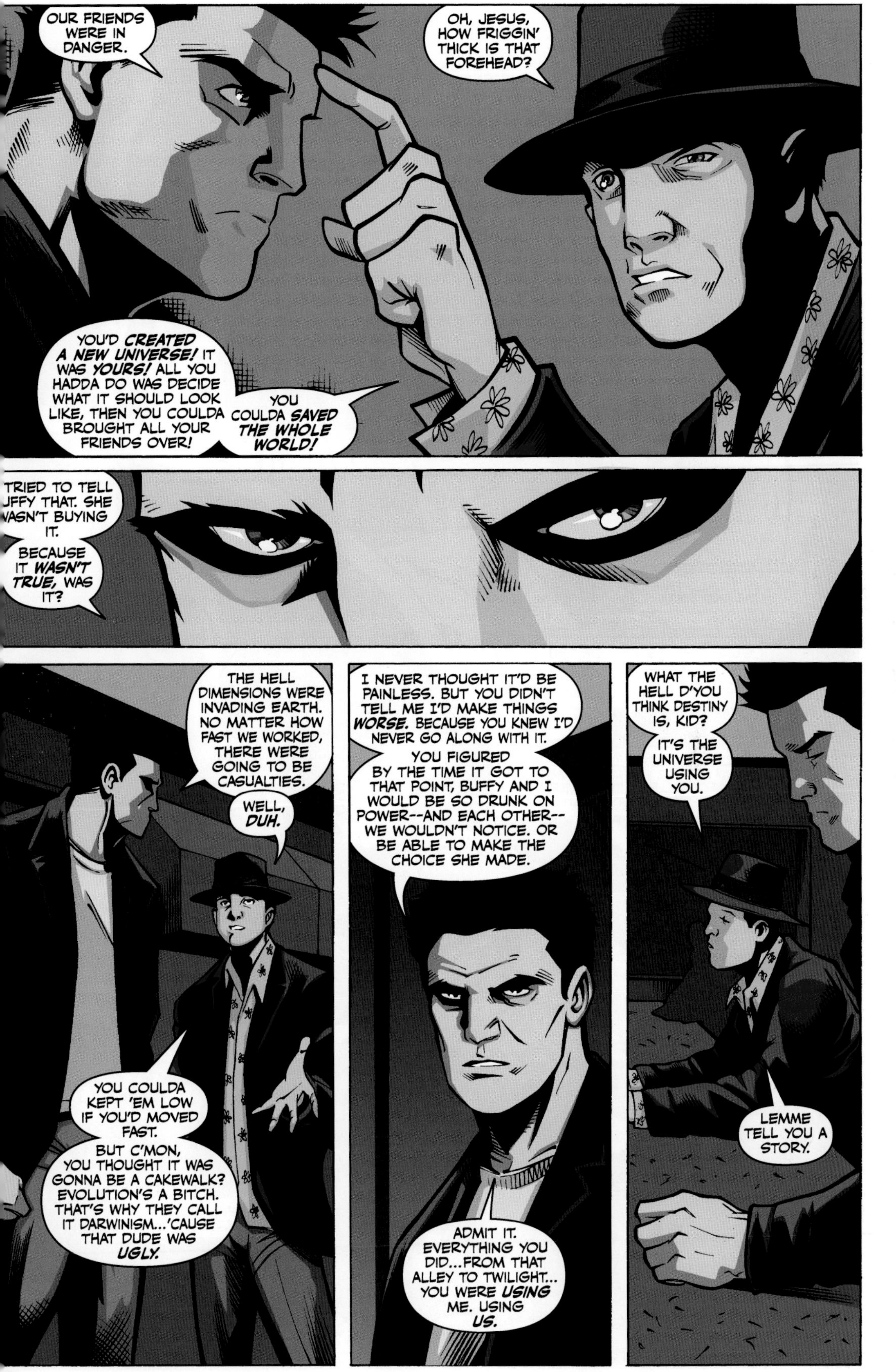
OUR FRIENDS WERE IN DANGER.
OH, JESUS, HOW FRIGGIN' THICK IS THAT FOREHEAD?
YOU'D **CREATED A NEW UNIVERSE!** IT WAS **YOURS!** ALL YOU HADDA DO WAS DECIDE WHAT IT SHOULD LOOK LIKE, THEN YOU COULDA BROUGHT ALL YOUR FRIENDS OVER!
YOU COULDA **SAVED THE WHOLE WORLD!**
TRIED TO TELL UFFY THAT. SHE WASN'T BUYING IT.
BECAUSE IT **WASN'T TRUE,** WAS IT?
THE HELL DIMENSIONS WERE INVADING EARTH. NO MATTER HOW FAST WE WORKED, THERE WERE GOING TO BE CASUALTIES.
WELL, **DUH.**
YOU COULDA KEPT 'EM LOW IF YOU'D MOVED FAST.
BUT C'MON, YOU THOUGHT IT WAS GONNA BE A CAKEWALK? EVOLUTION'S A BITCH. THAT'S WHY THEY CALL IT DARWINISM...'CAUSE THAT DUDE WAS **UGLY.**
I NEVER THOUGHT IT'D BE PAINLESS. BUT YOU DIDN'T TELL ME I'D MAKE THINGS **WORSE.** BECAUSE YOU KNEW I'D NEVER GO ALONG WITH IT.
YOU FIGURED BY THE TIME IT GOT TO THAT POINT, BUFFY AND I WOULD BE SO DRUNK ON POWER--AND EACH OTHER--WE WOULDN'T NOTICE. OR BE ABLE TO MAKE THE CHOICE SHE MADE.
ADMIT IT. EVERYTHING YOU DID...FROM THAT ALLEY TO TWILIGHT... YOU WERE **USING** ME. USING **US.**
WHAT THE HELL D'YOU THINK DESTINY IS, KID?
IT'S THE UNIVERSE USING YOU.
LEMME TELL YOU A STORY.

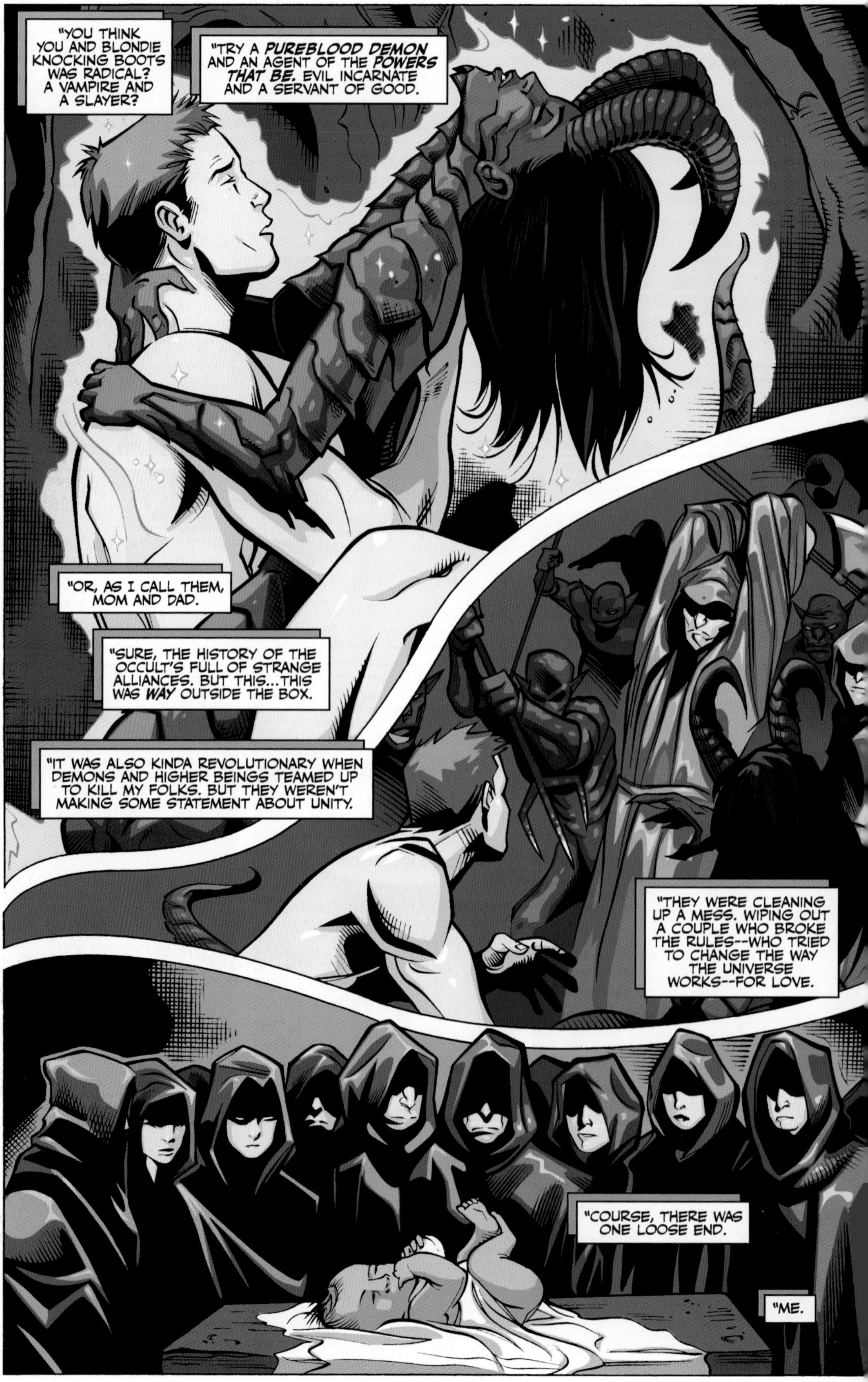
"YOU THINK YOU AND BLONDIE KNOCKING BOOTS WAS RADICAL? A VAMPIRE AND A SLAYER?
"TRY A *PUREBLOOD DEMON* AND AN AGENT OF THE *POWERS THAT BE.* EVIL INCARNATE AND A SERVANT OF GOOD.
"OR, AS I CALL THEM, MOM AND DAD.
"SURE, THE HISTORY OF THE OCCULT'S FULL OF STRANGE ALLIANCES. BUT THIS...THIS WAS *WAY* OUTSIDE THE BOX.
"IT WAS ALSO KINDA REVOLUTIONARY WHEN DEMONS AND HIGHER BEINGS TEAMED UP TO KILL MY FOLKS. BUT THEY WEREN'T MAKING SOME STATEMENT ABOUT UNITY.
"THEY WERE CLEANING UP A MESS. WIPING OUT A COUPLE WHO BROKE THE RULES--WHO TRIED TO CHANGE THE WAY THE UNIVERSE WORKS--FOR LOVE.
"COURSE, THERE WAS ONE LOOSE END.
"ME.

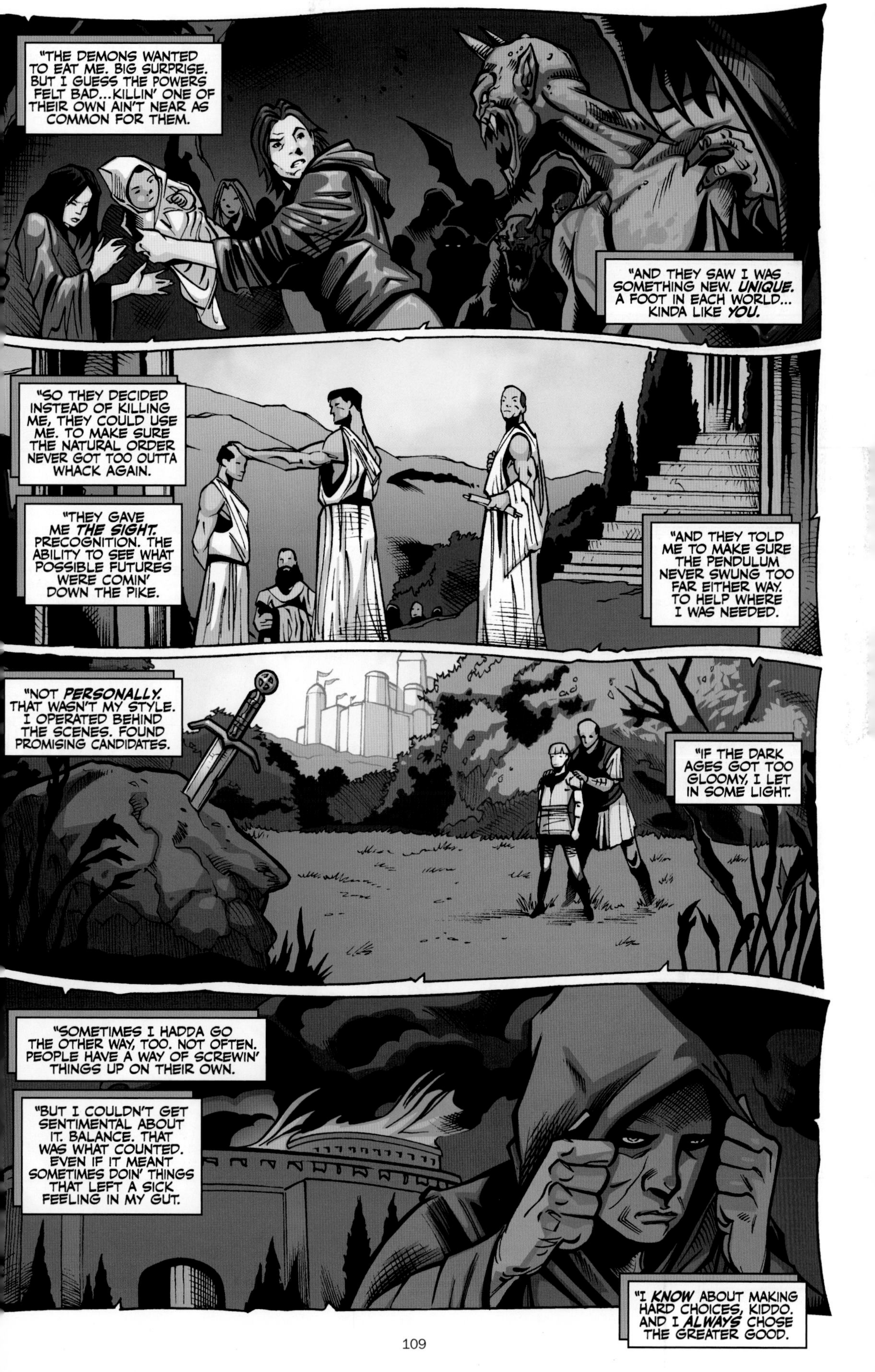
"THE DEMONS WANTED TO EAT ME. BIG SURPRISE. BUT I GUESS THE POWERS FELT BAD...KILLIN' ONE OF THEIR OWN AIN'T NEAR AS COMMON FOR THEM.
"AND THEY SAW I WAS SOMETHING NEW. UNIQUE. A FOOT IN EACH WORLD... KINDA LIKE YOU.
"SO THEY DECIDED INSTEAD OF KILLING ME, THEY COULD USE ME. TO MAKE SURE THE NATURAL ORDER NEVER GOT TOO OUTTA WHACK AGAIN.
"THEY GAVE ME THE SIGHT. PRECOGNITION. THE ABILITY TO SEE WHAT POSSIBLE FUTURES WERE COMIN' DOWN THE PIKE.
"AND THEY TOLD ME TO MAKE SURE THE PENDULUM NEVER SWUNG TOO FAR EITHER WAY. TO HELP WHERE I WAS NEEDED.
"NOT PERSONALLY. THAT WASN'T MY STYLE. I OPERATED BEHIND THE SCENES. FOUND PROMISING CANDIDATES.
"IF THE DARK AGES GOT TOO GLOOMY, I LET IN SOME LIGHT.
"SOMETIMES I HADDA GO THE OTHER WAY, TOO. NOT OFTEN. PEOPLE HAVE A WAY OF SCREWIN' THINGS UP ON THEIR OWN.
"BUT I COULDN'T GET SENTIMENTAL ABOUT IT. BALANCE. THAT WAS WHAT COUNTED. EVEN IF IT MEANT SOMETIMES DOIN' THINGS THAT LEFT A SICK FEELING IN MY GUT.
"I KNOW ABOUT MAKING HARD CHOICES, KIDDO. AND I ALWAYS CHOSE THE GREATER GOOD.

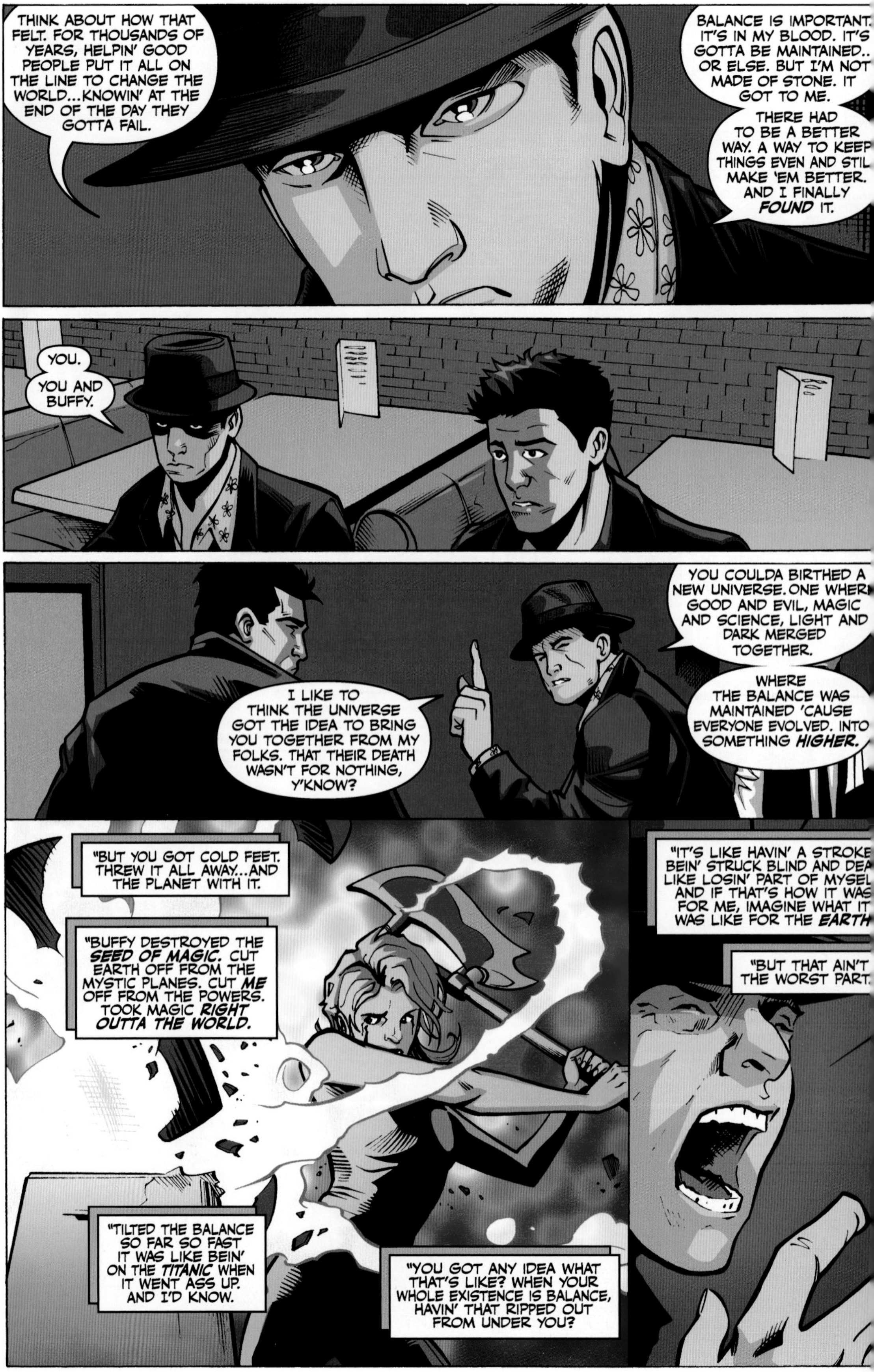

THINK ABOUT HOW THAT FELT. FOR THOUSANDS OF YEARS, HELPIN' GOOD PEOPLE PUT IT ALL ON THE LINE TO CHANGE THE WORLD...KNOWIN' AT THE END OF THE DAY THEY GOTTA FAIL.
BALANCE IS IMPORTANT. IT'S IN MY BLOOD. IT'S GOTTA BE MAINTAINED.. OR ELSE. BUT I'M NOT MADE OF STONE. IT GOT TO ME.
THERE HAD TO BE A BETTER WAY. A WAY TO KEEP THINGS EVEN AND STIL MAKE 'EM BETTER. AND I FINALLY FOUND IT.
YOU.
YOU AND BUFFY.
I LIKE TO THINK THE UNIVERSE GOT THE IDEA TO BRING YOU TOGETHER FROM MY FOLKS. THAT THEIR DEATH WASN'T FOR NOTHING, Y'KNOW?
YOU COULDA BIRTHED A NEW UNIVERSE. ONE WHER GOOD AND EVIL, MAGIC AND SCIENCE, LIGHT AND DARK MERGED TOGETHER.
WHERE THE BALANCE WAS MAINTAINED 'CAUSE EVERYONE EVOLVED. INTO SOMETHING HIGHER.
"BUT YOU GOT COLD FEET. THREW IT ALL AWAY...AND THE PLANET WITH IT.
"BUFFY DESTROYED THE SEED OF MAGIC. CUT EARTH OFF FROM THE MYSTIC PLANES. CUT ME OFF FROM THE POWERS. TOOK MAGIC RIGHT OUTTA THE WORLD.
"TILTED THE BALANCE SO FAR SO FAST IT WAS LIKE BEIN' ON THE TITANIC WHEN IT WENT ASS UP. AND I'D KNOW.
"YOU GOT ANY IDEA WHAT THAT'S LIKE? WHEN YOUR WHOLE EXISTENCE IS BALANCE, HAVIN' THAT RIPPED OUT FROM UNDER YOU?
"IT'S LIKE HAVIN' A STROKE BEIN' STRUCK BLIND AND DEA LIKE LOSIN' PART OF MYSEL AND IF THAT'S HOW IT WAS FOR ME, IMAGINE WHAT IT WAS LIKE FOR THE EARTH
"BUT THAT AIN'T THE WORST PART.

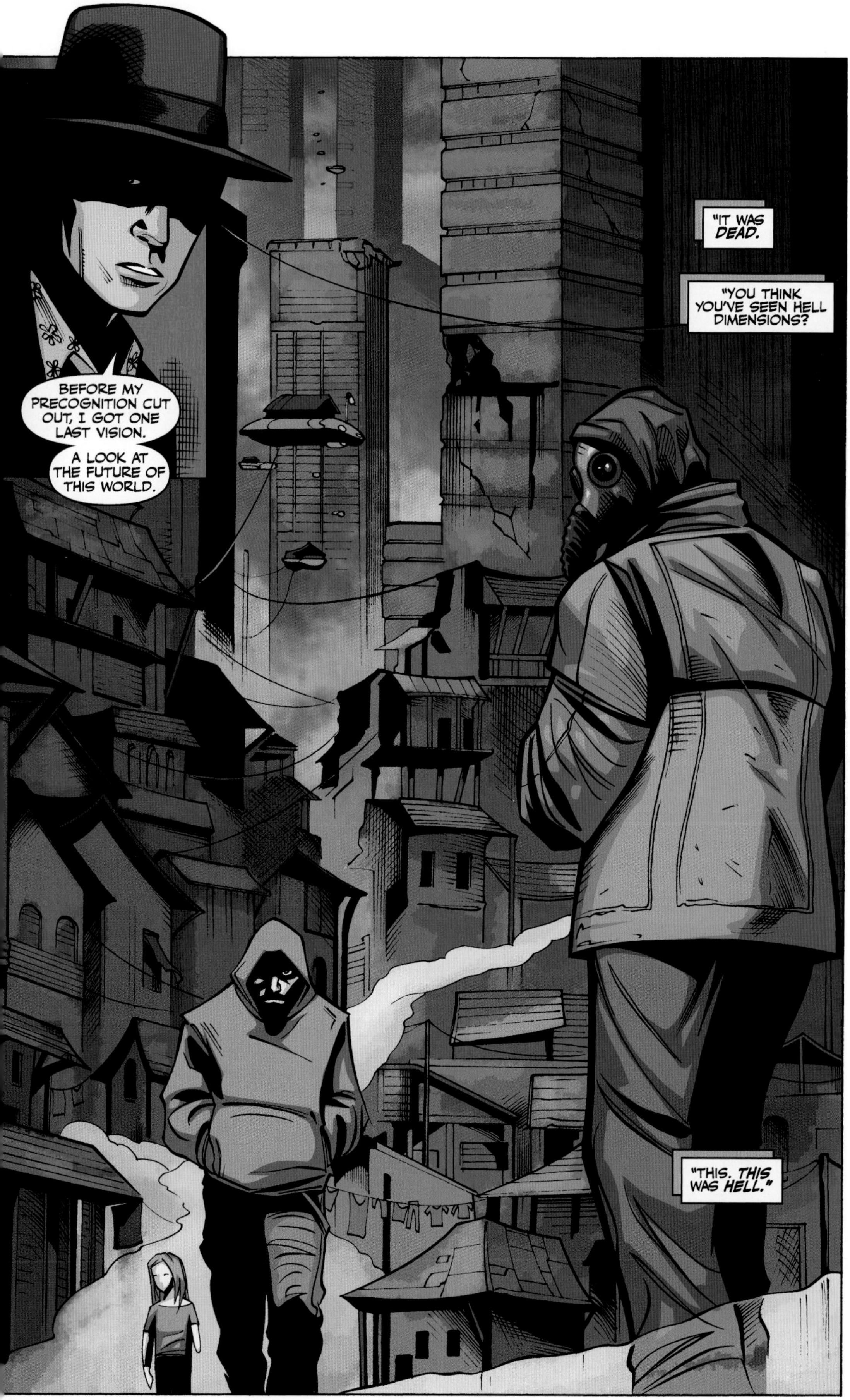

BEFORE MY PRECOGNITION CUT OUT, I GOT ONE LAST VISION.
A LOOK AT THE FUTURE OF THIS WORLD.
"IT WAS *DEAD.*
"YOU THINK YOU'VE SEEN HELL DIMENSIONS?
"THIS. *THIS* WAS *HELL.*"

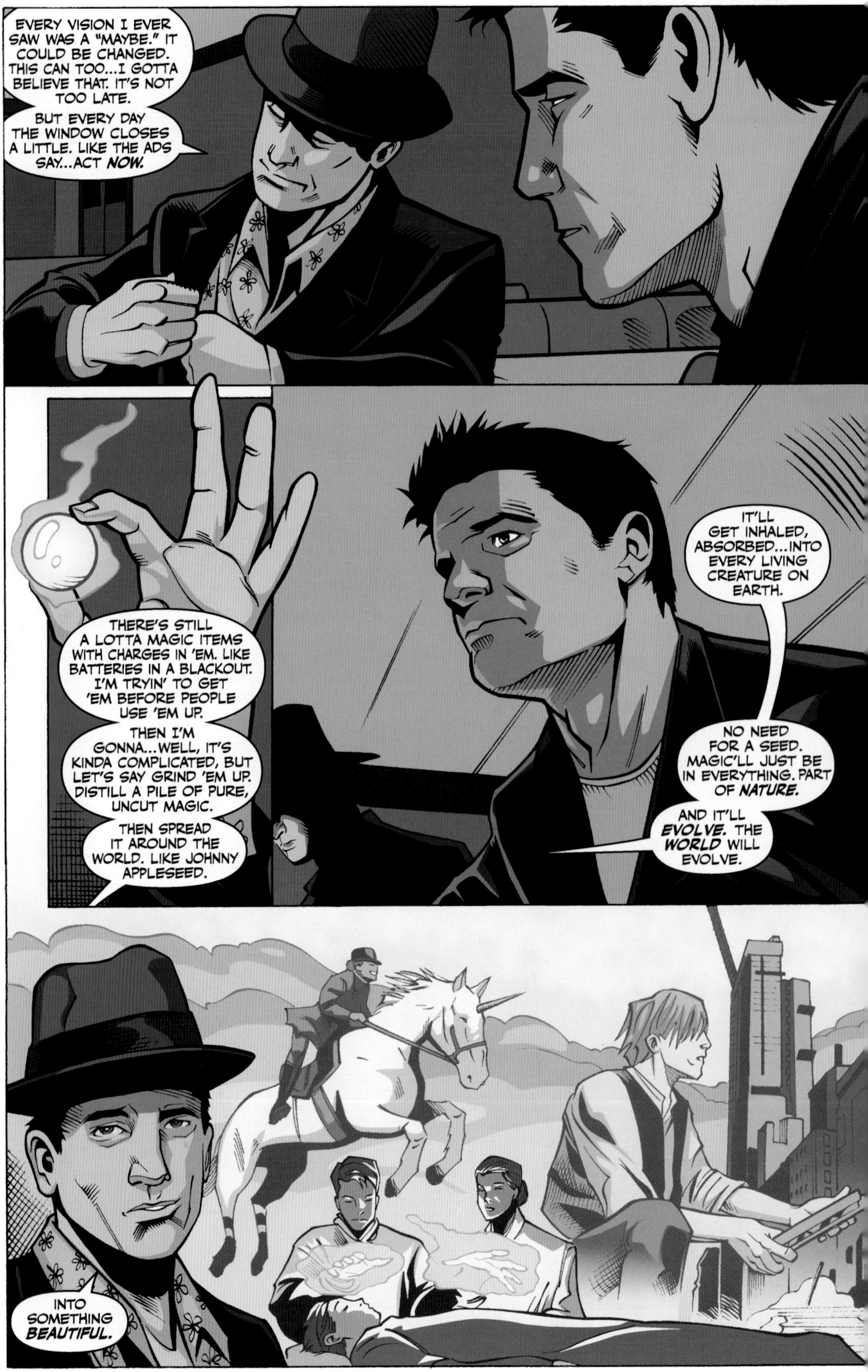
EVERY VISION I EVER SAW WAS A "MAYBE." IT COULD BE CHANGED. THIS CAN TOO...I GOTTA BELIEVE THAT. IT'S NOT TOO LATE.
BUT EVERY DAY THE WINDOW CLOSES A LITTLE. LIKE THE ADS SAY...ACT ***NOW.***
THERE'S STILL A LOTTA MAGIC ITEMS WITH CHARGES IN 'EM. LIKE BATTERIES IN A BLACKOUT. I'M TRYIN' TO GET 'EM BEFORE PEOPLE USE 'EM UP.
THEN I'M GONNA...WELL, IT'S KINDA COMPLICATED, BUT LET'S SAY GRIND 'EM UP. DISTILL A PILE OF PURE, UNCUT MAGIC.
THEN SPREAD IT AROUND THE WORLD. LIKE JOHNNY APPLESEED.
IT'LL GET INHALED, ABSORBED...INTO EVERY LIVING CREATURE ON EARTH.
NO NEED FOR A SEED. MAGIC'LL JUST BE IN EVERYTHING. PART OF ***NATURE.***
AND IT'LL ***EVOLVE.*** THE ***WORLD*** WILL EVOLVE.
INTO SOMETHING ***BEAUTIFUL.***

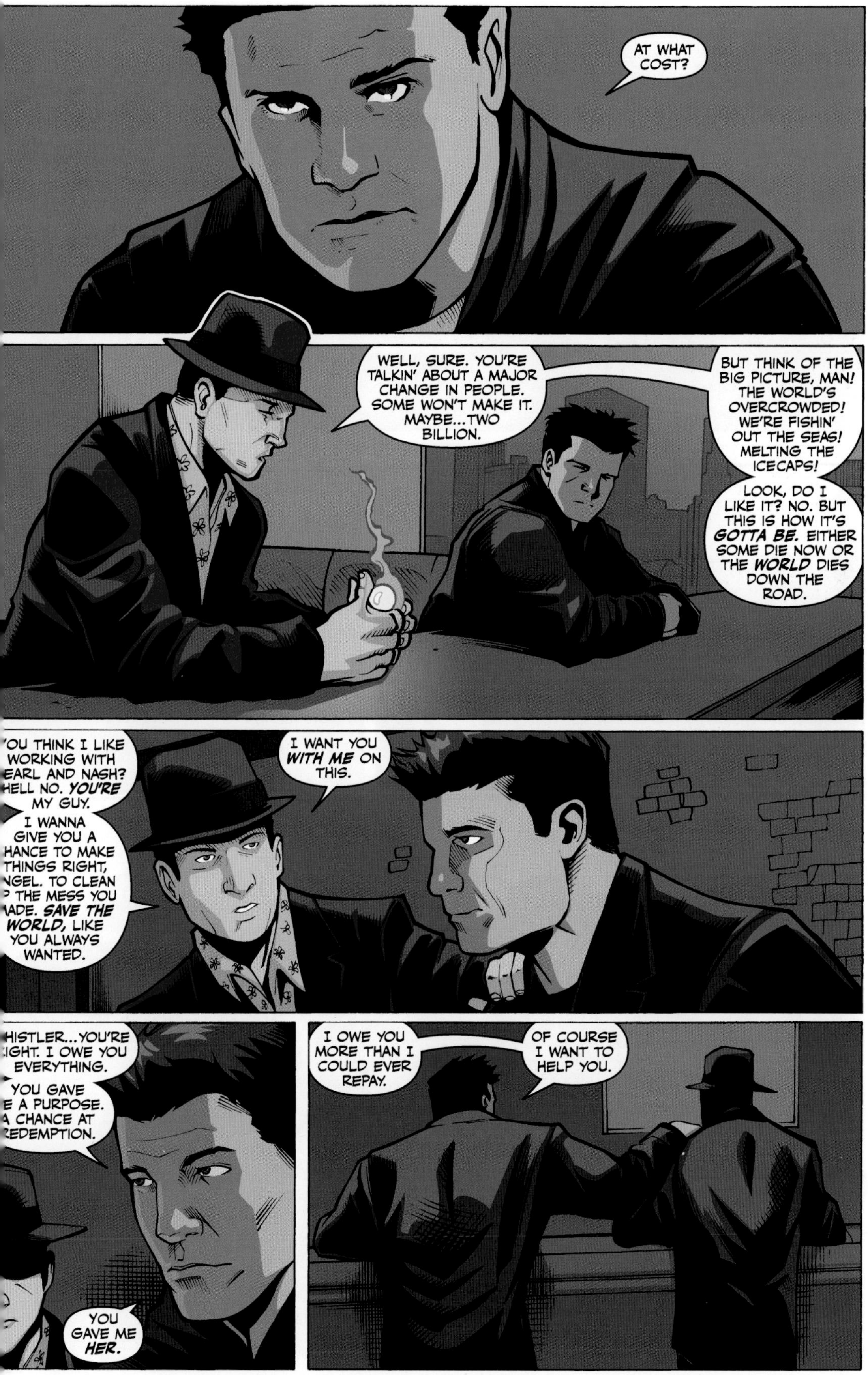

AT WHAT COST?
WELL, SURE. YOU'RE TALKIN' ABOUT A MAJOR CHANGE IN PEOPLE. SOME WON'T MAKE IT. MAYBE...TWO BILLION.
BUT THINK OF THE BIG PICTURE, MAN! THE WORLD'S OVERCROWDED! WE'RE FISHIN' OUT THE SEAS! MELTING THE ICECAPS!
LOOK, DO I LIKE IT? NO. BUT THIS IS HOW IT'S *GOTTA BE.* EITHER SOME DIE NOW OR THE *WORLD* DIES DOWN THE ROAD.
OU THINK I LIKE WORKING WITH EARL AND NASH? HELL NO. *YOU'RE* MY GUY.
I WANNA GIVE YOU A HANCE TO MAKE THINGS RIGHT, NGEL. TO CLEAN THE MESS YOU ADE. *SAVE THE WORLD,* LIKE YOU ALWAYS WANTED.
I WANT YOU *WITH ME* ON THIS.
HISTLER...YOU'RE IGHT. I OWE YOU EVERYTHING.
YOU GAVE E A PURPOSE. A CHANCE AT REDEMPTION.
YOU GAVE ME *HER.*
I OWE YOU MORE THAN I COULD EVER REPAY.
OF COURSE I WANT TO HELP YOU.

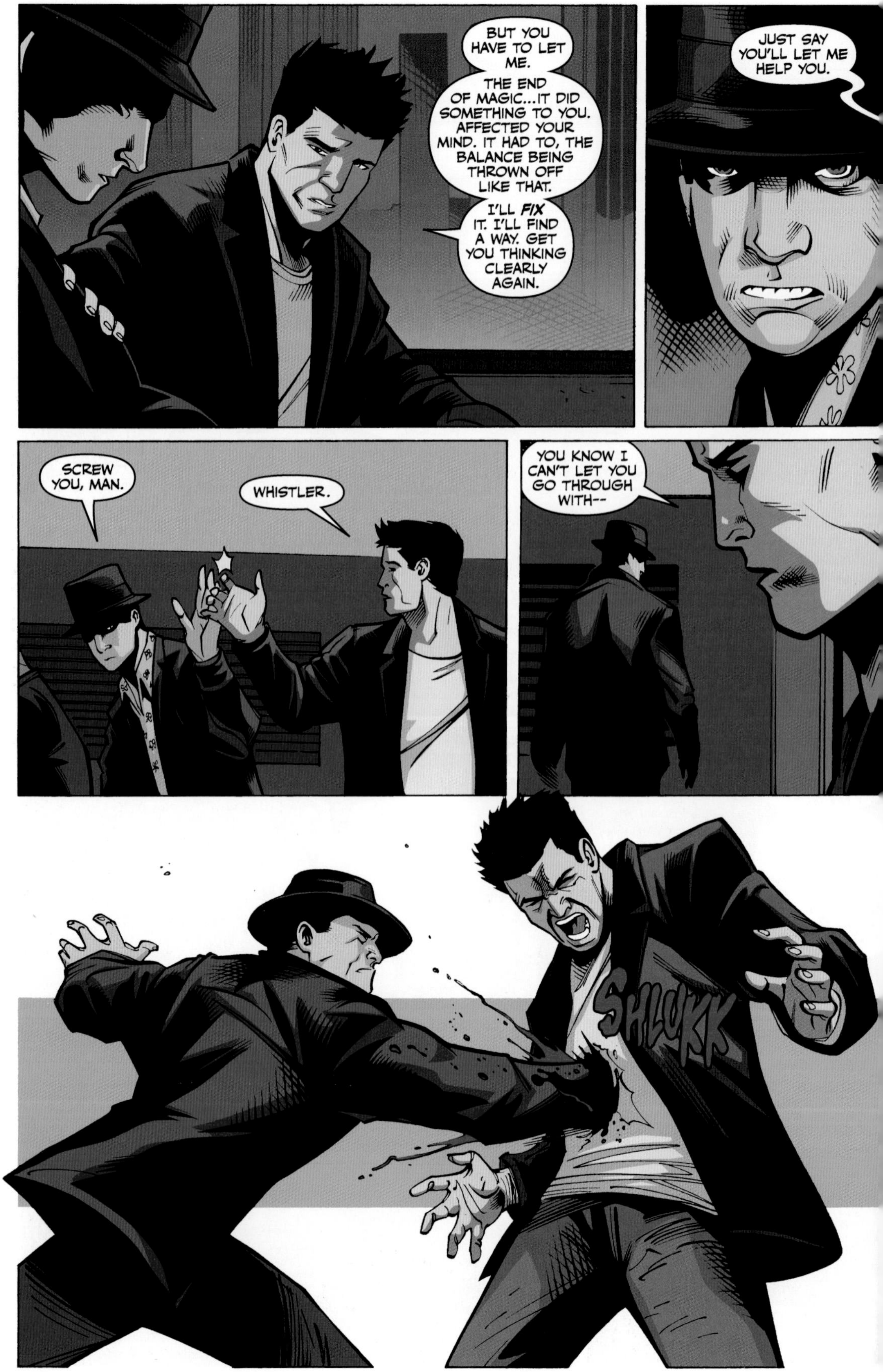

BUT YOU HAVE TO LET ME.
THE END OF MAGIC...IT DID SOMETHING TO YOU. AFFECTED YOUR MIND. IT HAD TO, THE BALANCE BEING THROWN OFF LIKE THAT.
I'LL FIX IT. I'LL FIND A WAY. GET YOU THINKING CLEARLY AGAIN.
JUST SAY YOU'LL LET ME HELP YOU.
SCREW YOU, MAN.
WHISTLER.
YOU KNOW I CAN'T LET YOU GO THROUGH WITH--
SHLUKK

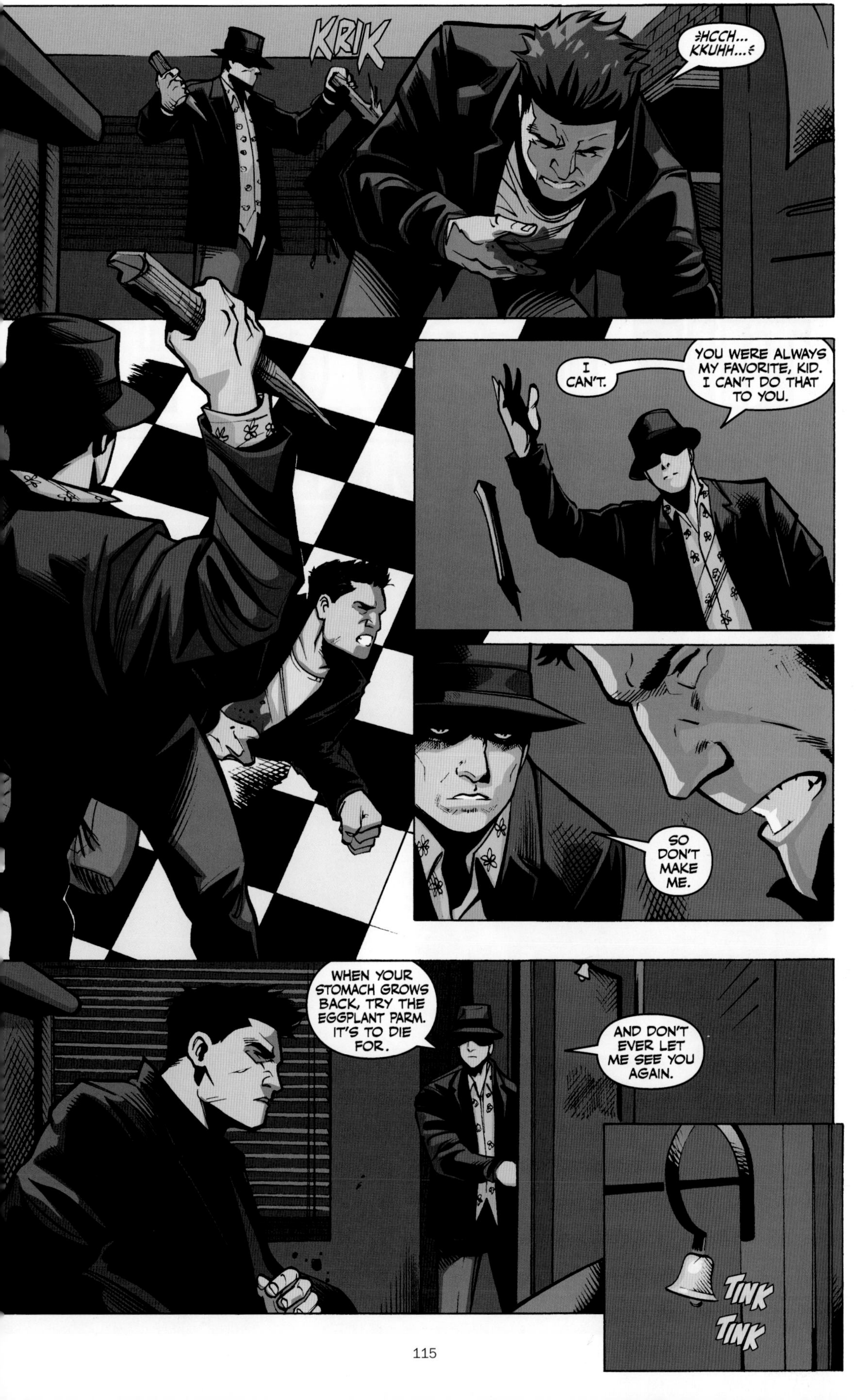
KRIK
HCCH... KKUHH...
YOU WERE ALWAYS MY FAVORITE, KID. I CAN'T DO THAT TO YOU.
I CAN'T.
SO DON'T MAKE ME.
WHEN YOUR STOMACH GROWS BACK, TRY THE EGGPLANT PARM. IT'S TO DIE FOR.
AND DON'T EVER LET ME SEE YOU AGAIN.
TINK
TINK

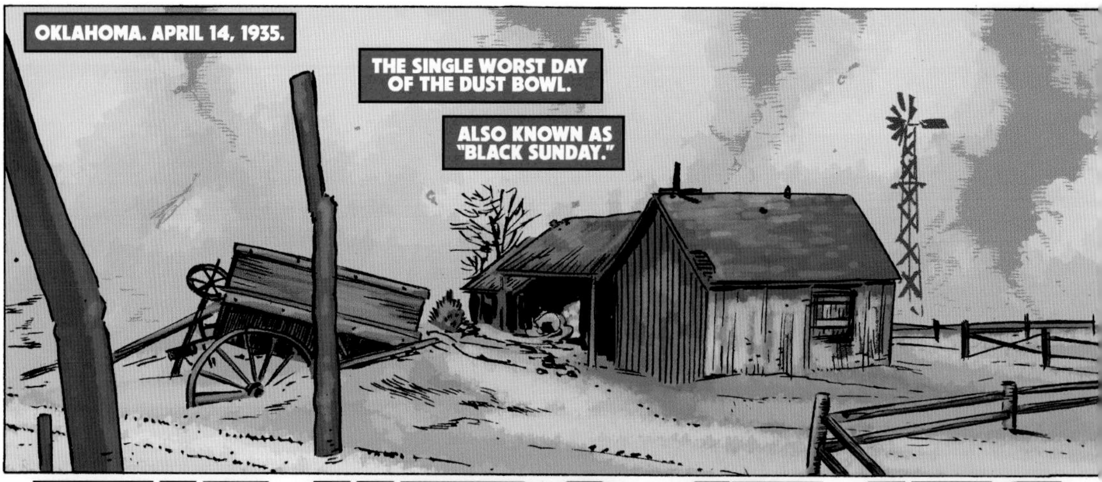
OKLAHOMA. APRIL 14, 1935.
THE SINGLE WORST DAY OF THE DUST BOWL.
ALSO KNOWN AS "BLACK SUNDAY."

THE HERO OF HIS OWN STORY

PART TWO: PEARL AND NASH

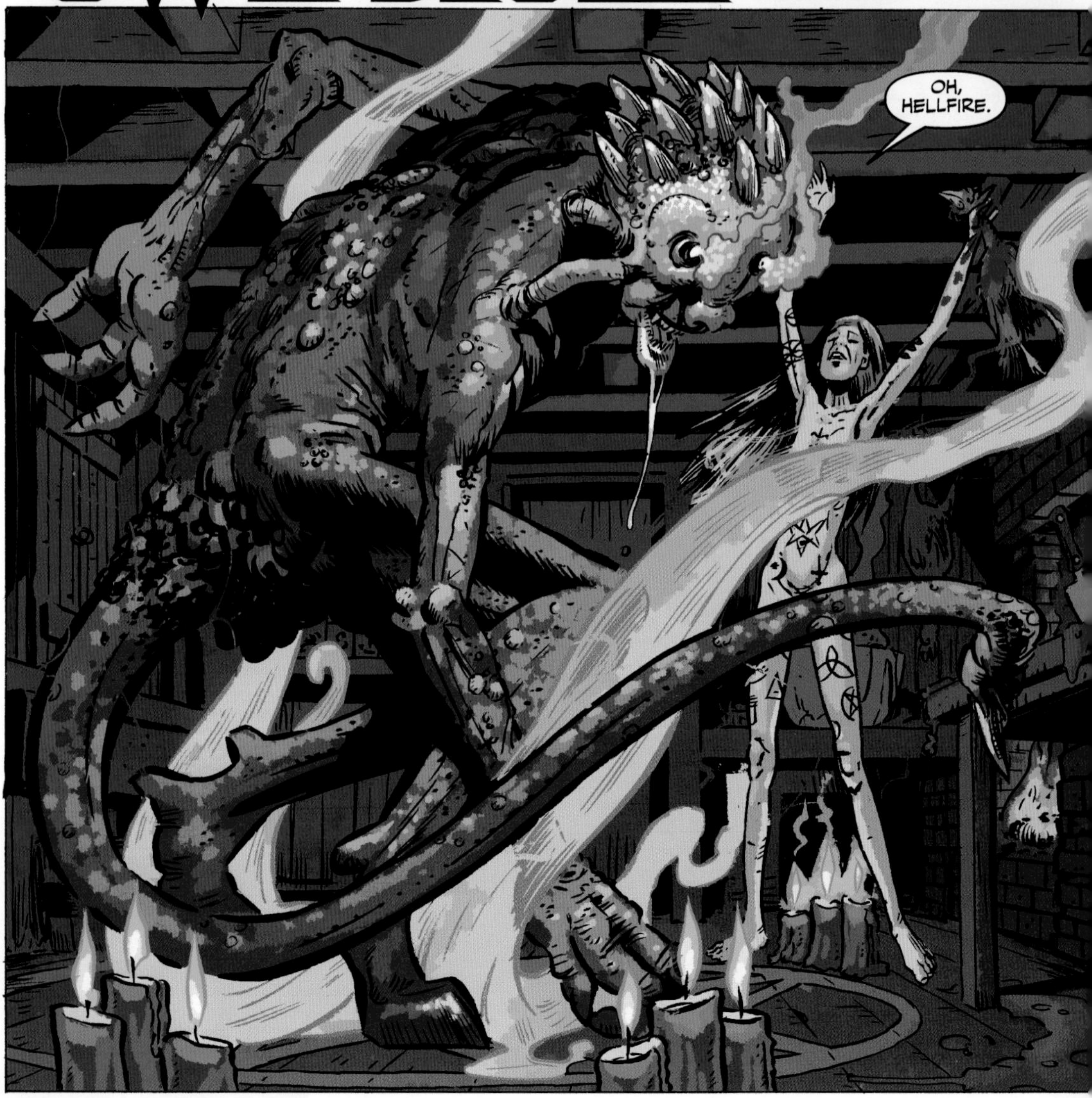
OH, HELLFIRE.

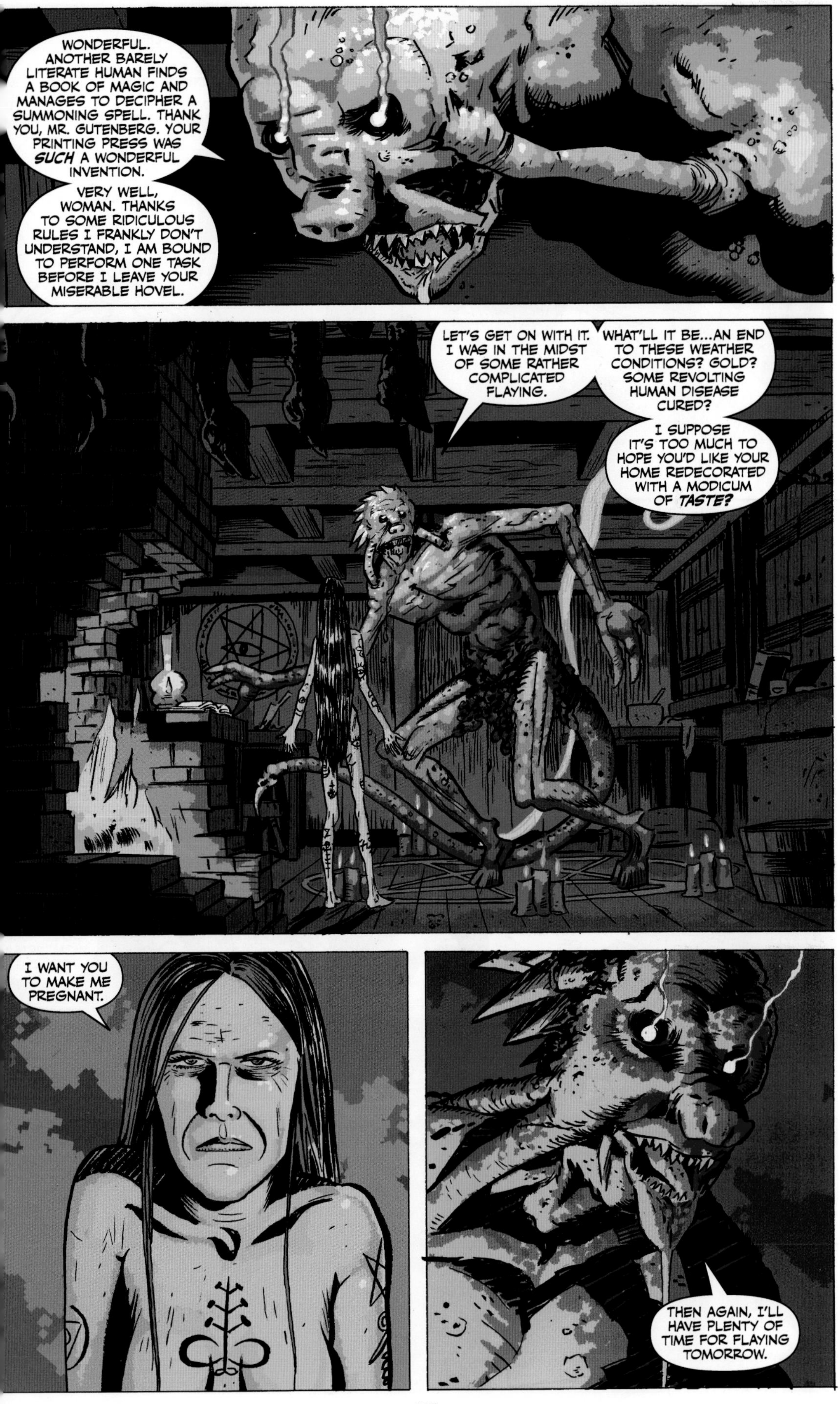
WONDERFUL. ANOTHER BARELY LITERATE HUMAN FINDS A BOOK OF MAGIC AND MANAGES TO DECIPHER A SUMMONING SPELL. THANK YOU, MR. GUTENBERG. YOUR PRINTING PRESS WAS *SUCH* A WONDERFUL INVENTION.
VERY WELL, WOMAN. THANKS TO SOME RIDICULOUS RULES I FRANKLY DON'T UNDERSTAND, I AM BOUND TO PERFORM ONE TASK BEFORE I LEAVE YOUR MISERABLE HOVEL.
LET'S GET ON WITH IT. I WAS IN THE MIDST OF SOME RATHER COMPLICATED FLAYING.
WHAT'LL IT BE...AN END TO THESE WEATHER CONDITIONS? GOLD? SOME REVOLTING HUMAN DISEASE CURED?
I SUPPOSE IT'S TOO MUCH TO HOPE YOU'D LIKE YOUR HOME REDECORATED WITH A MODICUM OF *TASTE?*
I WANT YOU TO MAKE ME PREGNANT.
THEN AGAIN, I'LL HAVE PLENTY OF TIME FOR FLAYING TOMORROW.

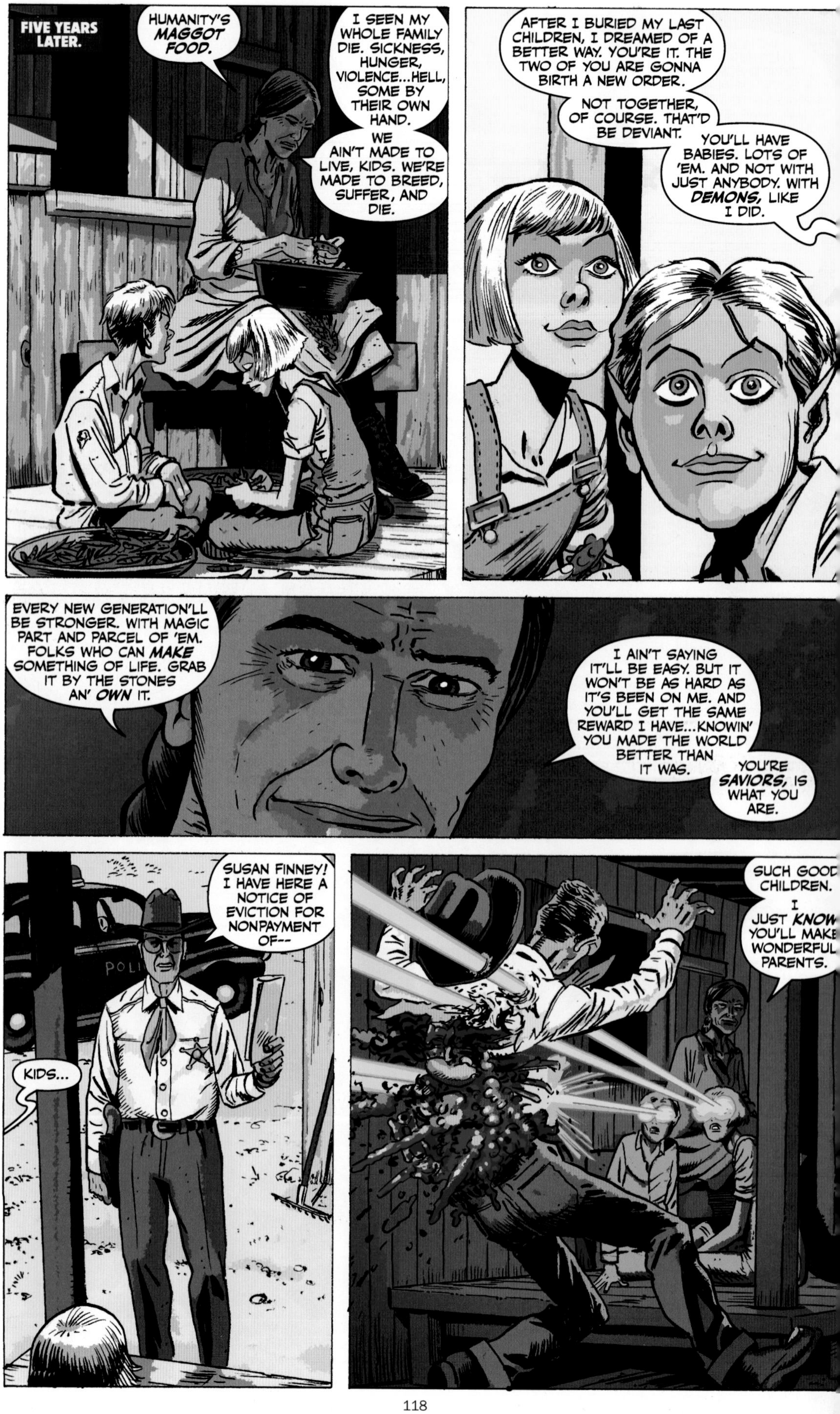

FIVE YEARS LATER.
HUMANITY'S *MAGGOT FOOD.*
I SEEN MY WHOLE FAMILY DIE. SICKNESS, HUNGER, VIOLENCE...HELL, SOME BY THEIR OWN HAND.
WE AIN'T MADE TO LIVE, KIDS. WE'RE MADE TO BREED, SUFFER, AND DIE.
AFTER I BURIED MY LAST CHILDREN, I DREAMED OF A BETTER WAY. YOU'RE IT. THE TWO OF YOU ARE GONNA BIRTH A NEW ORDER.
NOT TOGETHER, OF COURSE. THAT'D BE DEVIANT.
YOU'LL HAVE BABIES. LOTS OF 'EM. AND NOT WITH JUST ANYBODY. WITH *DEMONS,* LIKE I DID.
EVERY NEW GENERATION'LL BE STRONGER. WITH MAGIC PART AND PARCEL OF 'EM. FOLKS WHO CAN *MAKE* SOMETHING OF LIFE. GRAB IT BY THE STONES AN' *OWN* IT.
I AIN'T SAYING IT'LL BE EASY. BUT IT WON'T BE AS HARD AS IT'S BEEN ON ME. AND YOU'LL GET THE SAME REWARD I HAVE...KNOWIN' YOU MADE THE WORLD BETTER THAN IT WAS.
YOU'RE *SAVIORS,* IS WHAT YOU ARE.
SUSAN FINNEY! I HAVE HERE A NOTICE OF EVICTION FOR NONPAYMENT OF--
POLI
KIDS...
SUCH GOOD CHILDREN.
I JUST *KNOW* YOU'LL MAKE WONDERFUL PARENTS.

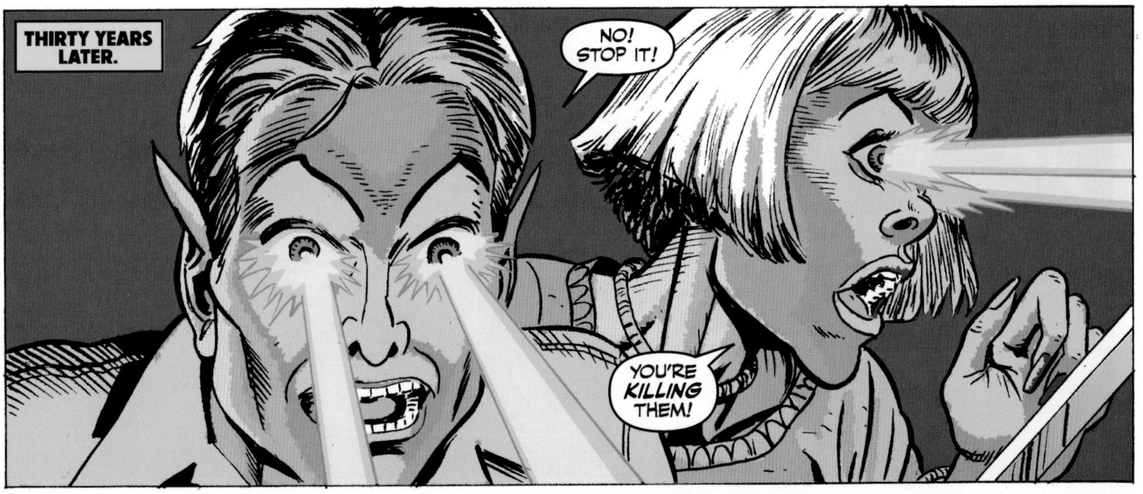
THIRTY YEARS LATER.
NO! STOP IT!
YOU'RE KILLING THEM!

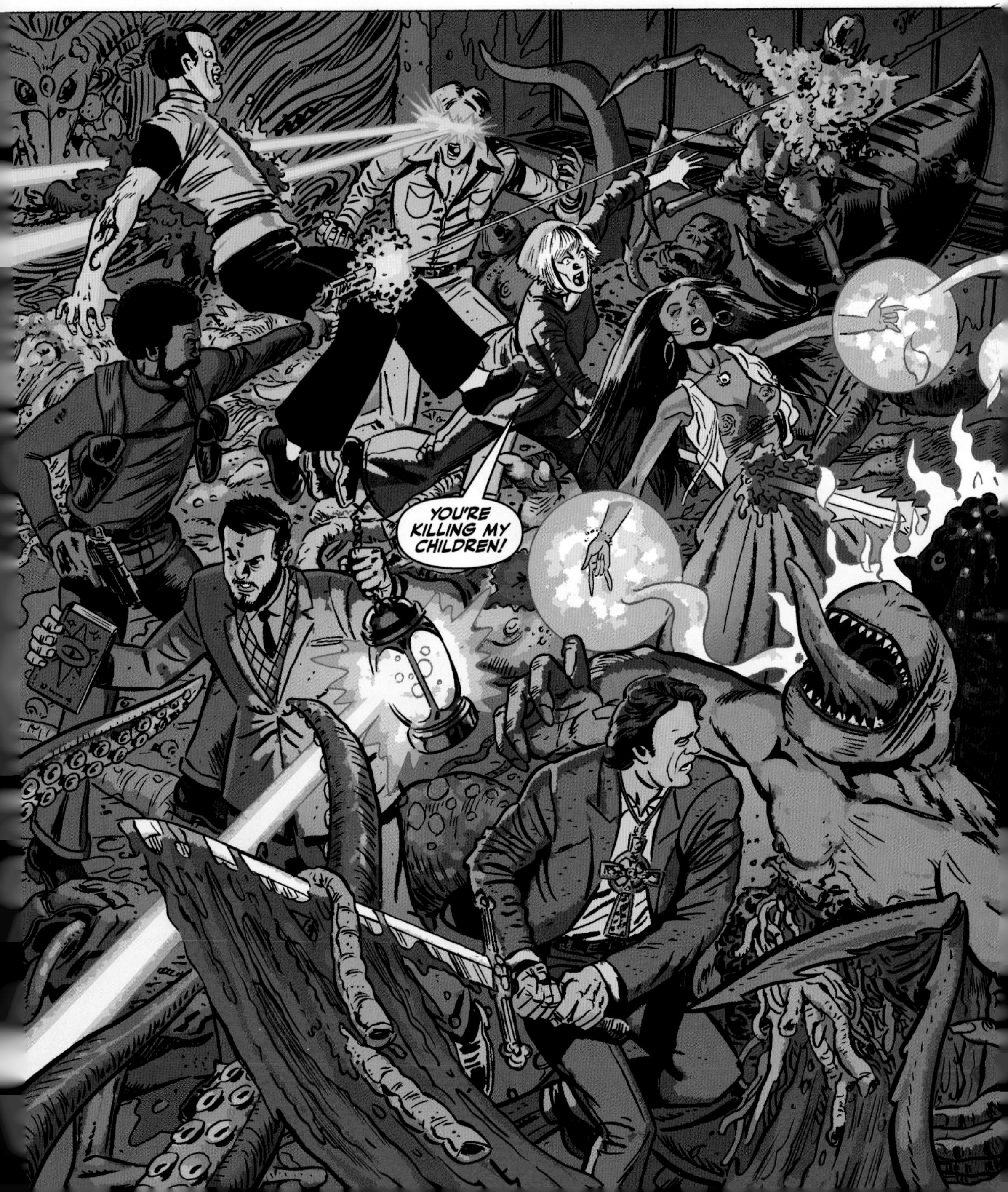
YOU'RE KILLING MY CHILDREN!

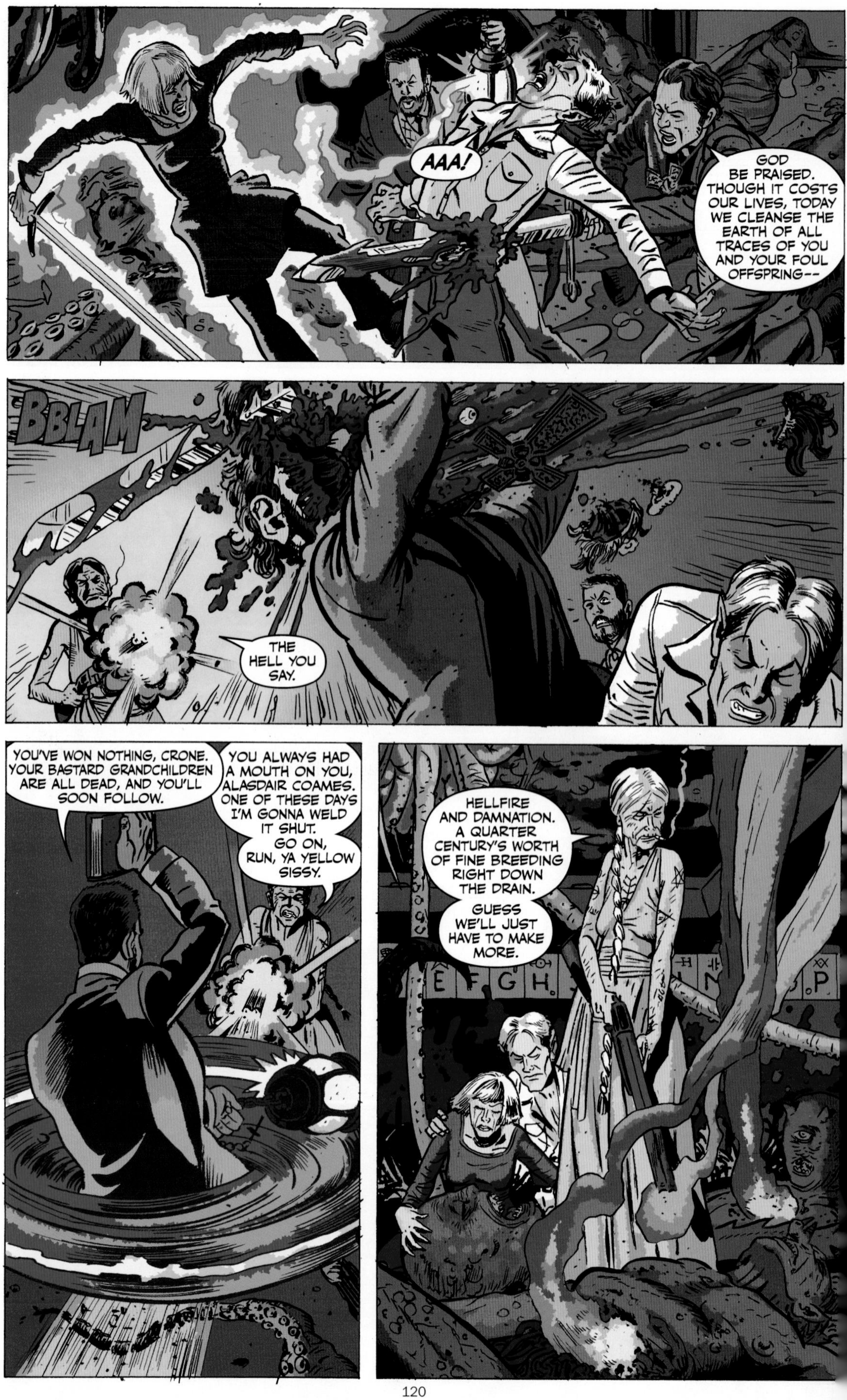
AAA!
GOD BE PRAISED. THOUGH IT COSTS OUR LIVES, TODAY WE CLEANSE THE EARTH OF ALL TRACES OF YOU AND YOUR FOUL OFFSPRING--
BBLAM
THE HELL YOU SAY.
YOU'VE WON NOTHING, CRONE. YOUR BASTARD GRANDCHILDREN ARE ALL DEAD, AND YOU'LL SOON FOLLOW.
YOU ALWAYS HAD A MOUTH ON YOU, ALASDAIR COAMES. ONE OF THESE DAYS I'M GONNA WELD IT SHUT.
GO ON, RUN, YA YELLOW SISSY.
HELLFIRE AND DAMNATION. A QUARTER CENTURY'S WORTH OF FINE BREEDING RIGHT DOWN THE DRAIN.
GUESS WE'LL JUST HAVE TO MAKE MORE.

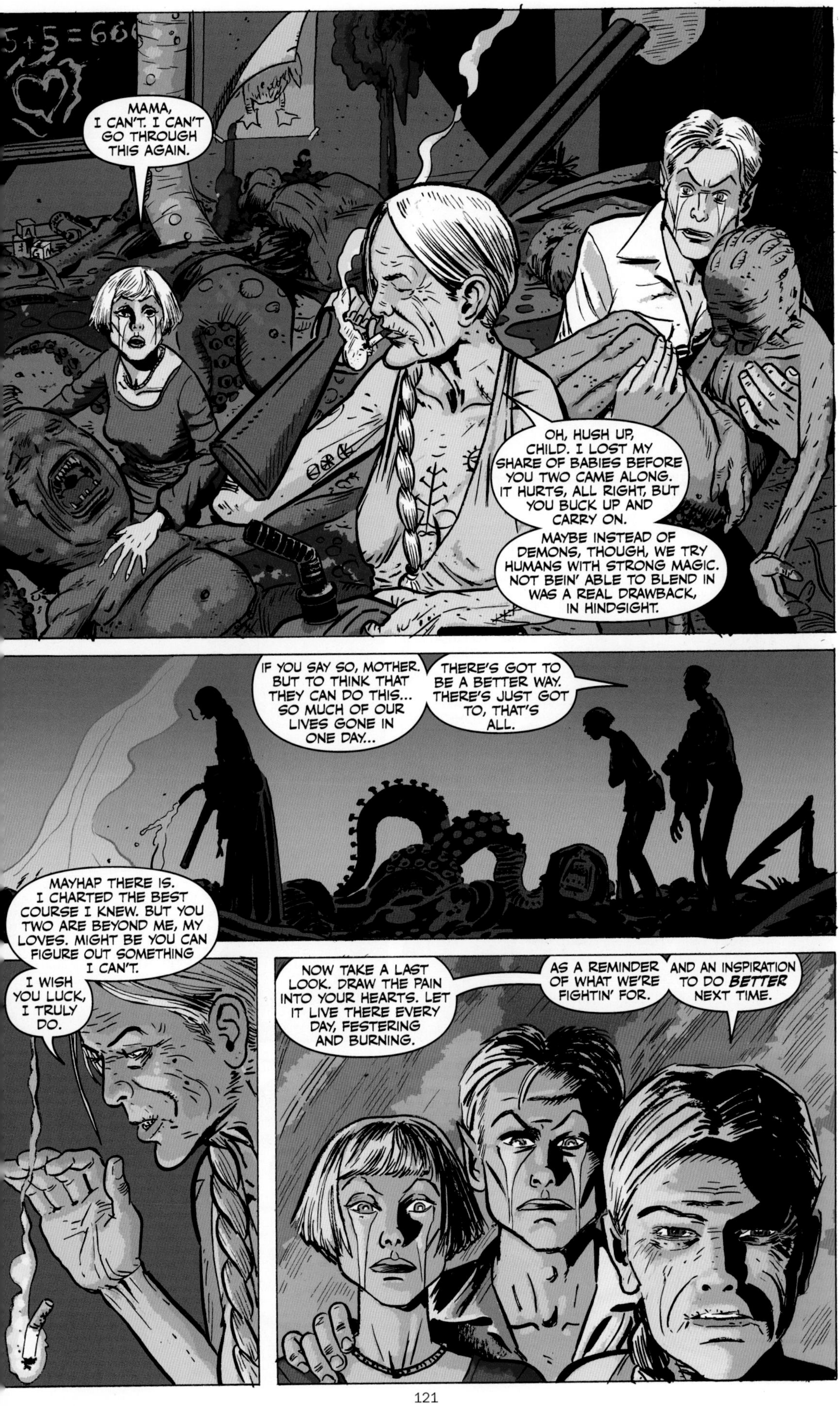
5+5=666
MAMA, I CAN'T. I CAN'T GO THROUGH THIS AGAIN.
OH, HUSH UP, CHILD. I LOST MY SHARE OF BABIES BEFORE YOU TWO CAME ALONG. IT HURTS, ALL RIGHT, BUT YOU BUCK UP AND CARRY ON.
MAYBE INSTEAD OF DEMONS, THOUGH, WE TRY HUMANS WITH STRONG MAGIC. NOT BEIN' ABLE TO BLEND IN WAS A REAL DRAWBACK, IN HINDSIGHT.
IF YOU SAY SO, MOTHER. BUT TO THINK THAT THEY CAN DO THIS... SO MUCH OF OUR LIVES GONE IN ONE DAY...
THERE'S GOT TO BE A BETTER WAY. THERE'S JUST GOT TO, THAT'S ALL.
MAYHAP THERE IS. I CHARTED THE BEST COURSE I KNEW. BUT YOU TWO ARE BEYOND ME, MY LOVES. MIGHT BE YOU CAN FIGURE OUT SOMETHING I CAN'T.
I WISH YOU LUCK, I TRULY DO.
NOW TAKE A LAST LOOK. DRAW THE PAIN INTO YOUR HEARTS. LET IT LIVE THERE EVERY DAY, FESTERING AND BURNING.
AS A REMINDER OF WHAT WE'RE FIGHTIN' FOR.
AND AN INSPIRATION TO DO *BETTER* NEXT TIME.

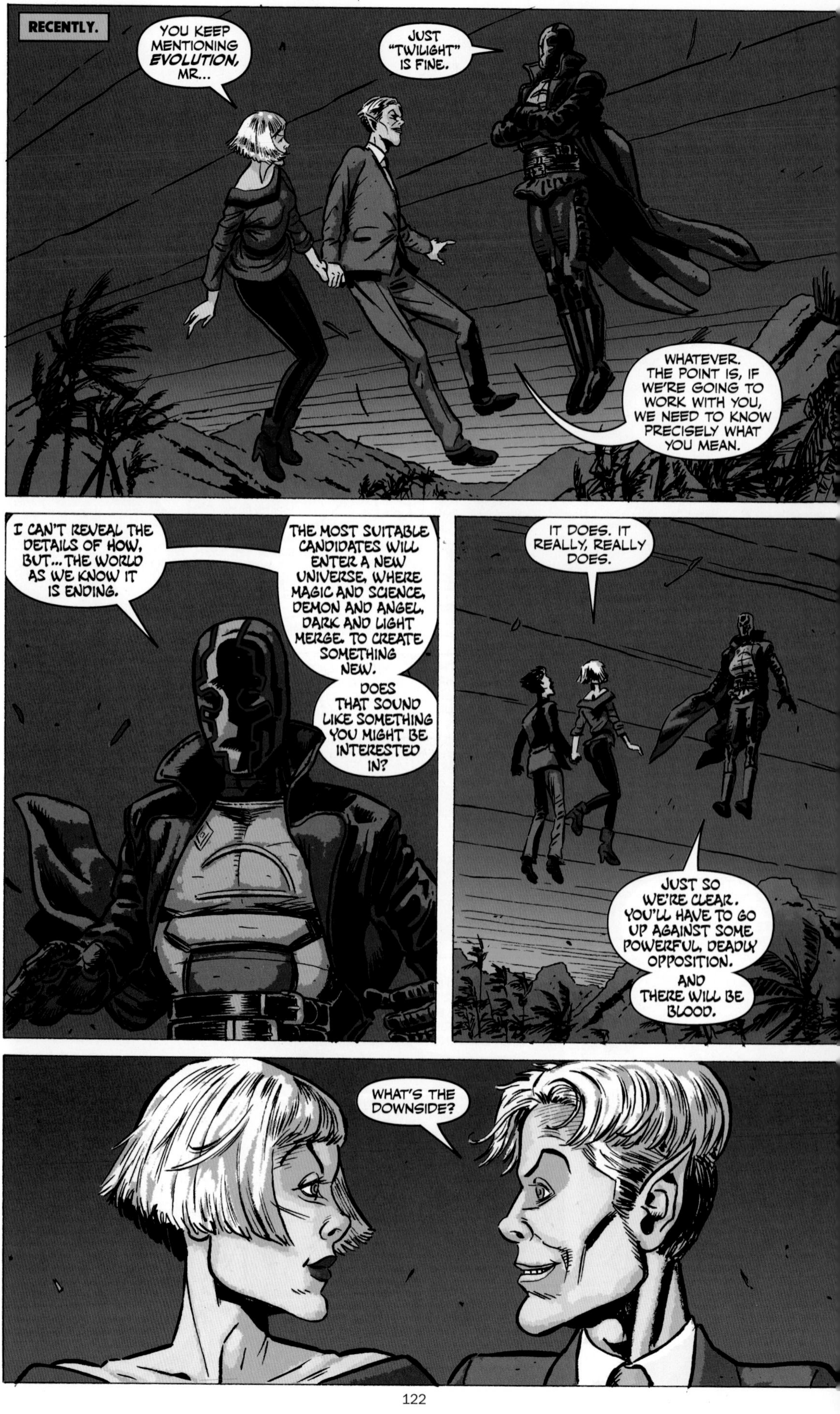

RECENTLY.
YOU KEEP MENTIONING EVOLUTION, MR...
JUST "TWILIGHT" IS FINE.
WHATEVER. THE POINT IS, IF WE'RE GOING TO WORK WITH YOU, WE NEED TO KNOW PRECISELY WHAT YOU MEAN.
I CAN'T REVEAL THE DETAILS OF HOW, BUT... THE WORLD AS WE KNOW IT IS ENDING.
THE MOST SUITABLE CANDIDATES WILL ENTER A NEW UNIVERSE, WHERE MAGIC AND SCIENCE, DEMON AND ANGEL, DARK AND LIGHT MERGE TO CREATE SOMETHING NEW.
DOES THAT SOUND LIKE SOMETHING YOU MIGHT BE INTERESTED IN?
IT DOES. IT REALLY, REALLY DOES.
JUST SO WE'RE CLEAR. YOU'LL HAVE TO GO UP AGAINST SOME POWERFUL, DEADLY OPPOSITION.
AND THERE WILL BE BLOOD.
WHAT'S THE DOWNSIDE?

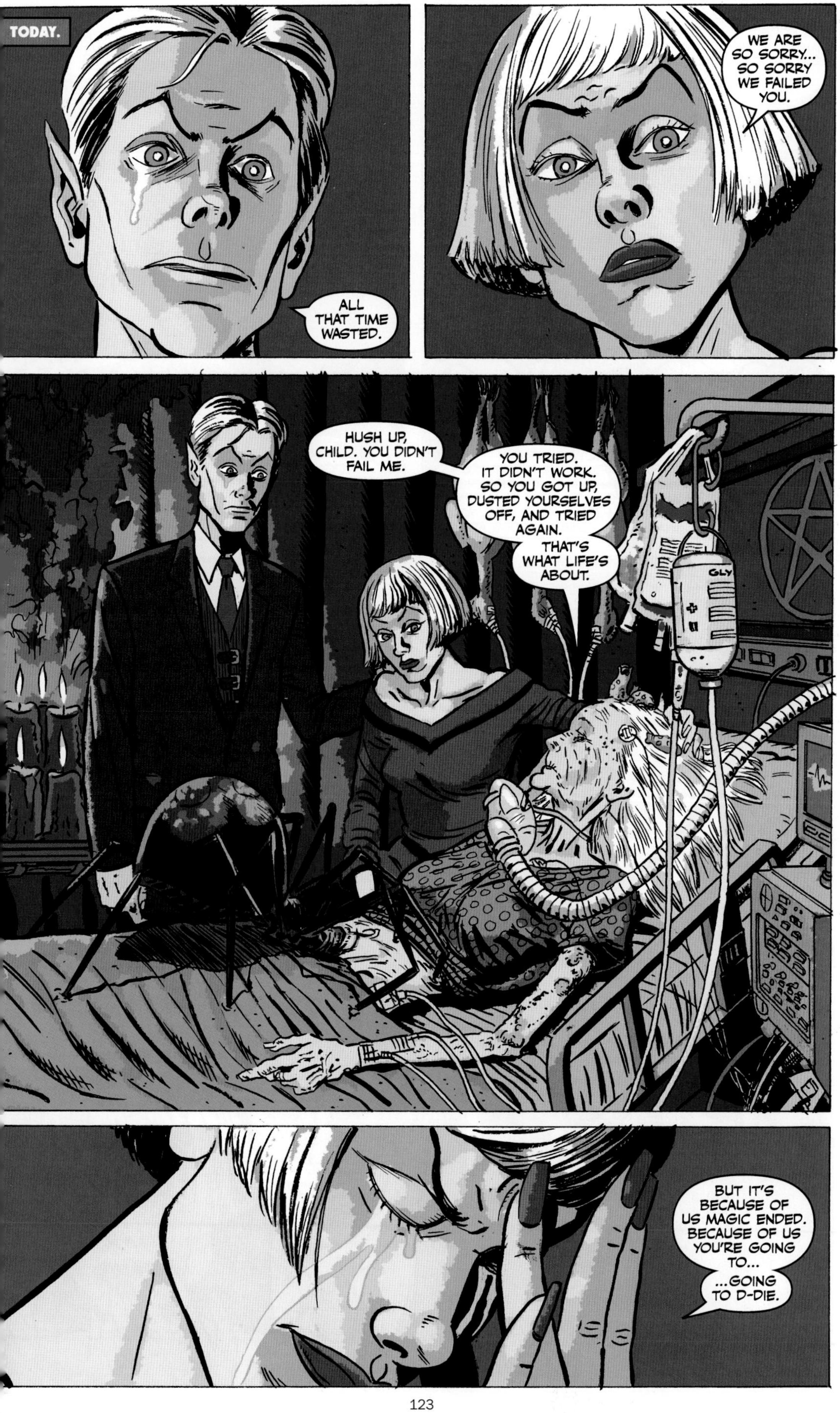
TODAY.
ALL THAT TIME WASTED.
WE ARE SO SORRY... SO SORRY WE FAILED YOU.
HUSH UP, CHILD. YOU DIDN'T FAIL ME.
YOU TRIED. IT DIDN'T WORK. SO YOU GOT UP, DUSTED YOURSELVES OFF, AND TRIED AGAIN.
THAT'S WHAT LIFE'S ABOUT.
GLY
BUT IT'S BECAUSE OF US MAGIC ENDED. BECAUSE OF US YOU'RE GOING TO...
...GOING TO D-DIE.

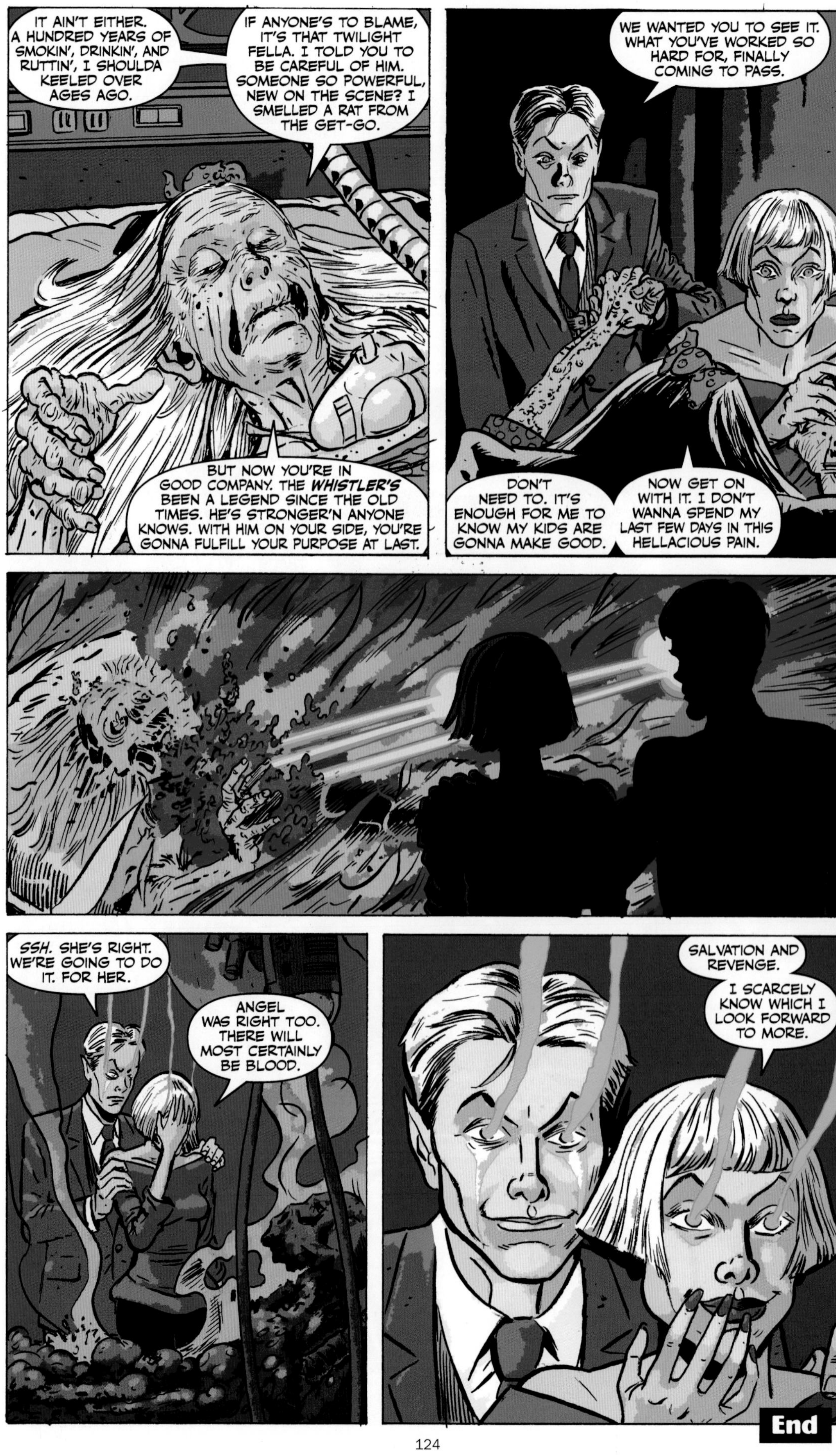
IT AIN'T EITHER. A HUNDRED YEARS OF SMOKIN', DRINKIN', AND RUTTIN', I SHOULDA KEELED OVER AGES AGO.
IF ANYONE'S TO BLAME, IT'S THAT TWILIGHT FELLA. I TOLD YOU TO BE CAREFUL OF HIM. SOMEONE SO POWERFUL, NEW ON THE SCENE? I SMELLED A RAT FROM THE GET-GO.
BUT NOW YOU'RE IN GOOD COMPANY. THE *WHISTLER'S* BEEN A LEGEND SINCE THE OLD TIMES. HE'S STRONGER'N ANYONE KNOWS. WITH HIM ON YOUR SIDE, YOU'RE GONNA FULFILL YOUR PURPOSE AT LAST.
WE WANTED YOU TO SEE IT. WHAT YOU'VE WORKED SO HARD FOR, FINALLY COMING TO PASS.
DON'T NEED TO. IT'S ENOUGH FOR ME TO KNOW MY KIDS ARE GONNA MAKE GOOD.
NOW GET ON WITH IT. I DON'T WANNA SPEND MY LAST FEW DAYS IN THIS HELLACIOUS PAIN.
SSH. SHE'S RIGHT. WE'RE GOING TO DO IT. FOR HER.
ANGEL WAS RIGHT TOO. THERE WILL MOST CERTAINLY BE BLOOD.
SALVATION AND REVENGE.
I SCARCELY KNOW WHICH I LOOK FORWARD TO MORE.
End

ANGEL & FAITH COVER GALLERY AND SKETCHBOOK

WITH NOTES FROM

REBEKAH ISAACS

Angel in bright, sunny LA weather provides an almost unlimited amount of fun possibilities! It seemed like it might be an appropriate time to throw some cheesecake in the mix for the issue #11 variant cover (as in the sketch featuring Faith in a bikini), but Editorial liked the depth of the composition of the first driving sketch best. It was great to get a chance to throw in an extra nod to the Angel TV show, in the form of our boy's '67 Plymouth Belvedere.

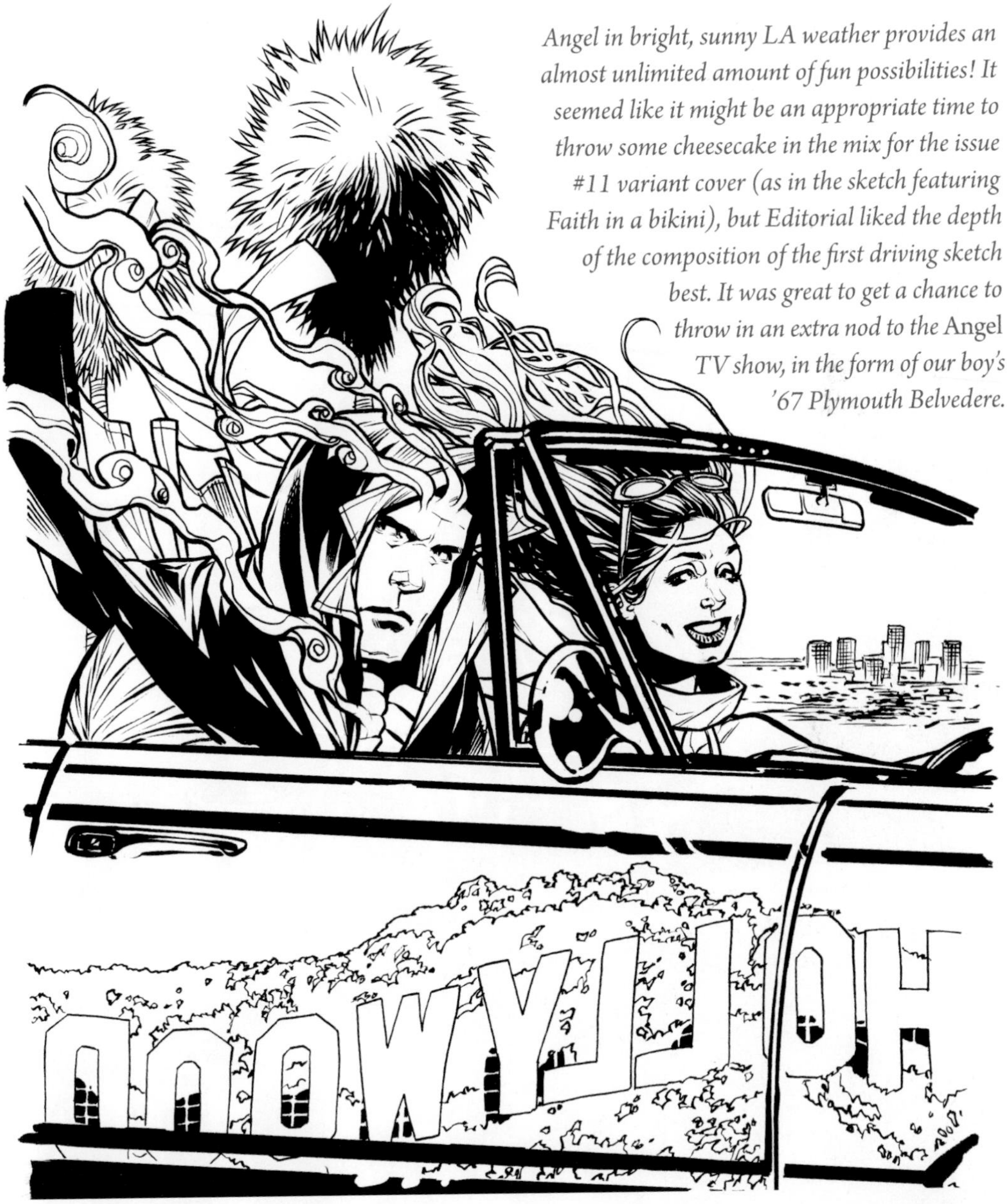

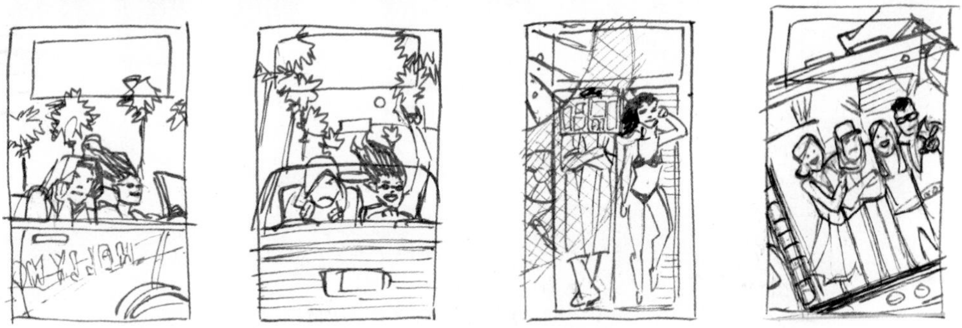

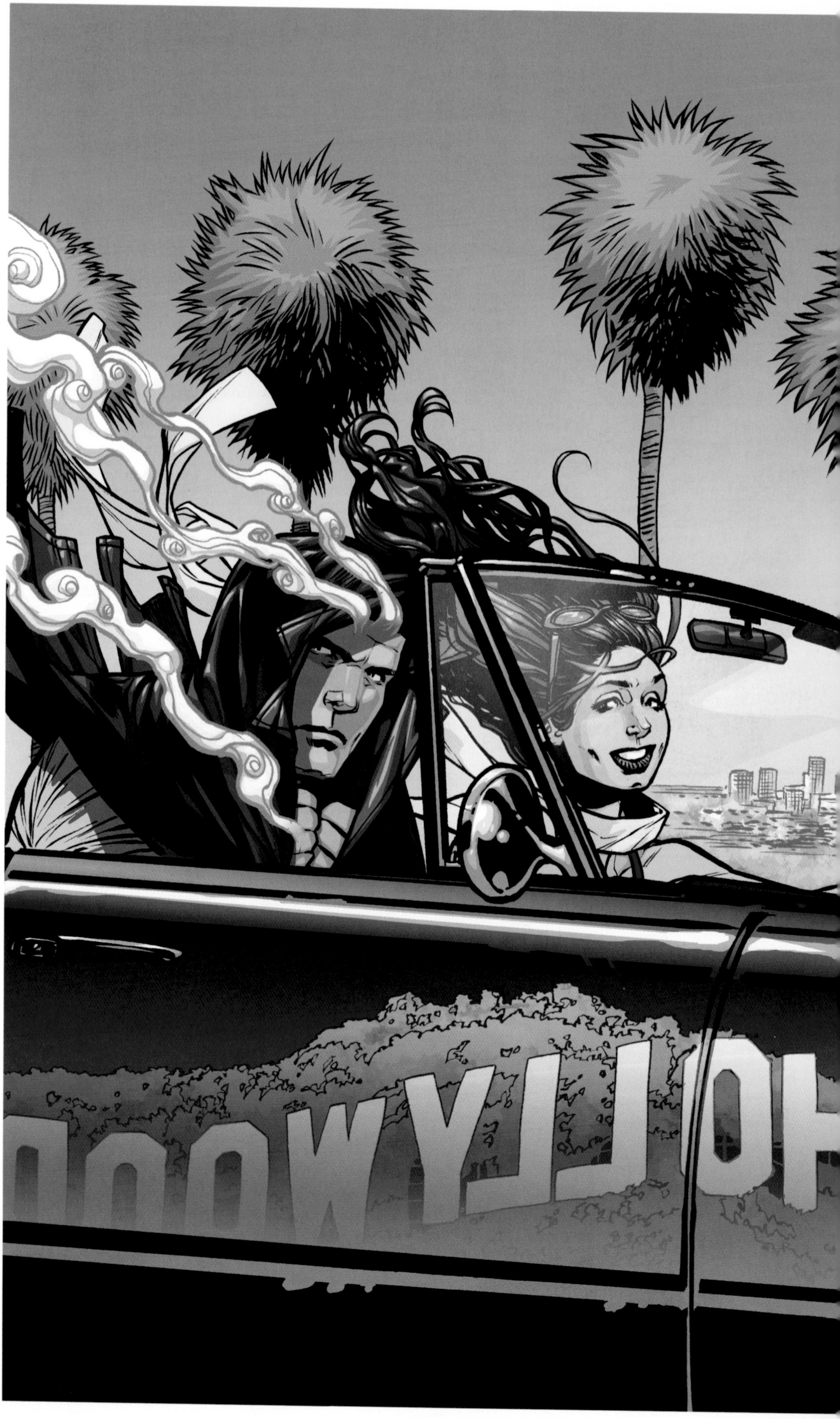

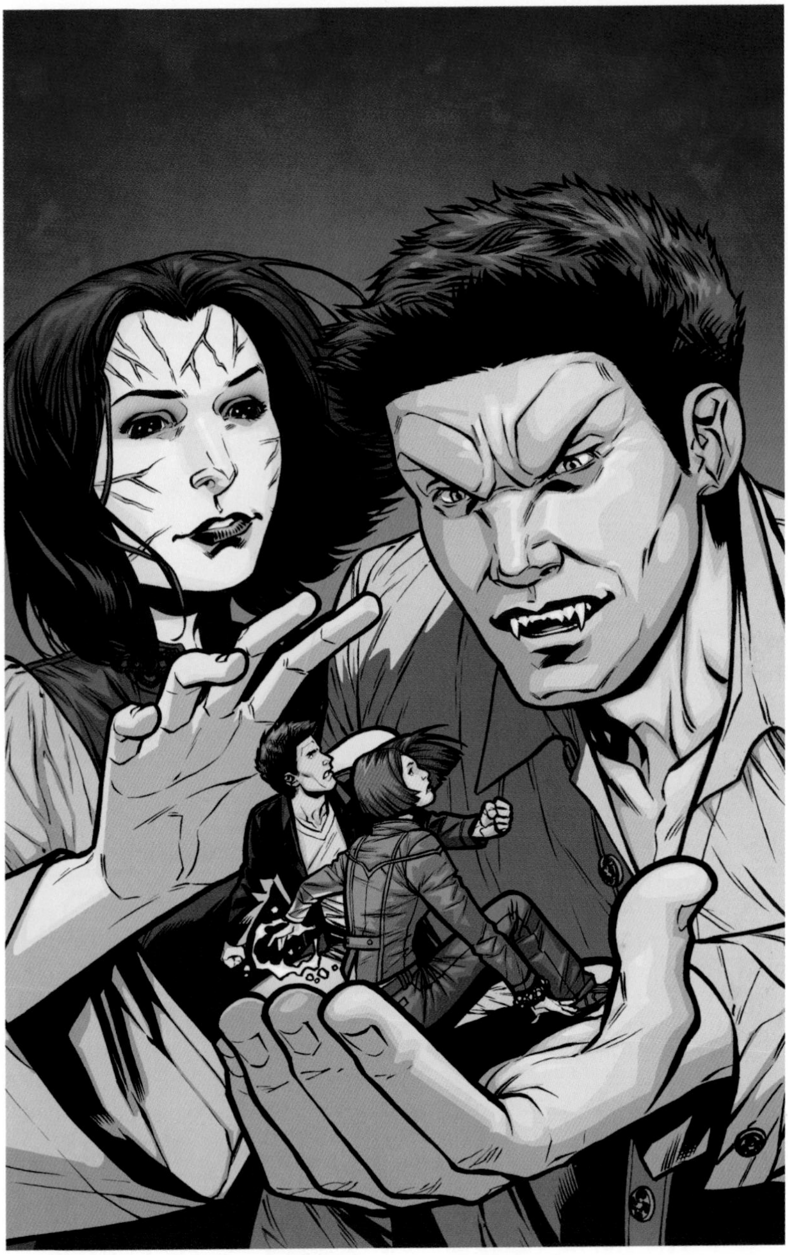

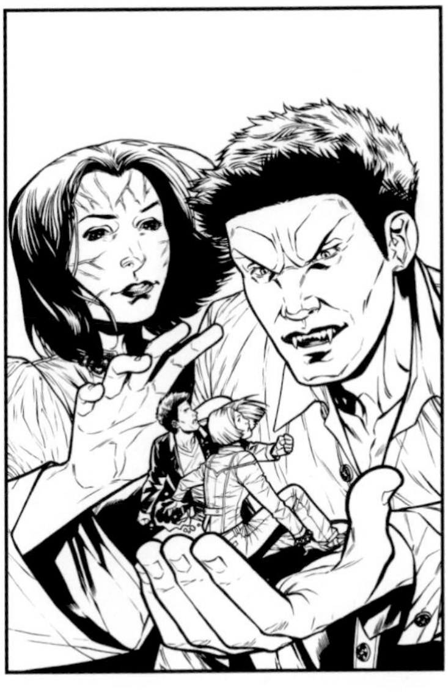

The issue #12 variant cover was my chance to do something a bit more conceptual and figurative than usual. I opted to show Dark Willow in her old hairstyle from the show, not with her asymetrical bob as she would later appear in the interior pages of the issue, since the Dark Willow here is symbolic of Willow's past and her fears of returning to that lack of control.

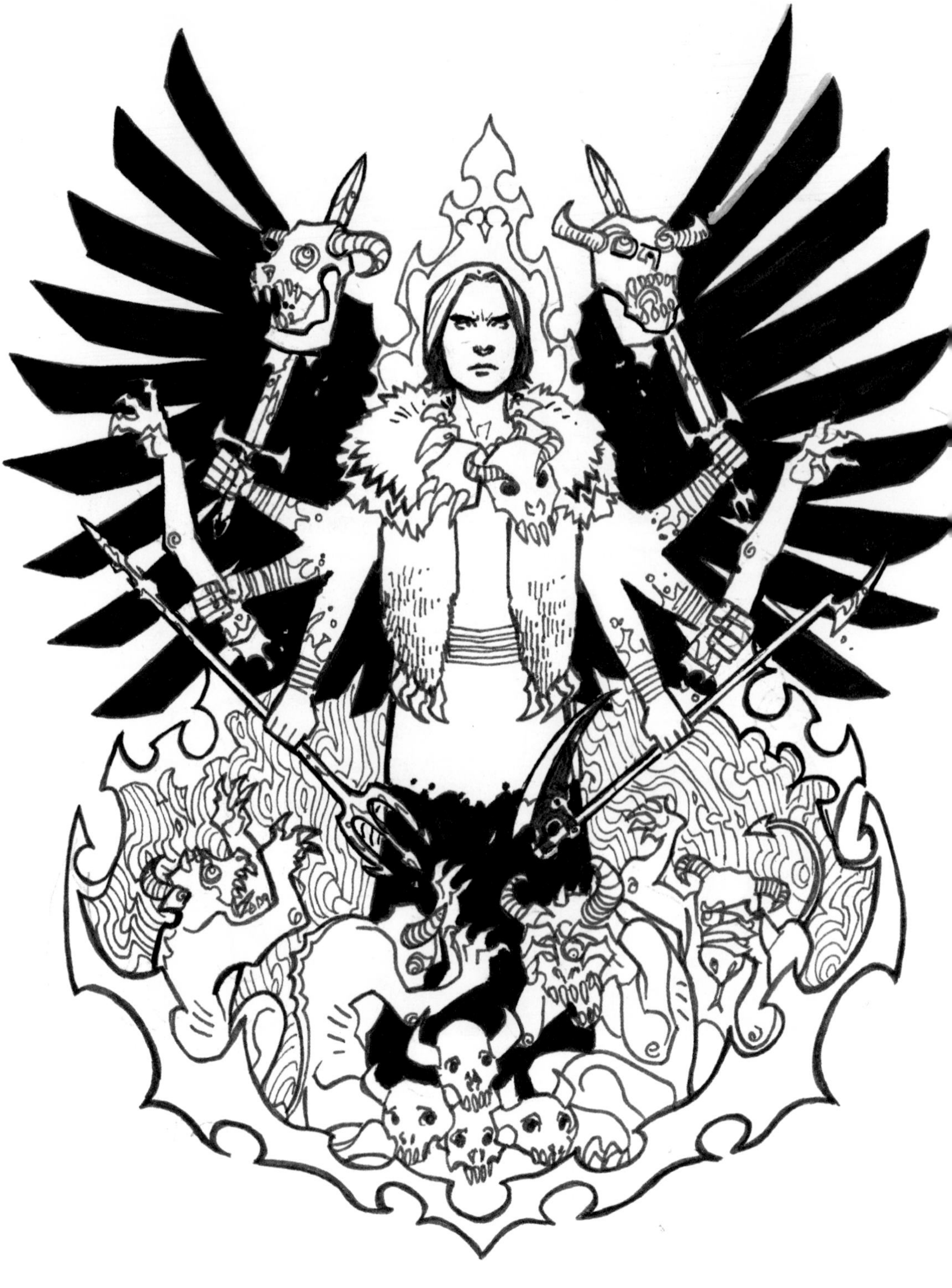

CONNOR THE DESTROYER

This painting of Connor as the Destroyer needed to have a bit of a primitive look, yet be detailed enough to keep the likeness recognizable. I looked at images of demons in medieval illuminated manuscripts for the little guys at Connor's feet. To give him a deified look I used a halo of flame inspired by ancient Hindu sculptures and friezes. In my humble opinion, Connor needs to get this as a tattoo.

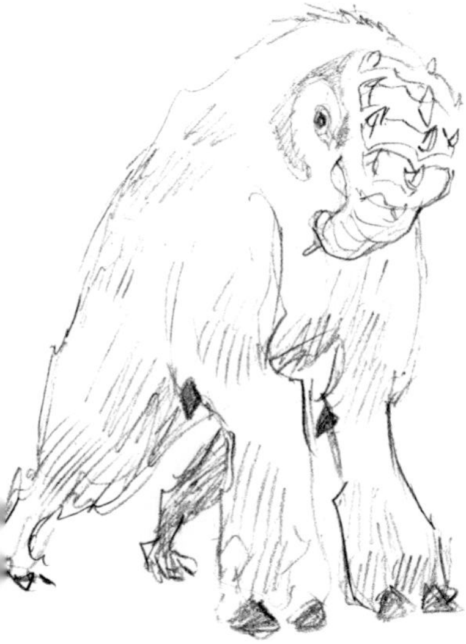

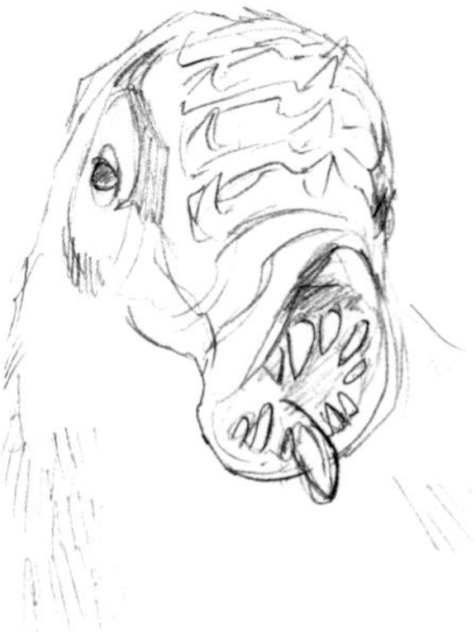

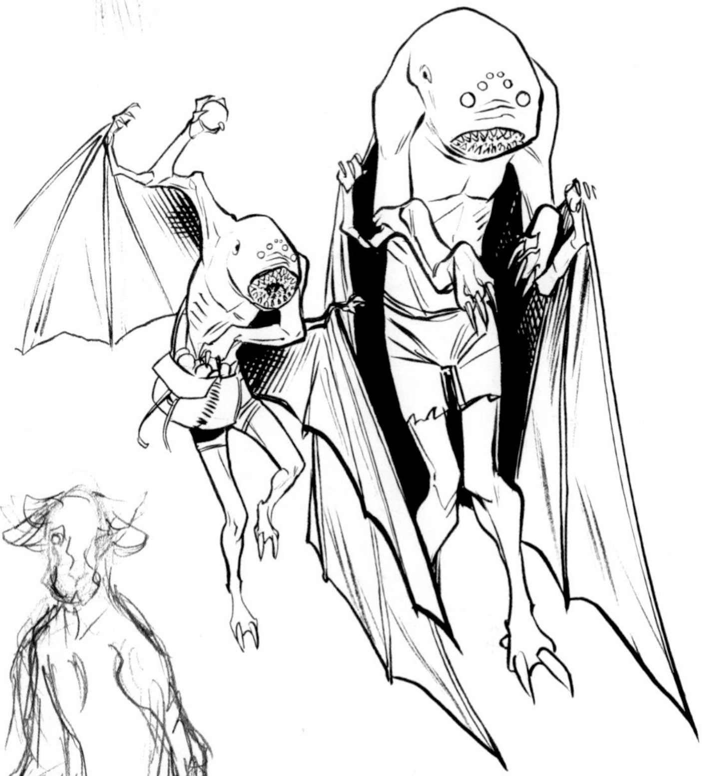

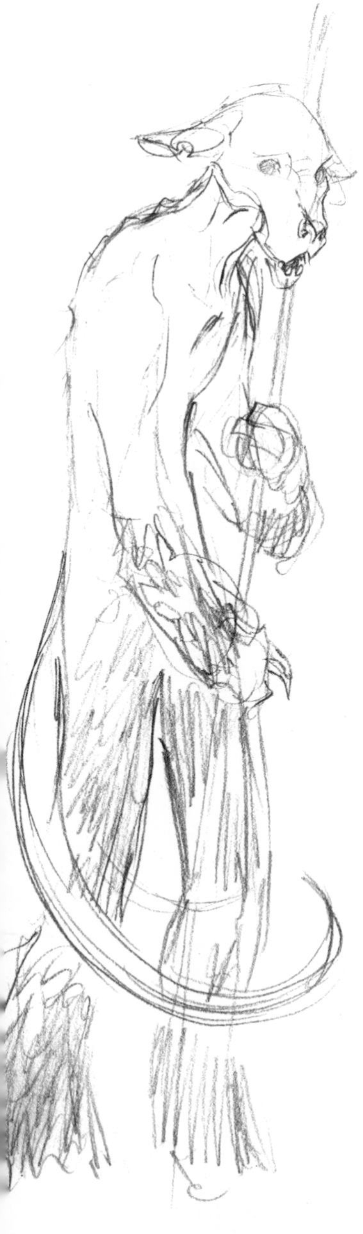

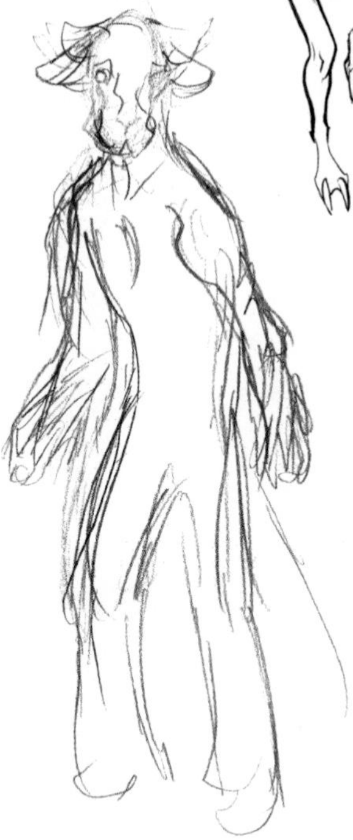

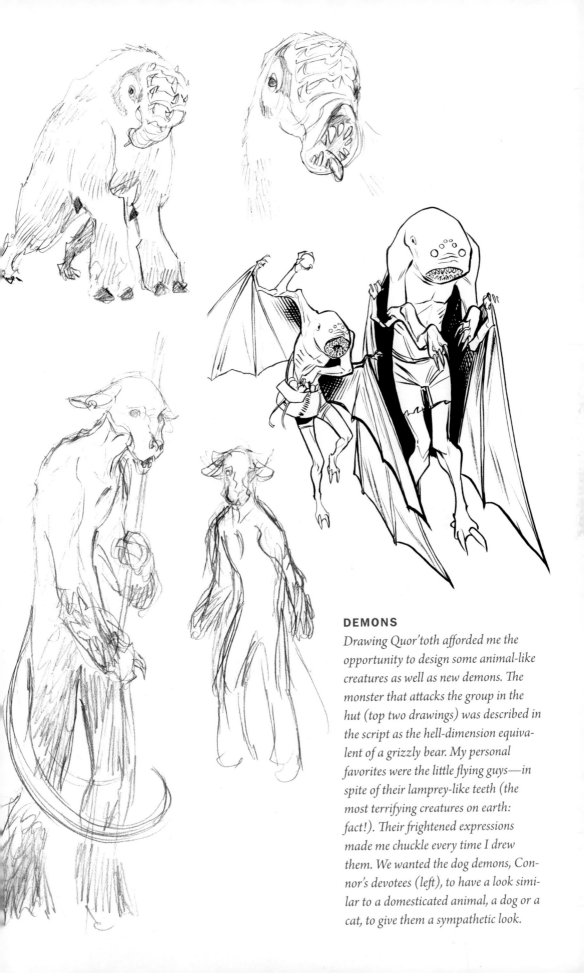

DEMONS

Drawing Quor'toth afforded me the opportunity to design some animal-like creatures as well as new demons. The monster that attacks the group in the hut (top two drawings) was described in the script as the hell-dimension equivalent of a grizzly bear. My personal favorites were the little flying guys—in spite of their lamprey-like teeth (the most terrifying creatures on earth: fact!). Their frightened expressions made me chuckle every time I drew them. We wanted the dog demons, Connor's devotees (left), to have a look similar to a domesticated animal, a dog or a cat, to give them a sympathetic look.

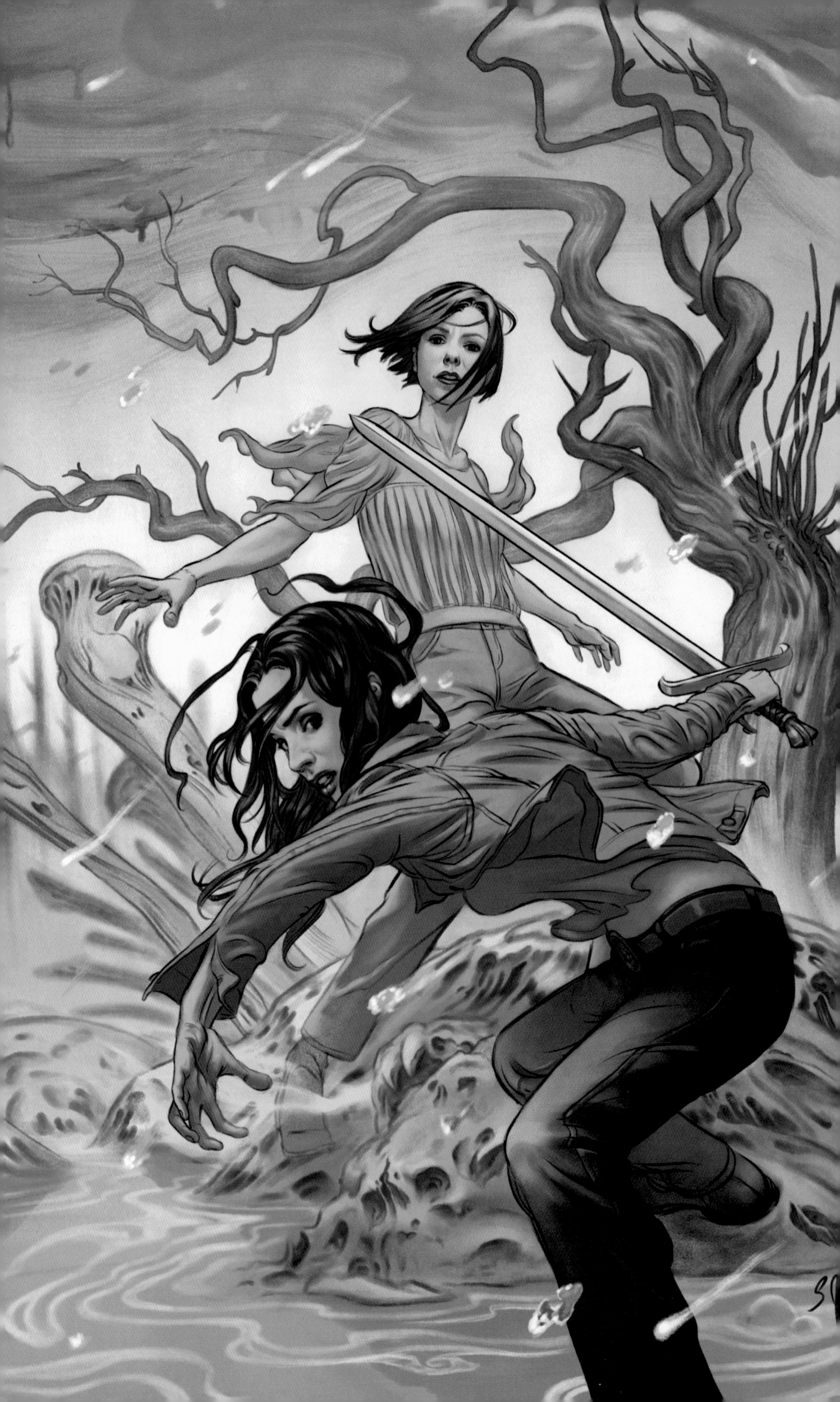

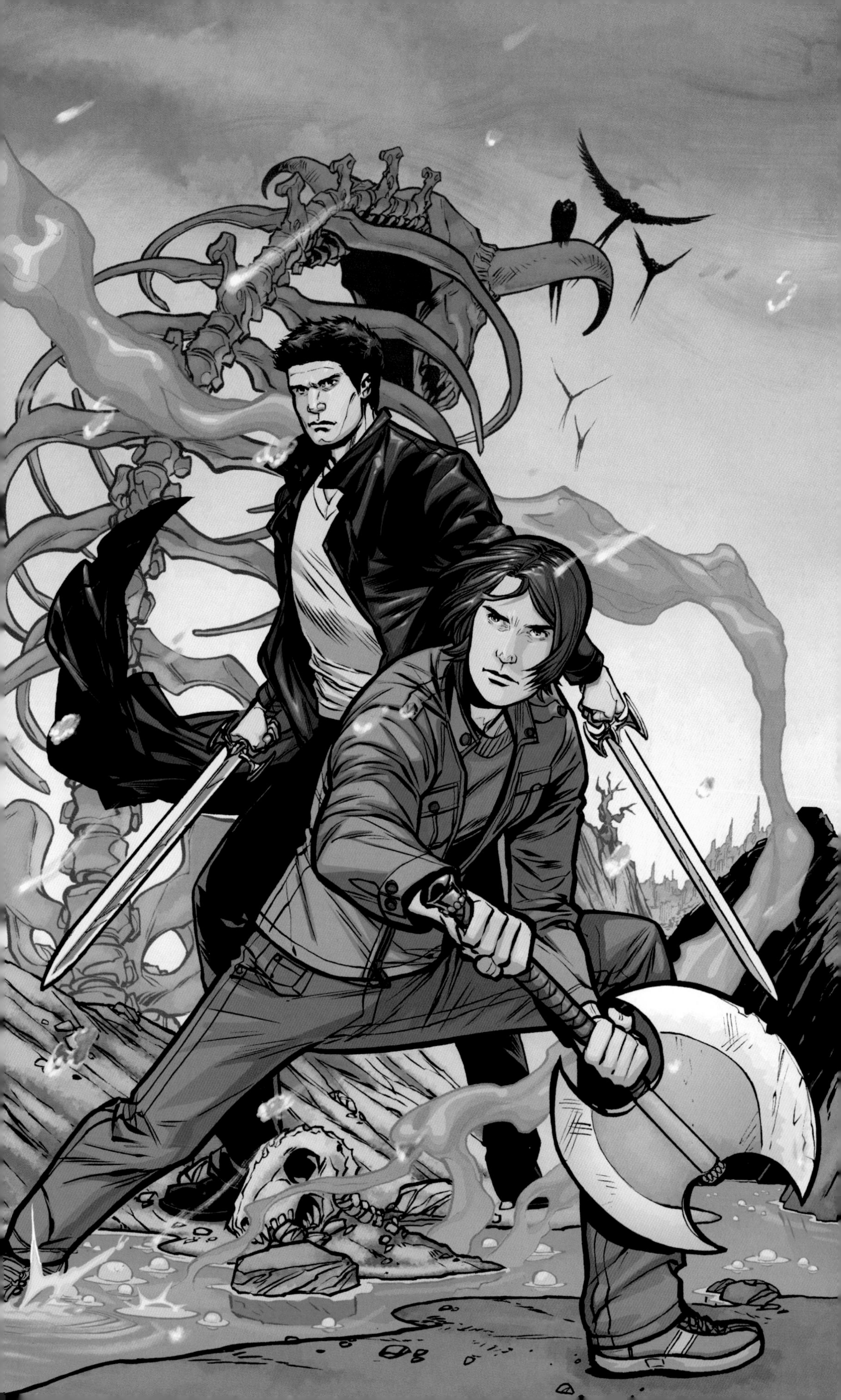

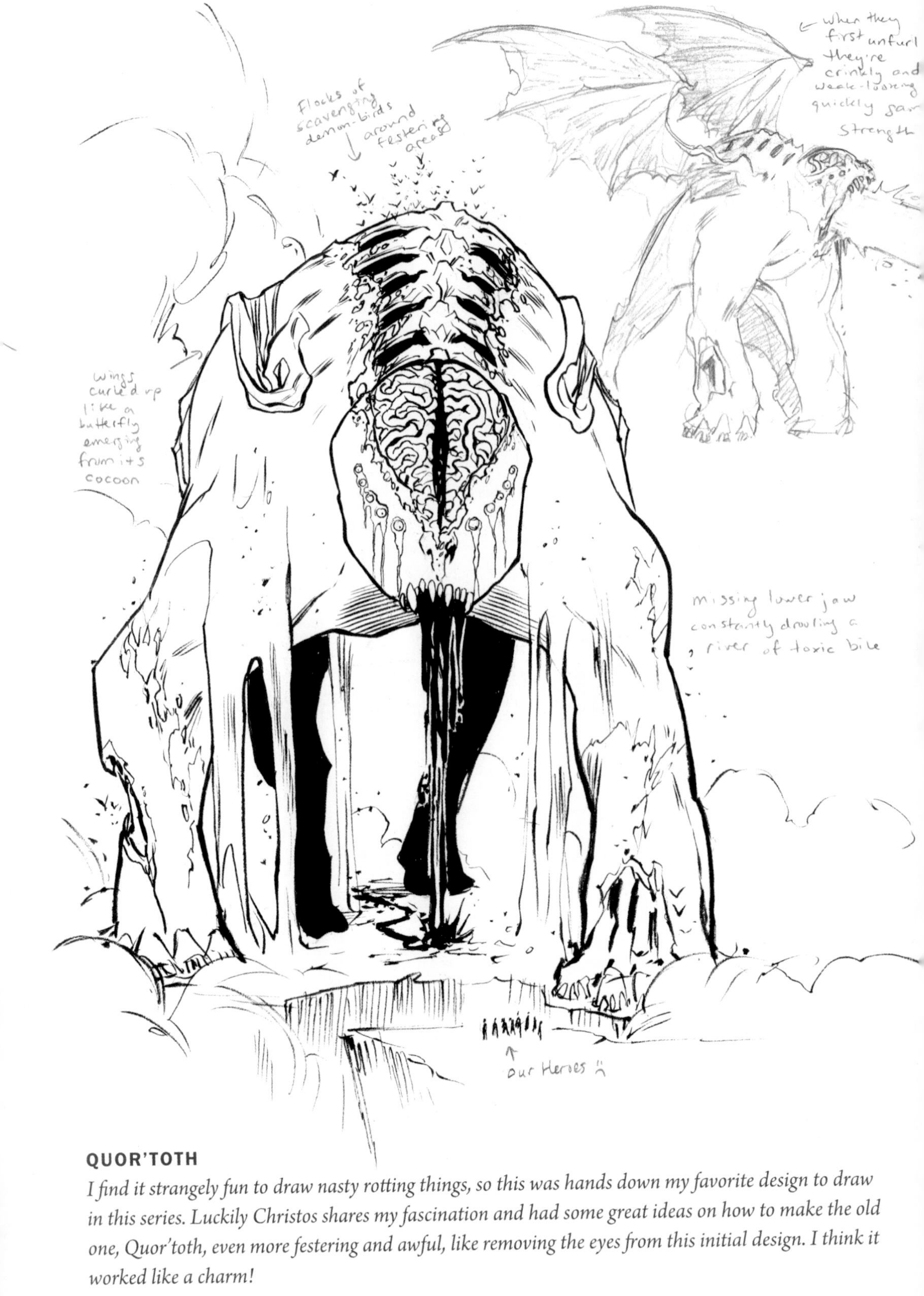

Flocks of scavenging demon-birds around festering areas
← when they first unfurl they're crinkly and weak-looking quickly gain strength
wings curled up like a butterfly emerging from it's cocoon
missing lower jaw constantly drooling a river of toxic bile
our Heroes

QUOR'TOTH

I find it strangely fun to draw nasty rotting things, so this was hands down my favorite design to draw in this series. Luckily Christos shares my fascination and had some great ideas on how to make the old one, Quor'toth, even more festering and awful, like removing the eyes from this initial design. I think it worked like a charm!

Preceding pages: *The standard and variant cover art for issue #13. On the left is Steve Morris's, on the right is my cover with colorist Dan Jackson. We all collaborated to make a single image across to covers.*

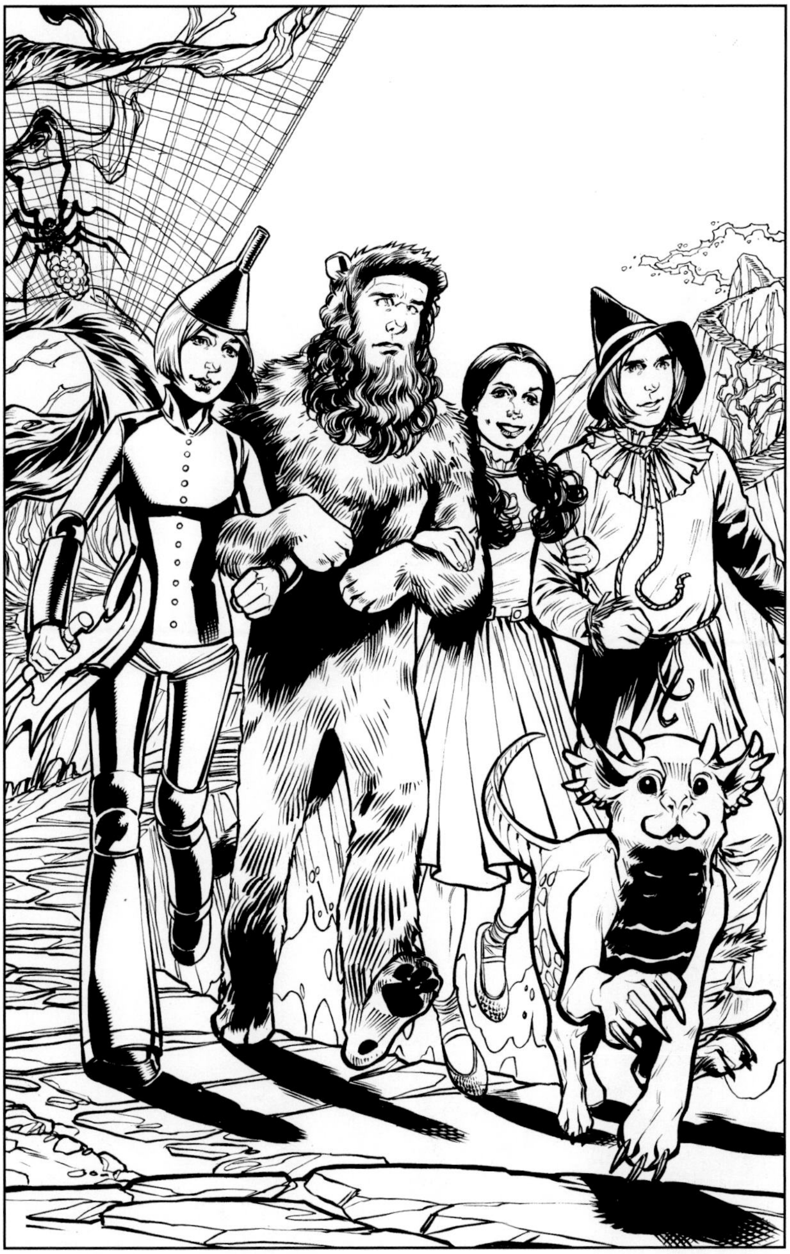

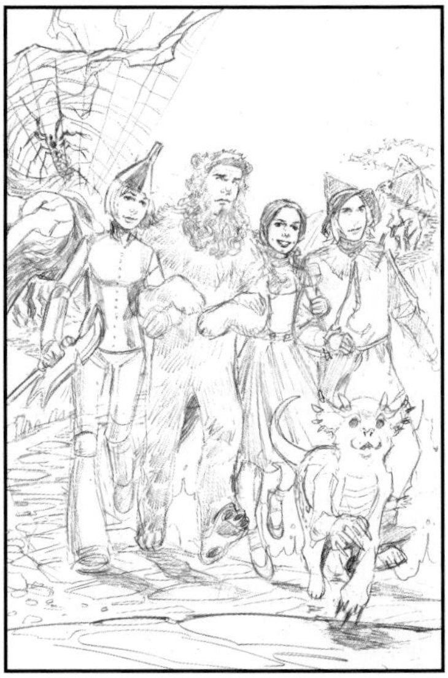

Most of the cover concepts given to me are pretty general, but the A&F editors are big Wizard of Oz *fans and I was more than happy to oblige when they requested an homage. The themes of the source material and our issue really couldn't fit more perfectly. Initially we thought we should just put the regular Toto in the foreground, but eventually decided to go with a demon puppy. He didn't need to have a specific look since we wouldn't see him in the actual issue, but since I was drawing this at the same time as designing Connor's demon acolytes, this little guy ended up being the basis for their eventual, more grown-up design. The final art appears on page 2 of this book.*

Following page: *The variant cover art for issue #15.*

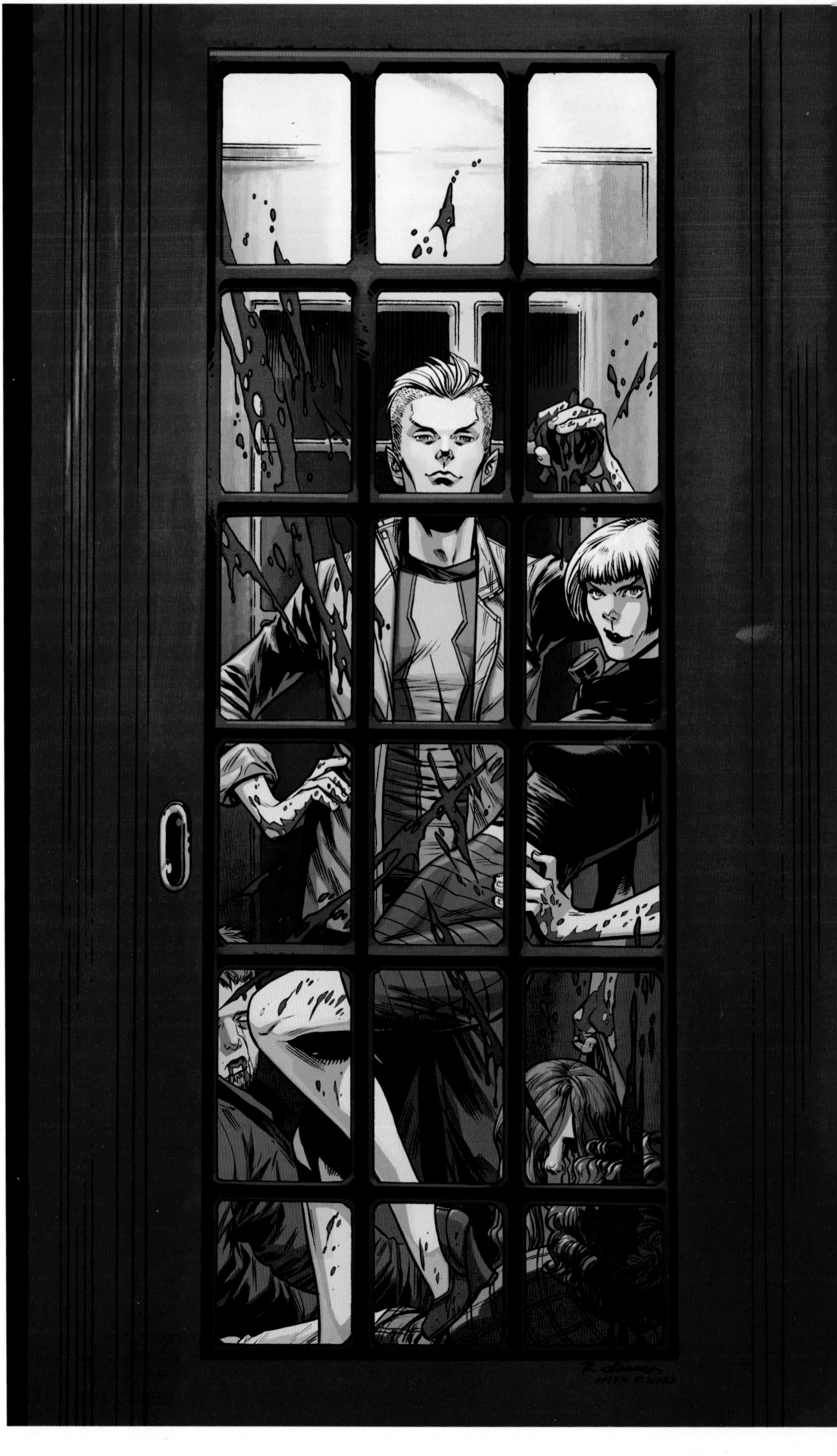

Buffy the Vampire Slayer™

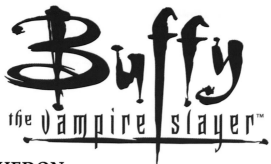

FROM JOSS WHEDON

BUFFY THE VAMPIRE SLAYER SEASON 8

VOLUME 1: THE LONG WAY HOME
Joss Whedon and Georges Jeanty
ISBN 978-1-59307-822-5 | $15.99

VOLUME 2: NO FUTURE FOR YOU
Brian K. Vaughan, Georges Jeanty, and Joss Whedon
ISBN 978-1-59307-963-5 | $15.99

VOLUME 3: WOLVES AT THE GATE
Drew Goddard, Georges Jeanty, and Joss Whedon
ISBN 978-1-59582-165-2 | $15.99

VOLUME 4: TIME OF YOUR LIFE
Joss Whedon, Jeph Loeb, Georges Jeanty, and others
ISBN 978-1-59582-310-6 | $15.99

VOLUME 5: PREDATORS AND PREY
Joss Whedon, Jane Espenson, Georges Jeanty, Cliff Richards, and others
ISBN 978-1-59582-342-7 | $15.99

VOLUME 6: RETREAT
Joss Whedon, Jane Espenson, Georges Jeanty, Karl Moline, and others
ISBN 978-1-59582-415-8 | $15.99

VOLUME 7: TWILIGHT
Joss Whedon, Brad Meltzer, and Georges Jeanty
ISBN 978-1-59582-558-2 | $16.99

VOLUME 8: LAST GLEAMING
Joss Whedon, Scott Allie, and Georges Jeanty
ISBN 978-1-59582-610-7 | $16.99

BUFFY THE VAMPIRE SLAYER SEASON 8 LIBRARY EDITION

VOLUME 1
ISBN 978-1-59582-888-0 | $29.99

VOLUME 2
ISBN 978-1-59582-935-1 | $29.99

VOLUME 3
ISBN 978-1-59582-978-8 | $29.99

VOLUME 4
ISBN 978-1-61655-127-8 | $29.99

BUFFY THE VAMPIRE SLAYER SEASON 9

VOLUME 1: FREEFALL
Joss Whedon, Andrew Chambliss, Georges Jeanty, and others
ISBN 978-1-59582-922-1 | $17.99

VOLUME 2: ON YOUR OWN
Andrew Chambliss, Scott Allie, Georges Jeanty, and others
ISBN 978-1-59582-990-0 | $17.99

ANGEL & FAITH

VOLUME 1: LIVE THROUGH THIS
Christos Gage, Rebekah Isaacs, and Phil Noto
ISBN 978-1-59582-887-3 | $17.99

VOLUME 2: DADDY ISSUES
Christos Gage, Rebekah Isaacs, and Chris Samnee
ISBN 978-1-59582-960-3 | $17.99

AVAILABLE AT YOUR LOCAL COMICS SHOP OR BOOKSTORE!
To find a comics shop in your area, call 1-888-266-4226. For more information or to order direct:
On the web: DarkHorse.com • E-mail: mailorder@darkhorse.com • Phone: 1-800-862-0052 Mon.–Fri. 9 AM to 5 PM Pacific Time

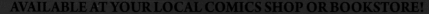

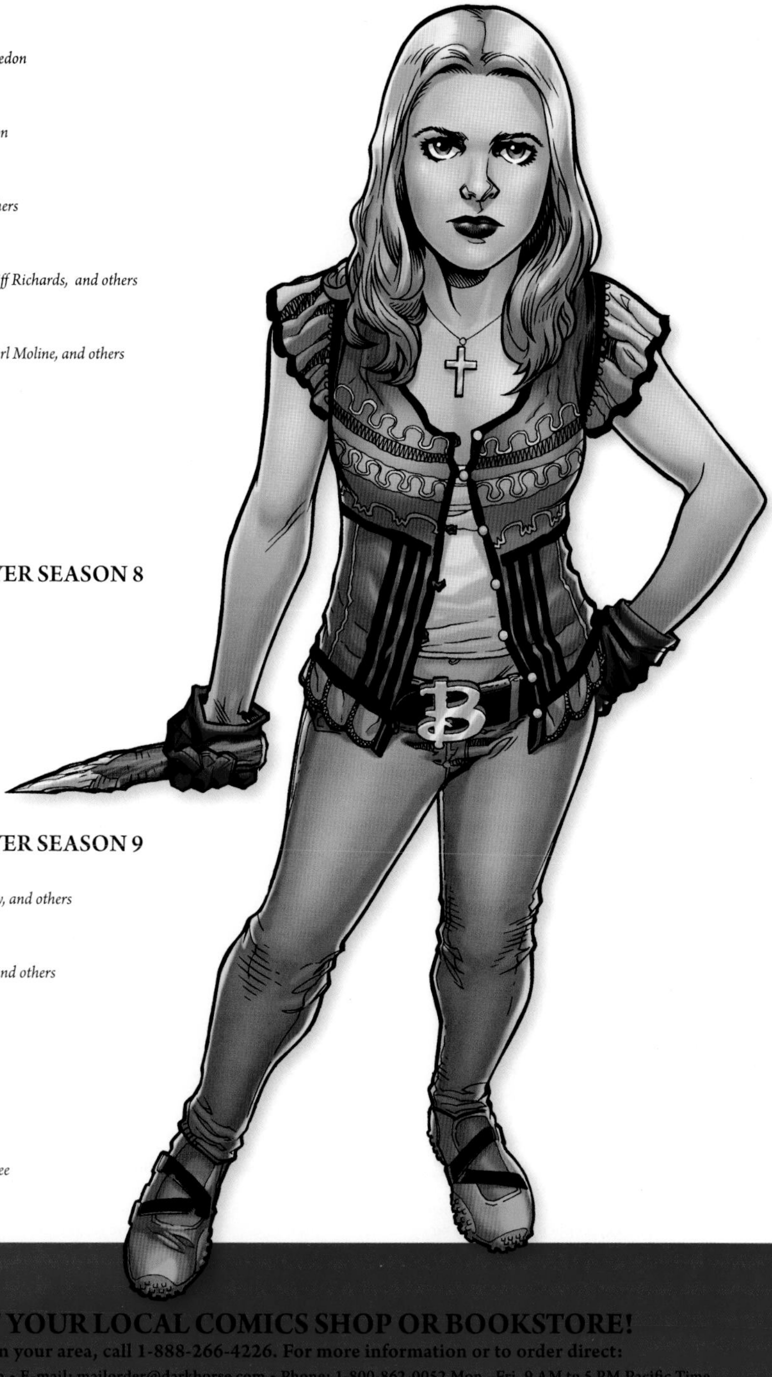

ALSO FROM JOSS WHEDON

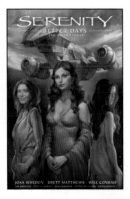

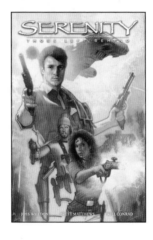

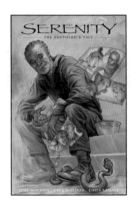

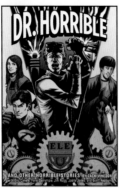

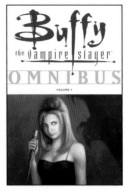

SERENITY
THOSE LEFT BEHIND
JOSS WHEDON BRETT MATTHEWS WILL CONRAD

SERENITY
BETTER DAYS
JOSS WHEDON BRETT MATTHEWS WILL CONRAD

SERENITY
THE SHEPHERD'S TALE
JOSS WHEDON ZACK WHEDON CHRIS SAMNEE

DR. HORRIBLE
AND OTHER HORRIBLE STORIES BY ZACK WHEDON

Buffy
the vampire slayer
OMNIBUS
VOLUME 1

BUFFY THE VAMPIRE SLAYER OMNIBUS
VOLUME 1
ISBN 978-1-59307-784-6 | $24.99
VOLUME 2
ISBN 978-1-59307-826-3 | $24.99
VOLUME 3
ISBN 978-1-59307-885-0 | $24.99
VOLUME 4
ISBN 978-1-59307-968-0 | $24.99
VOLUME 5
ISBN 978-1-59582-225-3 | $24.99
VOLUME 6
ISBN 978-1-59582-242-0 | $24.99
VOLUME 7
ISBN 978-1-59582-331-1 | $24.99

BUFFY THE VAMPIRE SLAYER: PANEL TO PANEL
ISBN 978-1-59307-836-2 | $19.99

ANGEL OMNIBUS
Christopher Golden, Eric Powell, and others
ISBN 978-1-59582-706-7 | $24.99

TALES OF THE SLAYERS
Joss Whedon, Amber Benson, Gene Colan, P. Craig Russell, Tim Sale, and others
ISBN 978-1-56971-605-2 | $14.99

TALES OF THE VAMPIRES
Joss Whedon, Brett Matthews, Cameron Stewart, and others
ISBN 978-1-56971-749-3 | $15.99

BUFFY THE VAMPIRE SLAYER: TALES HARDCOVER
ISBN 978-1-59582-644-2 | $29.99

FRAY: FUTURE SLAYER
Joss Whedon and Karl Moline
ISBN 978-1-56971-751-6 | $19.99

SERENITY VOLUME 1: THOSE LEFT BEHIND SECOND EDITION HARDCOVER
Joss Whedon, Brett Matthews, and Will Conrad
ISBN 978-1-59582-914-6 | $17.99

SERENITY VOLUME 2: BETTER DAYS AND OTHER STORIES HARDCOVER
Joss Whedon, Patton Oswalt, Zack Whedon, Patric Reynolds, and others
ISBN 978-1-59582-739-5 | $19.99

SERENITY VOLUME 3: THE SHEPHERD'S TALE HARDCOVER
Joss Whedon, Zack Whedon, and Chris Samnee
ISBN 978-1-59582-561-2 | $14.99

DR. HORRIBLE AND OTHER HORRIBLE STORIES
Joss Whedon, Zack Whedon, Joëlle Jones, and others
ISBN 978-1-59582-577-3 | $9.99

DOLLHOUSE VOLUME 1: EPITAPHS
Andrew Chambliss, Jed Whedon, Maurissa Tancharoen, and Cliff Richards
ISBN 978-1-59582-863-7 | $18.99

AVAILABLE AT YOUR LOCAL COMICS SHOP OR BOOKSTORE!
To find a comics shop in your area, call 1-888-266-4226.
For more information or to order direct visit DarkHorse.com or call 1-800-862-0052 Mon.–Fri. 9 AM to 5 PM Pacific Time.

DARK HORSE BOOKS
DarkHorse.com